Landscape Learning in the Pleistocene Great Basin

Landscape Learning
in the Pleistocene Great Basin

David B. Hunt

University of Utah Anthropological Papers No. 139

THE UNIVERSITY OF UTAH PRESS
Salt Lake City

The University of Utah Anthropological Papers
SERIES EDITORS: Brian F. Codding and Lisbeth A. Louderback

The Defiance House Man colophon is a registered trademark
of the University of Utah Press. It is based on a four-foot-tall
Ancient Puebloan pictograph (late PIII) near Glen Canyon, Utah.

LIBRARY OF CONGRESS CATALOGING-IN-PUBLICATION DATA

Names: Hunt, David B., author.
Title: Landscape learning in the Pleistocene Great Basin / David B. Hunt.
Other titles: University of Utah anthropological papers ; no. 139.
Description: Salt Lake City : The University of Utah Press, [2025] |
    Series: University of Utah anthropological papers ; 139 | Includes
    bibliographical references.
Identifiers: LCCN 2024016344 | ISBN 9781647692087 (paperback) | ISBN
    9781647692094 (ebook)
Subjects: LCSH: Hunting and gathering societies—Decision making. | Land
    settlement patterns, Prehistoric—Great Basin. | Excavations
    (Archaeology)—Great Basin. | Antiquities, Prehistoric—Great Basin. |
    Great Basin—Antiquities.
Classification: LCC GN388 .H833 2024 | DDC 979/.01—dc23/eng/20240902
LC record available at https://lccn.loc.gov/2024016344

Errata and further information on this and other titles available at UofUpress.com

DEDICATION

I dedicate this volume to my father, Dan Hunt,
who always encouraged me to seek adventure,
and to my mother, Norma Hunt,
who only wanted to hear about it after it was over.

Also, to Charlotte, Bridget, Ella, and Gemma,
whose adventures are just beginning.

Contents

Publisher's Note

Appendices A–G are available online at the University of Utah's J. Willard Marriott Digital Library:
https://collections.lib.utah.edu/ark:/87278/s6mntfnx

Figures

Tables

Equations

3.1. $\dfrac{1}{d^2}$

3.2. $D = E * \dfrac{1}{d^2}$

3.3. $\%LL = (1 - r_s^2) * 100$

3.4. $x_\omega = x \,(\mathrm{mod}\, 2\pi)$

3.5. $c(\theta; \mu, \rho) = \dfrac{1}{2\pi} \dfrac{1 - \rho^2}{1 + \rho^2 - 2\rho \cos(\theta - \mu)}, -\pi \leq \theta < \pi,\ \mu < 2\pi,\ 0 \leq \rho < 1$

4.1. $\displaystyle\int_i = \dfrac{Max\left(0, Slope_i^p\right)}{\sum_{i=1}^{8}\left(Max\left(0, Slope_j^p\right)\right)}$

4.2. $\mathrm{Accuracy} = \dfrac{TN + TP}{TN + FP + FN + TP}$

4.3. $\mathrm{Precision} = \dfrac{TP}{TP + FP}$

4.4. $\mathrm{Best\ Fit} = \dfrac{TP}{Observed} - \dfrac{FP}{Observed} + \dfrac{TP - FP}{Observed}$

Acknowledgments

This volume springs from my dissertation work at the University of Washington and I remain deeply grateful to my committee for their help and support: Don Grayson, Marcos Llobera, Charlotte Beck, Tom Jones, Darryl Holman, and Alan Gillespie. Don kindled my initial interest in the early colonization of the Americas, modelled the work of the scholar, and encouraged me throughout this process. This publication wouldn't have happened without his considerable guidance, support, and friendship. Marcos provided invaluable, encouraging support from the earliest stages of this journey and led me into the world of landscapes. Also, Charlotte and Tom's "Clovis and Western Stemmed: Population Migration and the Meeting of Two Technologies in the Intermountain West" (*American Antiquity* 75(1), 2017) influenced me far more than I would realize when I first read it in my tent during my initial field school. Collaborating with them both was a true honor.

Within the professional archaeology community, I found generous mentors and contributors. It is not an understatement to say that this project could not have been completed without the past work and present generosity of Craig Skinner. Great Basin archaeology is hard to imagine without the decades of obsidian and fine-grained volcanic (FGV) material research that he has amassed and freely shares. Similarly, without access to the Old River Bed (ORB) data provided by David Madsen, David Page, Daron Duke, Tom Jones, and Charlotte Beck, none of this work would be possible. Richard Holmer, Kathleen Hull, Richard Talbot, and Alex Nyers (Northwest Research Obsidian Studies Laboratory) also graciously provided datasets from their past work that is incorporated here. I am also grateful to Richie Rosencrance for his permission to use his excellent WST point type image (in Chapter 1).

The process of permitting archaeological work across two states initially appeared daunting, but Kris Carambelas (Utah Public Lands Office), Anna Camp (Nevada State Museum), and Bryan Hockett (Bureau of Land Management, Nevada) provided amazing guidance that streamlined the process. The staff at various field offices (Chris Merritt, Deb Miller, Kristine Curry [School and Institutional Trust Land Administration, Utah], Roy Plank, Michael Sheehan, Wes Willoughby, Harry Konwin, and Lucinda Dockstader) were all exceptionally helpful and a pleasure to work with. I'm also thankful to Chris Robinson of the Pahvant Ensign Ranches for allowing me to survey on their private ranchland.

Importantly, I also thank my field work volunteers. Brad Allen enthusiastically embraced weeks of walking through the desert for little more than dried mangos. And Wendy Hunt will always have my gratitude and admiration for bravely putting on her snake gaiters and heading into unknown brush, some of which we later realized was full of black widow spiders, to assist me fulfill a dream. Without the two of you, I would probably still be out there wandering around Topaz Mountain.

I am grateful for two anonymous reviewers and Dr. David Meltzer for their detailed comments on the manuscript. Justin Bracken, Anya Martin, and Jessica Booth's production team provided gracious editorial, copy editing, and presentation guidance from start to finish. This work has been vastly improved as a result of their combined efforts and professionalism.

This research was supported by funding from the Quaternary Research Center (QRC) at University of Washington.

Background and Research Objective

INTRODUCTION

As prehistoric hunter-gatherers moved into new and previously unknown regions, they were presented with a challenge that their descendants rarely faced: specifically, the challenge of discovering, for the first time, where critical resources, like food, water, and the raw materials needed to make tools, could be found on this entirely new landscape. While their descendants would benefit from the accumulation of this knowledge over time, these first colonizers were forced to learn a new landscape from scratch (Kelly, 1995; Kelly & Todd, 1988; Meltzer, 2002, 2021). Today, looking archaeologically at the traces of these endeavors, we can start to ask how initial colonization behaviors may have differed from those of the long-time occupations that followed—occupations by residents who inherited a learned landscape—and what information we might glean from these differences.

In North America, the earliest evidence of coastal migrations into the Americas, south of glacial ice, is likely lost to rising sea levels since the Last Glacial Maximum (LGM). However, moving inland, into areas such as the Great Basin, we may still be able to examine colonization events on unknown landscapes and begin to quantify behaviors that have long been qualitatively suspected. Within the Great Basin, the occupation of regions by people using Western Stemmed Tradition (WST) tools provides an opportunity for such an examination.

WESTERN STEMMED TRADITION

The WST is the earliest well-defined, lithic technological complex within western North America and is defined by the presence of a diverse variety (Figure 1.1) of stemmed points (Beck & Jones, 2009; Bryan, 1980;

Duke, 2011; Erlandson et al., 2011; Grayson, 2011; Haynes, 2007; Heizer & Hester, 1978; Kelly, 1978; Pendleton, 1979; Rosencrance, 2019; Smith et al., 2019; Swanson et al., 1964; Tuohy, 1974; Tuohy & Layton, 1977; Warren, 1967; Willig & Aikens, 1988). Increasingly, researchers are looking to the people using WST technology, and its stemmed point predecessors, as likely candidates of a coastal colonization into the Americas (Beck & Jones, 2010; Davis et al., 2022; Smith et al., 2019). These characteristics make WST archaeological data particularly promising when attempting to quantify colonization behaviors.

With a geographic range that extends from the west coast to the Rocky Mountains (Figure 1.2), the WST is most closely associated with the pluvial lakes of the Great Basin at the Terminal Pleistocene/Early Holocene (TP/EH) boundary (Beck & Jones, 2009; Grayson, 2011). WST points and sites are occasionally discovered in caves or rockshelters that formed along these lake margins, but more frequently are found in valley bottoms and on valley edges in what would have been low-lying wetland areas (Grayson, 1993, 2011; Madsen, 2007; Smith et al., 2019; Smith & Barker, 2017.

The earliest secure radiocarbon date for the WST is recorded at the Cooper's Ferry site (Davis et al., 2019, 2022), in central Idaho, with a stemmed point base discovered below bone dated to ~13,460 cal BP (11,630 ± 80 ^{14}C yr BP). Within the Great Basin, WST points make their earliest well-dated appearance at the Paisley Caves, in Oregon, with a minimum age of ~13,000 cal BP (11,070 ± 25 ^{14}C yr BP; Jenkins et al., 2012, 2013; Waters & Stafford, 2007). At Paulina Lake, also in Oregon, a stratum containing WST points sets the latest date for the WST at ~7,870 cal BP (7,080 ± 80 ^{14}C yr BP), coincident with a period of significant population decrease in the Great

FIGURE 1.1. Type specimens for WST projectile point types: (*a–b*) Haskett points, Haskett site; (*c*) Cougar Mountain, Cougar Mountain Cave; (*d–f*) Lind Coulee Types 1, 2, 3, Lind Coulee site; (*g*) Windust/square, Granite Point; (*h*) Windust, Marmes Rockshelter; (*i*) Parman, Parman Localities; (*j*) Lake Mohave, Lake Mojave; (*k*) Silver Lake, Lake Mojave; (*l*) Bonneville, Old River Bed delta; (*m*) Stubby, Old River Bed delta. Note that different Haskett and Lind Coulee types are consolidated into single types now. Images (*j*) and (*k*) are courtesy of Ed Knell, and (*l*) and (*m*) are courtesy of Daron Duke. Figure 1.1 image courtesy of Richie Rosencrance. Reprinted from McDonough et al. 2024: Figure 2.2.

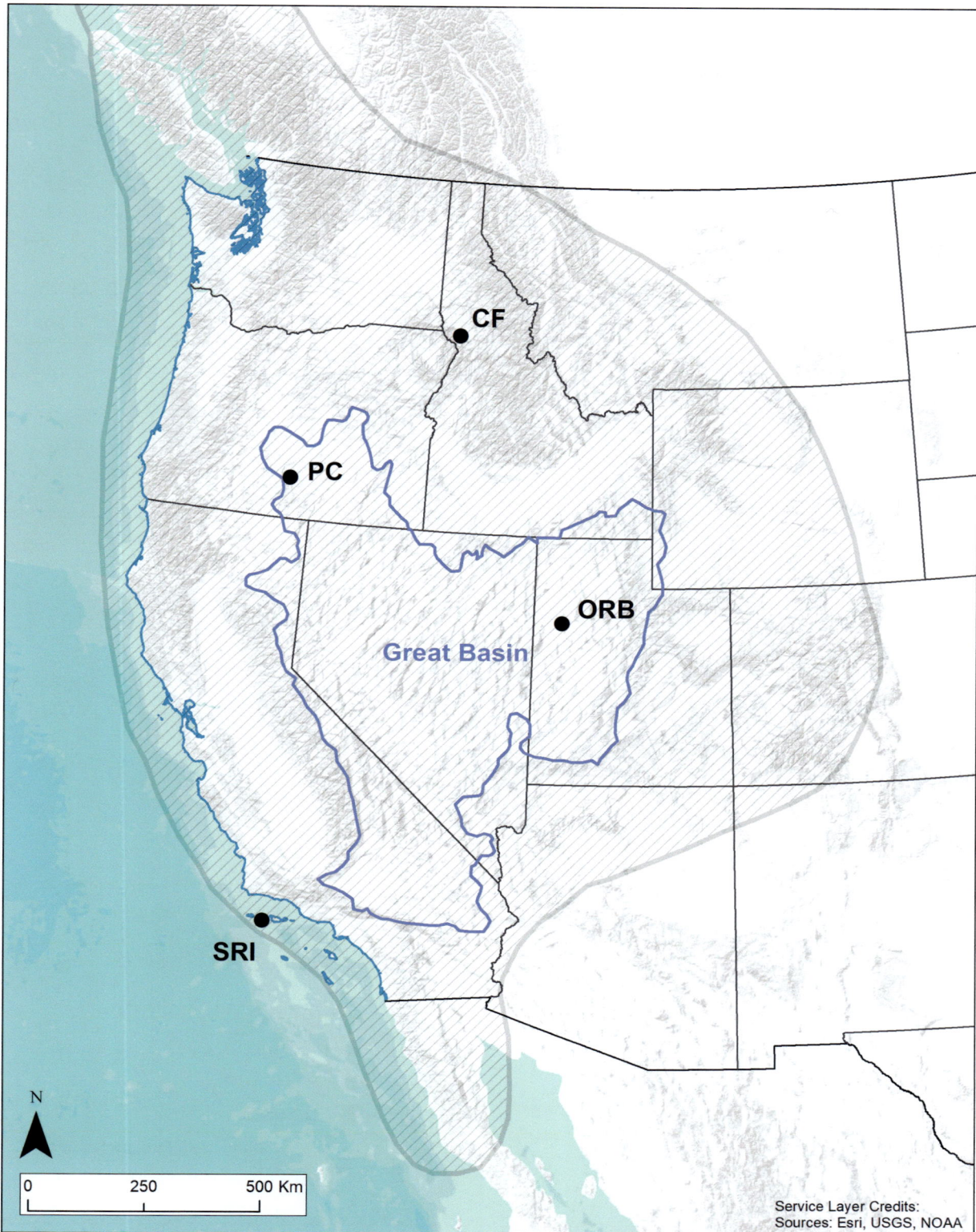

FIGURE 1.2. Distribution of Western Stemmed Tradition (WST) diagnostic tool types (gray hatched region, after Madsen, 2016), mentioned WST sites [CF: Cooper's Ferry; PC: Paisley Caves; SRI: Santa Rosa Island], and the Old River Bed (ORB) delta study area. Light blue outline indicates the hydrographic Great Basin boundary (after Grayson, 2011).

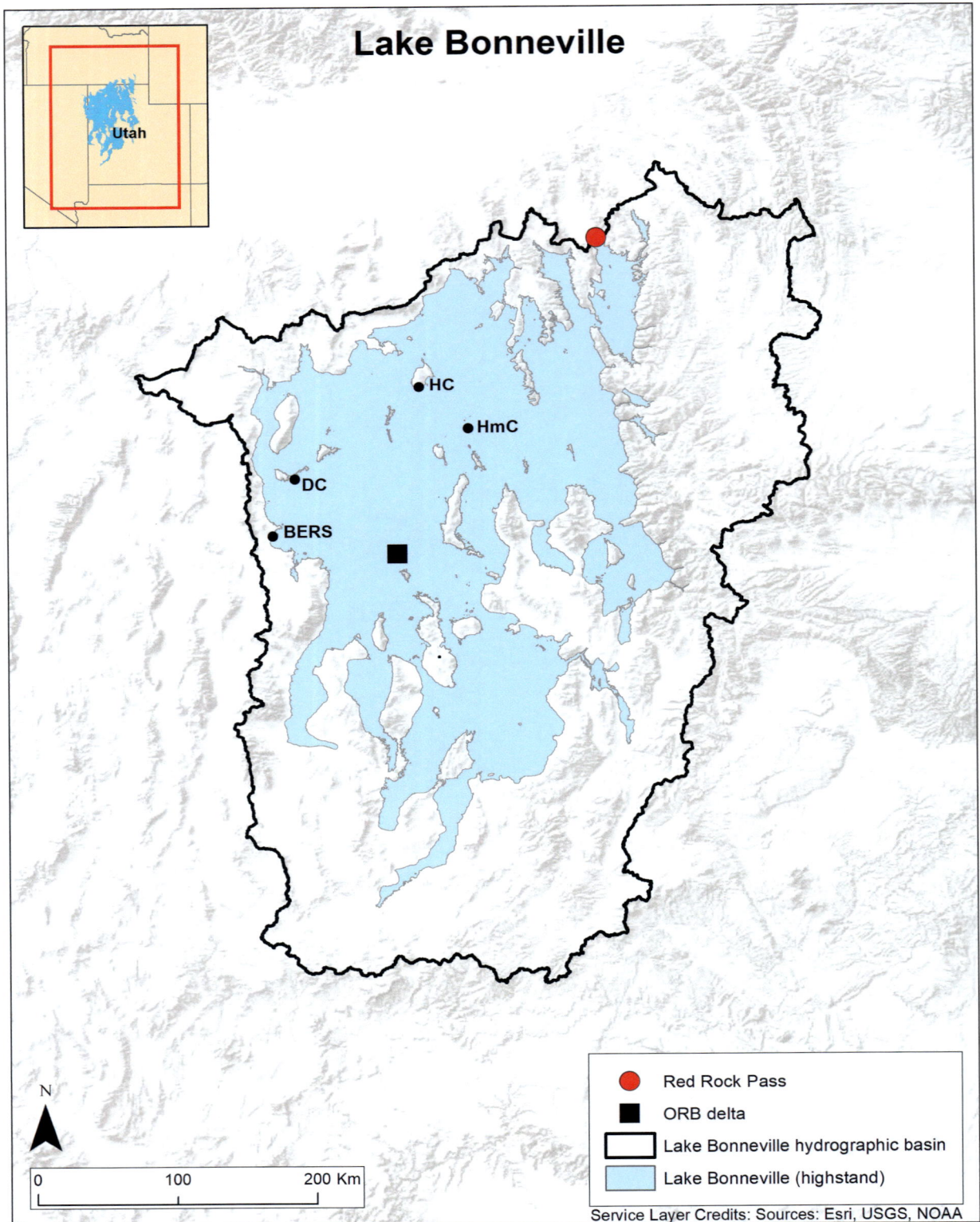

FIGURE 1.3. Lake Bonneville highstand (Chen & Maloof, 2017a) in relation to the Bonneville hydrographic basin and WST-aged occupation sites. Key: BERS: Bonneville Estates Rockshelter; DC: Danger Cave; HC: Hogup Cave; HmC: Homestead Cave.

Basin and the onset of the arid Middle Holocene (Beck & Jones, 1997; Connolly, 1999; Grayson, 2011; Louderback et al., 2011; Smith & Barker, 2017). As a result, we know that the WST spanned a great deal of time, at least ~5,590 cal BP years (~11,630–7,080 ^{14}C yr BP) in and around the Great Basin.

A problem arises in that the majority of Great Basin stemmed point sites are found in the remnants of now-extinct pluvial lake wetlands. All that remains at these former wetland areas are the fine silts and clays of basin bottoms that, once dry, are subject to deflationary erosion as these sediments are stripped from the surface by wind. Heavier objects, such as stone tools and debitage, remain on the surface, often for millennia, resulting in confounding or entirely absent stratigraphic contexts, making absolute dating difficult. As a result, most Great Basin stemmed points have been found at "undated, largely uninformative…surficial sites" (Davis et al., 2012, p. 48; see also Beck & Jones, 1997; Smith and Barker, 2017). Thus, temporally sequencing many individual WST sites and their diagnostic artifacts is currently difficult, often unattainable, and leaves Great Basin archaeologists with few traditional methods for piecing together site chronologies (Beck & Jones, 1997; Goebel & Keene, 2013; Graf, 2007).

We are faced, then, with both a paucity of datable, stratigraphically intact WST sites and an abundance of undatable WST surface sites, usually appearing as lithic scatters spread over large, formerly littoral, areas. These lithic scatters are typically devoid of datable organic artifacts, long destroyed by millennia of exposure to winds and the elements. Nonetheless, these sites provide an opportunity to extract valuable information about potential colonizing events and the earliest occupations in the Great Basin. As a result, archaeologists continually strive to distill additional information about how these earliest peoples, and continental colonizers, interacted with new, previously uninhabited, and unknown landscapes.

LANDSCAPE LEARNING

To help address problems like these, this volume tests a new method for quantifying the level of landscape knowledge represented within a specific archaeological site. It is proposed that this approach, in turn, could then be used to rank archaeological sites in terms of relative occupancy on a given landscape. I do this by exploring the landscape learning theoretical framework, which considers how human colonizers of a new land collectively acquire and share knowledge about their new environment.

Landscape learning is the dynamic cultural process of landscape interaction, adaptation, and knowledge accumulation. It involves the exploration of topography, the discovery of critical resources, and the adoption of new adaptive strategies within a previously unknown region. Landscape learning is often implicitly assumed in the literature but is poorly understood for such a critical behavioral component of the colonization process. As a result, recent models have attempted to qualify the cultural and social components of landscape learning (Fitzhugh, 2004; Meltzer, 2021; Rockman, 2009; Rockman & Steele, 2003). Here I endeavor to go further and to quantify one of the most basic components of such learning. In particular, I attempt to provide quantitative answers to two key questions with regard to toolstone acquisition and learning: "What did they know?" and "When did they know it?" (Mandryk, 2003, p. xiii). If this process can be successfully quantified, perhaps we can then place previously undatable sites in, at least, relative chronological order. The landscape learning model is described more fully in Chapter 2.

METHODOLOGY TESTING

To determine if landscape learning can be detected and quantified across discrete temporal ranges, I use the results of archaeological research at the Old River Bed (ORB) delta in Utah as a testbed (Madsen, Schmitt, et al., 2015). At the ORB delta, hundreds of WST sites and artifacts are strongly associated with individual, chronologically ordered distributaries within an extinct river delta complex. The ORB data affords the opportunity to detect landscape learning within known chronological time slices by analyzing lithic material sourcing, testing the utilization of prominent resources, and investigating what these patterns tell us about the accumulation of landscape knowledge and the colonization process. Importantly, the first appearance of the WST and its temporal span coincide well with the emergence and lifespan of the ORB delta.

Study Region

Lake Bonneville was the largest of the Great Basin pluvial lakes (Figure 1.3), with a depth (~300 m) and a surface area (50,500 km²) rivaling the size of modern-day Lake Michigan (Atwood et al., 2016, p. 19; Currey et al., 1984). Lake Bonneville reached its highstand, ~1552 m above sea level (ASL), around 18,000 cal BP as it topped the lowest edge (the Zenda threshold) of its basin (Oviatt & Shroder, 2016; Shroder et al., 2016, p. 78). While people would eventually occupy the caves and rockshelters created by Lake Bonneville wave erosion (e.g., Bonneville Estates Rockshelter and Danger Cave), there is no evidence of human occupation coincident with the

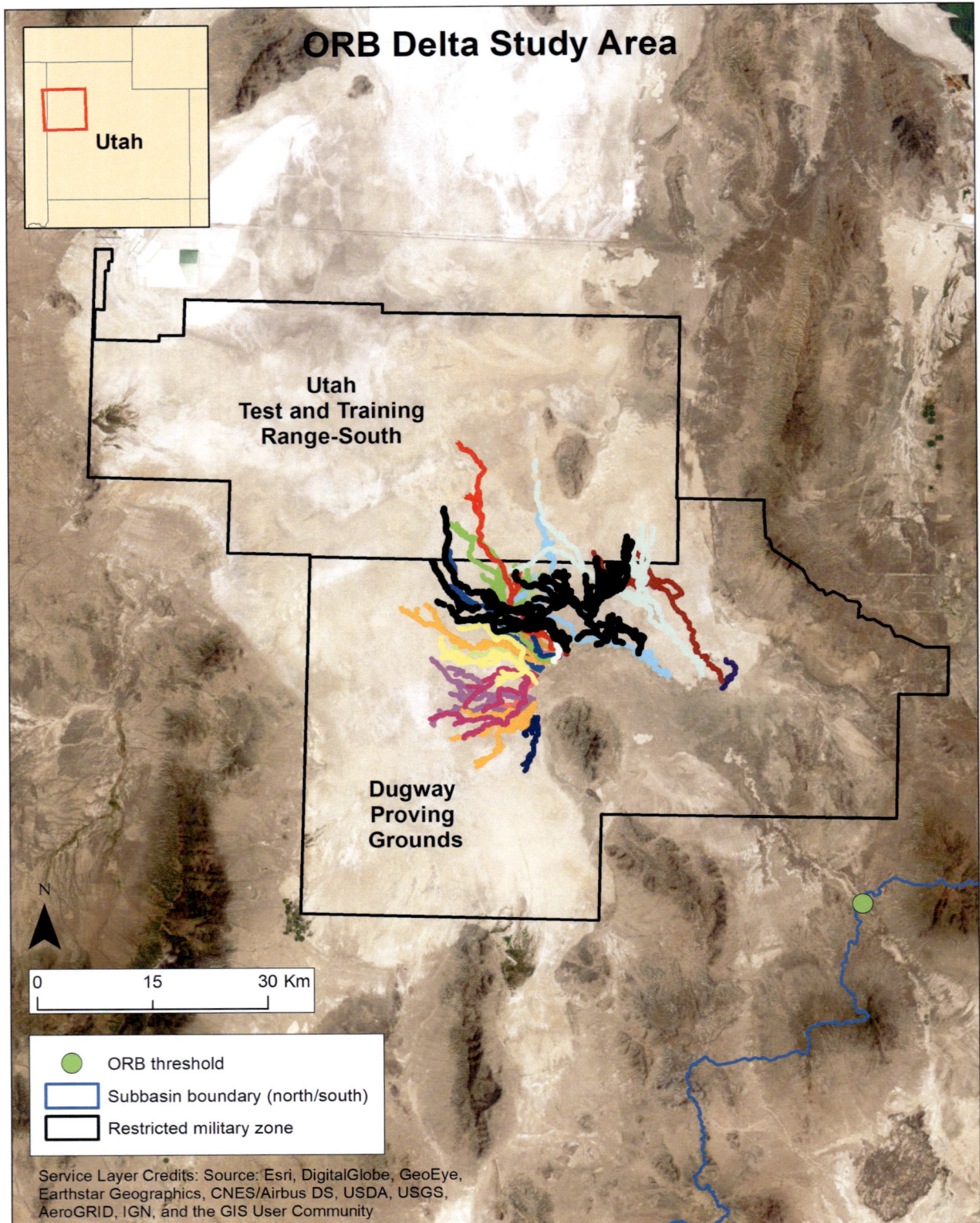

FIGURE 1.4. The Old River Bed (ORB) delta study region today with ORB channels shown according to assigned color name (after Madsen, Schmitt, et al., 2015). See also Appendix A, Tables A.1 and A.2 (https://collections.lib.utah.edu/ark :/87278/s6mntfnx). Channel data by David Page (personal communication, August 22, 2018).

Bonneville shoreline at this level or time (Beck & Jones, 1997; Graf, 2007; Jennings, 1957; Rhode et al., 2005).

Around 18,000 cal BP, the edge of the Bonneville Basin near Red Rock Pass, Idaho, collapsed, resulting in a cataclysmic flood outside the basin and a new shoreline within, the Provo shoreline, 125 m below the Bonneville shoreline (Hart et al., 2004; Oviatt & Shroder, 2016; Shroder et al., 2016). This shoreline fluctuated around 1450 m ASL for about 3,000 years. Between 15,000 and 13,000 cal BP, evaporation outpaced lake input and the lake level fell an additional 200 m. During this regression and around 14,000 cal BP (~12,000 ^{14}C yr BP), as the lake dropped below ~1,390 m ASL, the northern subbasin was cut off from the southern subbasin (Hart et al., 2004; Oviatt & Shroder, 2016). The last remaining connection between the northern and southern subbasins was a point of overflow at the Old River Bed threshold (Figure 1.4). Lake Bonneville continued its regression, arriving at elevations similar to modern-day Great Salt Lake levels (~1280 m ASL) around 13,000 cal BP (Oviatt & Shroder, 2016). This change is coincident with the timing of the first signs of human occupation in the basin. At Bonneville Estates Rockshelter (Figure 1.3), the earliest unequivocal human occupation is dated to ~13,000 cal BP (11,010 ^{14}C yr BP), with a WST occupation evident from ~12,800–12,000 cal BP (10,800–10,300 ^{14}C yr BP; Graf, 2007; Hockett, 2015; Rhode et al., 2005).

Following the separation of the northern and southern subbasins, a fanlike series of river distributaries formed, that meandered across the dried lake sediments of the northern subbasin (the Great Salt Lake basin) as the higher (~100 m) southern subbasin (the Sevier basin) drained to lower elevations (Madsen, 2016; Madsen, Schmitt, et al., 2015). The resultant Old River Bed delta, termed the ORB delta (Figure 1.4), created a new wetland environment coinciding with both the timing of the earliest inhabitations of the Great Basin and the appearance of the WST. Over the course of about 3,600 cal years (~11,500–8,800 ^{14}C yr BP), various distributaries formed and went extinct, creating a datable sequence of riverine habitats (Madsen, Schmitt, et al., 2015). Once the Sevier basin finally dried, the drainage ceased, people moved away, and the region has remained dry until present, placing the extinct delta into a sort of stasis. This stasis was protected and aided in the mid-twentieth century when the region was incorporated into the U.S. Army Dugway Proving Ground and the Utah Test and Training Range—South, restricted military zones for testing modern weapons that have effectively protected the delta's archaeological resources from development and illicit artifact collection.

WST in the ORB

Madsen (2016) and other researchers (Clark et al., 2016; Duke & Young, 2007; Madsen, Schmitt, et al., 2015; Oviatt et al., 2003; Page, 2008, 2015a, 2015b; Page & Duke, 2015; Rhode et al., 2005; Schmitt et al., 2007; Skinner, 2021) have studied the ORB delta's geomorphological origins and have surveyed, collected, and analyzed the archaeological remains found along its individual distributaries. Madsen, Schmitt, et al. (2015) documented 23 individual distributaries (color-coded in Figure 1.4; see Table A.1) and over 230 WST sites within the ORB delta. Ten of these distributaries have been reliably radiocarbon-dated through analysis of organic sediments, plant remains, or mollusk shells indicative of wetland environments, and are associated with Paleoindian sites, predominantly WST projectile point types (see Appendix A). A few Archaic era projectile point forms appear in the overall dataset, but these are generally considered to be intrusive objects that were deposited after the wetlands had dried (Beck & Jones, 2015). The extinction of the wetlands around ~9,800 cal BP (8,800 ^{14}C yr BP) ensured the WST record along the distributary channels was not significantly overlain by later human groups. As few charcoal or organic materials were recovered from the ORB delta archaeological sites, all site ages are relative estimates derived from the associated distributary dates, beginning around ~13,000 cal BP (11,300 ^{14}C yr BP; Madsen, Oviatt, et al., 2015).

Individual sites have been classified according to the distributary channel to which they belong, and according to whether they are on the channel margin or within the channel itself (Madsen et al., 2015). Sites on the margins are considered contemporaneous with the flow of the river, situated to exploit channel resources when it flowed, while sites within the channel are assumed to postdate the time the channel flowed. The majority of these artifacts (n = 2,288, but see Appendix A) fall within the broader WST typology and were classified to specific tool type (Beck & Jones, 2015; Charlotte Beck, personal communication, May 31, 2018).

The majority of the ORB delta artifacts are composed of obsidian or fine-grained volcanic (FGV) material that have been geochemically identified to regional lithic sources (Page, 2015a). Figure 1.5 presents the general locations of the 16 known lithic sources utilized during the WST occupation of the ORB delta (see Table A.42). Chapters 3 and 4 explore resource extents for these sources. As noted above, the overall study area covers roughly 284,000 km² using the lithic source points in Figure 1.5 to form a polygon, about twice the area that Tolan-Smith (2003) argues could have

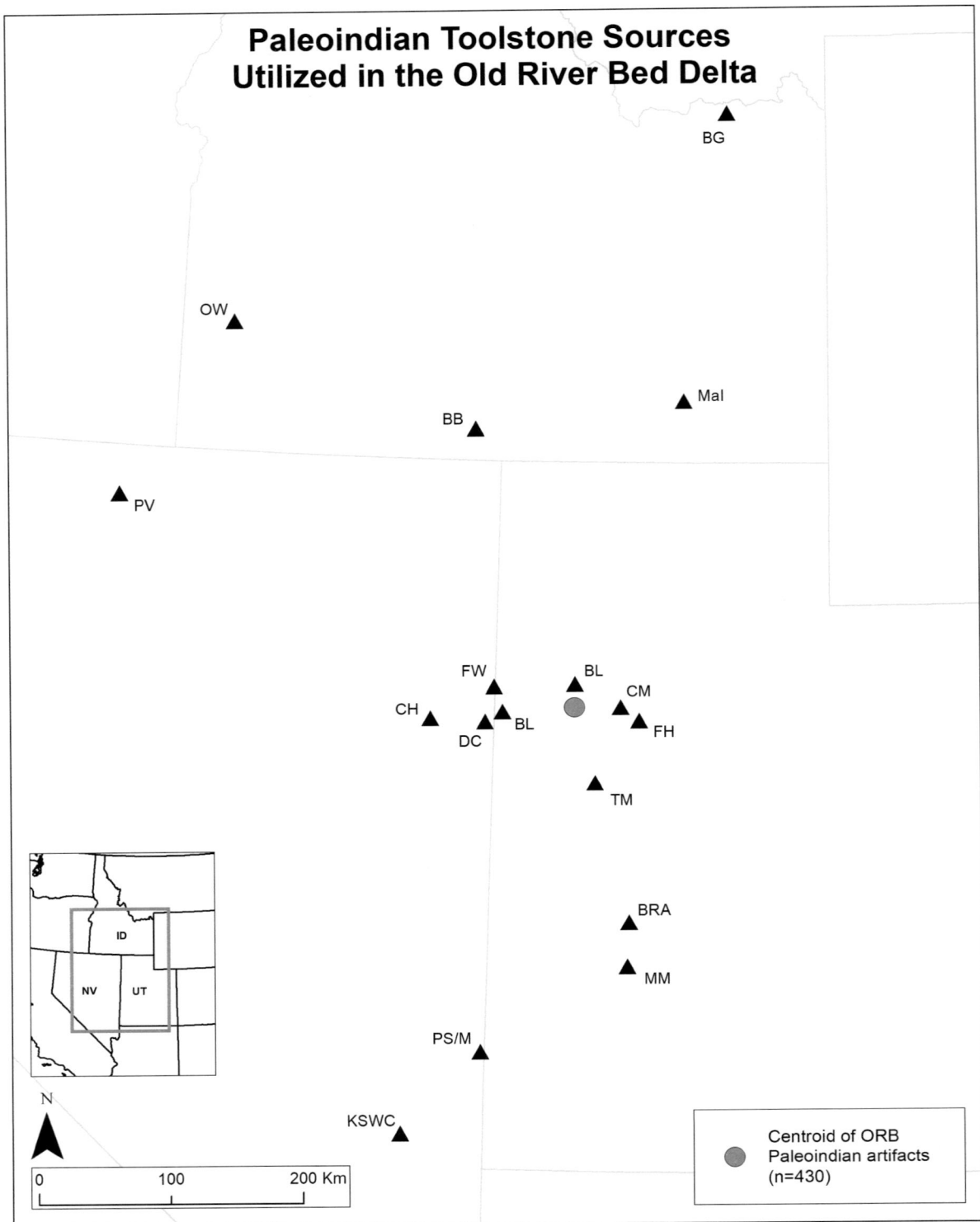

FIGURE 1.5. Rough locations of obsidian and fine-grained volcanic (FGV) toolstone sources utilized by Paleoindian people occupying the Old River Bed delta channels. Key: Badlands (BL), Brown's Bench (BB), Bear Gulch (BG), Black Rock Area (BRA), Currie Hills (CH), Cedar Mountain (CM), Deep Creek (DC), Ferguson Wash (FW), Flat Hills (FH), Kane Springs Wash Caldera (KSWC), Malad (Mal), Mineral Mountains (MM), Owyhee (OW), Panaca Summit/Modena (PS/M), Paradise Valley (PV), Topaz Mountain (TM) (Skinner 2021, see Appendix D, Table D.2, https://collections.lib .utah.edu/ark:/87278/s6mntfnx).

required one to two millennia to fully learn (see Chapter 2). The relationship between these artifacts and their lithic sources are well-defined and key to the potential success of my methodologies.

Importantly, the association of multiple sites with each of the ten dated channels provides the means to create pooled assemblages with significant temporal distinction. While the artifact counts for many sites are small (*mean* = 15.5), the expectation that sites within the same temporal period will exhibit the same level of landscape familiarization can be leveraged here. By pooling artifacts associated with each dated channel, statistically valid sample groups can be created for comparison across discrete date ranges.

Finally, the WST archaeological data from the ORB delta allows me to test landscape learning in the context of a colonizing event as the delta essentially emerged as "new land" with the recession of Lake Bonneville and the formation of an extensive wetland in the ORB delta. The results in Madsen, Oviat, and Young (2015) support this view as two of the earliest channels (Mocha and Manga, undated but underlying Gold) have no known sites and the Gold channel, which first appeared around ~13,200 cal BP (11,300 ^{14}C yr BP), presents only two WST sites. As younger channels emerge, the number of sites and their density increases, especially beginning with the large Black channel around ~12,900 cal BP (spanning ~11,000–10,300 ^{14}C yr BP), and the archaeological record reflects continuous habitation throughout the remaining lifecycle of the delta (Madsen, Oviatt, et al. 2015:43).

BOOK STRUCTURE

The research presented in this volume explores the landscape learning model and describes original methodologies designed to measure the accumulation of landscape knowledge. I attempt to answer the following question:

Can landscape learning be detected in the archaeological record and then be used to place assemblages in relative chronological order?

In Chapter 2, I explain the landscape learning theoretical framework, the opportunity it provides to archaeologists working with surface sites, and how we may be able to use it to measure what people knew and when they knew it as they explored unknown landscapes.

In Chapter 3, I define the Discoverability equation, a measure of prominence, and argue that lithic resource discovery can be modeled using the Discoverability equation. This model expands on Brantingham's (2003, p. 487; 2006) "neutral model of stone raw material procurement," demonstrating that resource size on the landscape increases encounter rate. The methods in this chapter provide a theoretical means to quantify the likelihood of an encounter with a lithic resource patch in a neutral model, a value that can act as a baseline measure. I also describe methods to then compare observed values against this expected baseline and to track change in landscape learning over time.

While most of the lithic resources utilized in the ORB delta are known, at least in general locational terms, we do not currently know their geological extent. We do not know the actual exposure size of these resources which, because of alluvial and colluvial action, can manifest as extensive (hundreds of square kilometers) secondary extents. Chapter 4 describes original methods for predicting these extents, demonstrates the predictions for five sources utilized at the ORB delta, reports on the actual extents observed during three seasons of survey, and calculates the effectiveness of these prediction methods.

Chapter 5 predicts the exposure values for the remaining ORB delta lithic resources, based on the success of Chapter 4. Combined, the surveyed and predicted extents from Chapters 4 and 5 provide the distance (d) and exposure (E) variables for calculating the Discoverability results in Chapter 6.

Chapter 6 examines the early archaeology of the ORB within the context of the landscape learning model developed here. The goal of this examination is to determine whether that model has the potential of placing undated lithic assemblages created by human foragers entering a novel landscape into relative chronological order.

Appendices (https://collections.lib.utah.edu/ark:/87278/s6mntfnx): Appendix A explains the cleaning, merging, and filtering of several ORB delta data sources. The result of this work is a subset of Paleoindian artifacts for testing. Additional appendices represent supporting data tables and X-ray fluorescence (XRF) lab reports following field sampling.

Note: Where radiocarbon dates are presented from previously published literature, calibrated calendar dates have been calculated for uniformity. These dates were calculated using OxCal 4.4.4 (Bronk Ramsey, 2021; Reimer et al., 2020).

2

Theoretical Framework
The Landscape Learning Model

While learning the lay of the land is critical to the success of any foraging group entering a novel landscape, the processes by which foragers familiarize themselves with, and adapt to, a new landscape are not well-understood (Anthony, 1997; Beaton, 1991; Kelly, 2003a; Kelly & Todd, 1988; Meltzer, 2002; Rockman & Steele, 2003). Understanding these processes is particularly challenging today because all historically known hunter-gatherers have long resided in their homelands (Meltzer, 2002, 2003). There are, however, four generalized expectations about what these initial colonization processes may have looked like:

1. Environmental knowledge is acquired cumulatively, building a shared community knowledge base over time, but environmental factors, such as unpredictable patchy resources or difficult terrain, may variably affect the speed and breadth of this knowledge accumulation (Golledge, 2003; Meltzer, 2002; Rockman, 2003, 2013; Roebroeks, 2003).

2. Colonizers act to mitigate risk as they enter unknown lands. For example, colonizers are expected to carry with them critically needed material from known territories, until new, reliable sources are found. In contexts where trade is an unlikely factor, the presence of "exotic" material, such as nonlocal toolstone, in an archaeological assemblage is expected to signal the earliest forays into new land (Fitzhugh, 2004; Kelly & Todd, 1988; Rockman, 2003).

3. Over time, as a natural result of rising landscape knowledge, archaeological assemblages will increasingly exhibit the use of local materials as environ-mental familiarization grows (Fitzhugh, 2004; Mandryk, 2003; Meltzer, 2002).

4. Finally, regional archaeological sites within the same temporal period are expected to exhibit the same level of landscape familiarization, reflecting the aggregation of individual knowledge, through social interaction, into the community knowledge base (Kelly, 2003b; Meltzer, 2003; Rockman, 2003, 2013; Tolan-Smith, 2003).

These expectations are codified into the landscape learning model, a model principally advanced by Rockman (Rockman, 2009, 2013; Rockman & Steele, 2003). Within this model, Rockman defines environmental knowledge in three basic forms: locational, limitational, and social. Locational knowledge involves understanding the topography of the land and the location of resources on that topography. Locational knowledge is considered the easiest and fastest form of landscape knowledge to acquire and is biased towards prominent landmarks and large, fixed, nonorganic resources such as lithic sources (Kelly, 2003a; Rockman, 2003). This study focuses on such fixed, inorganic resources which only needed to be learned once by a community. While people colonizing a new territory likely would initially focus on learning the locations of reliable food patches (both plant and animal), these patches would also be highly variable (seasonal and mobile). In the Great Basin, the locations of food patches probably also have changed significantly between the Pleistocene and today, and understanding these patch locations may no longer be possible, while fixed lithic sources remain to this day. Modelling the landscape learning of fixed resources provides the added benefit of determining the baseline, or minimum, amount of time needed to learn that landscape.

However, not all resource patches are immediately evident to migrants, and it takes time and experience to accumulate detailed landscape knowledge at increasingly finer geographic scales (Meltzer, 2003). Limitational knowledge involves an understanding of the "usefulness and reliability" (Rockman, 2003, p. 5) of the resources at hand. These limitational parameters include issues of boundaries (both physical and social), seasonality and climate, and an overall economic familiarity (e.g., toolstone quality) with the landscape. Social knowledge involves the transmission of this knowledge, both horizontally (within the group and with external groups) and vertically (between generations), that allows the group as a whole to reduce risk and adapt to the new environment (Rockman, 2009). In this volume, I focus primarily on Rockman's locational knowledge as an indicator of landscape knowledge in general, and specifically as a potential gauge of the length of human residence on the landscape.

Landmark prominence is a key factor in the acquisition of locational knowledge. While Rockman does not define *prominence* directly, topographical prominence can be defined as an example of a "landscape affordance" (Llobera, 2001, p. 1007) or as the means by "which the environment lends or offers itself for action" (Kirchhoff, 2009, p. 5). Prominence affects the detection of a resource, and over time, changes in the detection and utilization of resources reflect processes of social change on that landscape (Llobera, 2001). This perspective, in turn, allows us to link increasing affordance detection (i.e., increasing local resource knowledge and use) with increasing social knowledge, and thus gauge the overall socialization and landscape learning process occurring on the landscape. Importantly, the detection and utilization of these affordances by people is reflected in their material culture and the resultant archaeological record.

For the purposes of this research, prominence will be expressed as a function of the surface exposure of a lithic resource on the landscape (see Chapter 4 for a complete definition of "exposure"). During the locational phase of landscape learning, the model expects that the most prominent, or "most detectable," resources will be discovered in rank-order and utilized in corresponding proportions. For newcomers, who lack the benefits of time on the landscape and local social networks, less prominent (i.e., less exposed and less dis-

coverable) resources are expected to be overlooked. As a result, we can expect that lithic assemblages produced by these earliest colonizers will reflect a high bias towards the most easily discovered lithic sources and correspondingly low spatial organization and efficiency (Kelly, 1995). This bias should decrease, and spatial optimization increase, as landscape learning increases, eventually peaking at "complete" landscape learning which, for the purposes of this study, is represented by the complete knowledge of the lithic source landscape.

Principles of the landscape learning model have found utility in evaluating the process of landscape familiarization or socialization by immigrants, specifically with regard to lithic sources (Fitzhugh, 2004; Fitzhugh & Trusler, 2009; Rockman, 2009; Ford, 2011; but see also Kitchel, 2018). Fitzhugh (2004) focuses on a phase of the colonization process referred to as "regionalization" (after the colonization stages outlined in Spiess et al. [1998]: pioneering, migration, regionalization), a period characterized by increasing local resource familiarization and decreasing dependence on resources from the migrants' home range (e.g., exotic toolstone). While the initial pioneering and migration forays into a region may remain archaeologically invisible, due to scarcity and initial low populations, the stages of regionalization occur across a broad continuum, from an early "settling in" (Fitzhugh, 2004, p. 14) period, where environmental knowledge is low and uncertainty high, to late stages marked by deep knowledge of the region, including its relevant resources and their specific qualities. Regionalization can then be expressed in terms of increasing certainty in, and knowledge of, the terrain and in the optimization and utilization of local resources over homeland resources. As settling in advances, migrants increasingly replace exotic, previously trusted resources with suitable, readily available, and efficiently acquired local substitutes.

This research specifically centers on developing methodologies to detect and quantify changes in locational knowledge over time, measured by the utilization of prominent resources. Following the landscape learning model, if assemblages were created within distinct temporal periods, I expect to see lithic resource knowledge within those periods act as a "proxy measure of landscape knowledge" (Kitchel, 2018, p. 871), increasing over time. Successfully utilizing this model requires a method to consistently measure lithic resource knowledge within a given archaeological assemblage and another method to then compare these values between assemblages, methods which are proposed and tested here. This approach is dependent on a means to set a neutral "baseline" (Fitzhugh, 2004, p. 14) against which to compare regional landscape knowledge as it is acquired over time. The methods to establish this baseline, to measure lithic resource knowledge within a specific assemblage, and to then compare landscape learning levels over time, are the subject of Chapter 3.

However, significant questions of temporal and spatial scale are not well addressed within the landscape learning model. The issue of scale is largely untested within this model and represents a significant and problematic variable. How quickly do people learn a landscape and how broadly? Ford (2011) attempted to use the landscape learning model within the context of the occupation of the Ivane Valley of New Guinea between 43,000–49,000 cal BP but demonstrated what archaeologically appears as an almost instantaneous adaptation to local toolstone. In this case, the Ivane Valley likely is too small (<50 km^2) to detect landscape learning archaeologically within the large temporal span (~6000 years) examined. In contrast, Tolan-Smith (2003) suggests that, following a 7000-year abandonment during the last ice age, the landscape of England (~130,000 km^2, Kellner 2022) was relearned and that landscape learning may be visible on scales of several millennia. England is roughly half the size of my study region (~284,000 km^2, see "WST in the ORB," Chapter 1) and Tolan-Smith's example may provide a useful guide to gauge spatial and temporal scale expectations.

If successful, applying these methods may yield otherwise inaccessible information about how people behave and adapt as they encounter unknown lands for the first time. They may specifically reveal information about the rate of landscape knowledge acquisition and provide a means to compare the levels of landscape learning between assemblages. Most importantly, comparing the levels of landscape lithic resource knowledge across assemblages may provide a means to place otherwise undatable lithic assemblages into relative chronological order.

3   The Discoverability Model

Building models from first principles is a critical step in any research program aimed at understanding such complex spatio-temporal processes as foraging movements.
(Turchin, 2006, p. 453)

INTRODUCTION

Operationalizing the landscape learning theoretical framework requires the creation of two original methodologies. The first involves quantifying the prominence, or what I will call "discoverability," of patchy resources in terms of the locational attributes of surface exposure and distance. As will be shown, the discoverability value represents the likelihood of a random walker, with no landscape knowledge, encountering a resource patch. These values will be used as a means for setting a "neutral" baseline against which to compare landscape learning over time. The second methodology provides a means to quantify levels of landscape learning for an assemblage in order to compare that assemblage, and other assemblages, to the baseline.

All examples shown or described in this chapter are available in the form of Python code/programs or Jupyter Notebooks located on a GitHub repository. See "Repository and Software" at the end of this chapter for online access.

DEFINING PROMINENCE/DISCOVERABILITY

Brantingham (2003) created a "neutral model" computer simulation for modeling how an unbiased agent, moving via a simple (or Brownian) random walk on an unbiased landscape would accumulate lithic material in its toolkit, as a proxy for understanding assemblage formation. The goal of the model was to help understand what natural, probabilistic patterns of lithic acquisition could be expected when the agent "does not seek to optimize any specific currency" (p. 492). In this way, the neutral model creates a baseline acquisition pattern, devoid of human adaptive behaviors. With such a baseline, variation from that baseline can then be used to provide insight into human adaptations to the landscape.

Brantingham (2003; see also Tobler, 1970) demonstrated that as the distance of a lithic source from the starting point of a search (the central place or home site) increases, the proportion of that specific raw material observed in the final assemblage decreases exponentially, an example of the distance decay effect (Equation 3.1):

$$\frac{1}{d^2} \qquad\qquad (Eq.\ 3.1)$$

This factor is useful for calculating how patches at varying distances from a central point may be encountered in varying rates. Further, it is proposed here that Brantingham's neutral model can be expanded by biasing, or modulating, an additional environmental variable, the size of the target (e.g., a lithic source/patch), without negatively affecting the overall neutral nature of Brantingham's original model.

Natural lithic sources vary greatly in size and are not uniformly distributed on the landscape. Obsidian sources in the Great Basin, for example, may be concentrated in dense flows or scattered as nodules in vast fields spread by explosive volcanic action. Defining a patch can be problematic because lithic sources may be spread out widely or the same flow may be exposed in multiple locations. Obsidian is also subject to colluvial and alluvial action, potentially creating enormous secondary distributions as erosion moves obsidian cobbles and pebbles downslope. Along the shores of Pleistocene Great Basin lakes, tertiary distribution may have further moved obsidian pebbles laterally as the secondary distributions were tumbled by wave action. The result of these natural forces is that, for many Great Basin obsidian sources, the full distribution extent may be spread across hundreds of square kilometers of exposure.

I propose that this *exposure* (E), the entire exposed surface distribution area of a lithic source, plays a key role in the discoverability of that source by mobile foragers. Even if the erosional distributions consist of pebbles too small to make tools, the presence of these distributions would have acted as a "signal" to alert hunter-gatherers that crucial toolstone resources were close at hand. Ethnographic studies report that hunter-gatherers are astute students of their environment, valuing environmental knowledge and attention to even the most subtle changes in the terrain and its appearance (Blurton Jones & Konner, 1976; Foster & Foster, 2000; Kelly, 1995). Hunter-gatherers would have quickly noticed the appearance of these distinctive sediments as they foraged and could easily follow them uphill to their sources (Meltzer, 2003). Original methods to predict the areal estimation of these exposures are detailed in Chapters 4 and 5.

The size of a source's exposure and its distance from a site will affect the probability of its detection—its *discoverability*—by a walker on an unlearned landscape. It follows that the sources that have been discovered will also affect the resultant compositions of hunter-gatherer lithic assemblages. The discoverability (D) of a lithic source is then expressed in terms of exposure (E) and distance (d) relative to a site/assemblage. In its simplest terms, this can be expressed as shown in Equation 3.2:

$$D = E * \frac{1}{d^2} \qquad \text{(Eq. 3.2)}$$

I propose that for any given site (or assemblage) in an otherwise neutral landscape, if one knows: (a) all the lithic toolstone sources in the region (the lithic universe), (b) the distances between the site and those sources, and (c) the exposure areas of the sources, the site's *expected* lithic assemblage composition can be calculated. This site-specific baseline is referred to as the *discoverability list* (or *Dlist*). This baseline represents

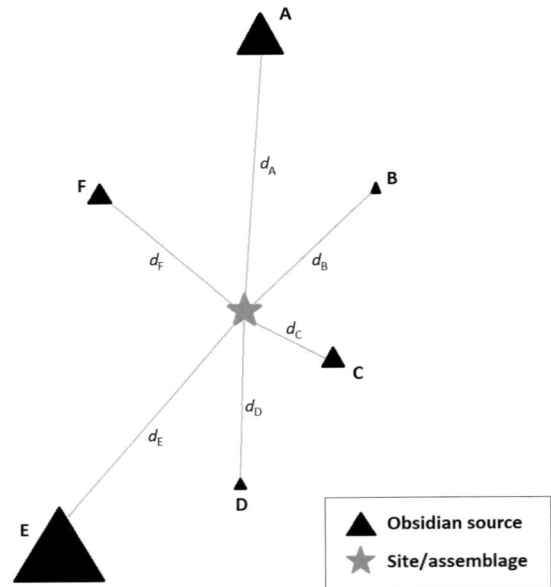

FIGURE 3.1. Illustration of the relationship between source exposures and distances relative to a given site/assemblage.

the resource proportions we would expect a random walker from a central place to encounter and accumulate on a wholly unlearned landscape, a "coming into the country" state of discoverability (Kelly & Todd, 1988).

The first step is calculating the discoverability value (Equation 3.2) for each source using the distances relative to a specific site. Figure 3.1 illustrates the relationship of six sources (A–F) to a single site/assemblage. The sources vary in size (exposure) and distances from the site.

From these values, the site's discoverability rank-order list (the *Dlist*) is created—the normalized, ranked list of lithic source proportions one would expect to find in a site assemblage in a neutral model. Table 3.1 demonstrates the calculation of the discoverability values and normalized proportions for the site in Figure 3.1.

Table 3.2 illustrates the expected lithic source proportions—a *Dlist*—based on the ranking of the normalized discoverability values.

The *Dlist* will, of course, vary from site to site, as the distances to sources will vary and affect the calculated discoverability value. Figure 3.2 illustrates how the distances vary for each of three sites operating within the same lithic universe of six sources.

Contrasting with this metric are the actual "observed" proportions of lithic material from a site. These proportions are known from the archaeological record, normalized to 100 percent, and make up the *observed list (Olist)*. The expected distribution (*Dlist*) can then be compared

TABLE 3.1. Calculation of the Discoverability (*D*) Values and Normalized Proportions.

Lithic Universe	*d* (km)	$\frac{1}{d^2}$	*E* (km²)	*D*	Normalized Proportions (100*D/∑D)
Source A	100	0.0001	14	0.0014	4.3%
Source B	50	0.0004	0.5	0.0002	0.6%
Source C	20	0.0025	7	0.0175	53.4%
Source D	75	0.00018	2	0.0004	1.1%
Source E	125	0.000064	100	0.0064	19.5%
Source F	60	0.00028	25	0.0069	21.2%
				0.0328	

TABLE 3.2. The Rank-Order Discoverability List, or *Dlist*.

Source	Expected Proportions (*Dlist*) (100*D/∑D)	Rank
Source C	53.4%	1
Source F	21.2%	2
Source E	19.5%	3
Source A	4.3%	4
Source D	1.1%	5
Source B	0.6%	6

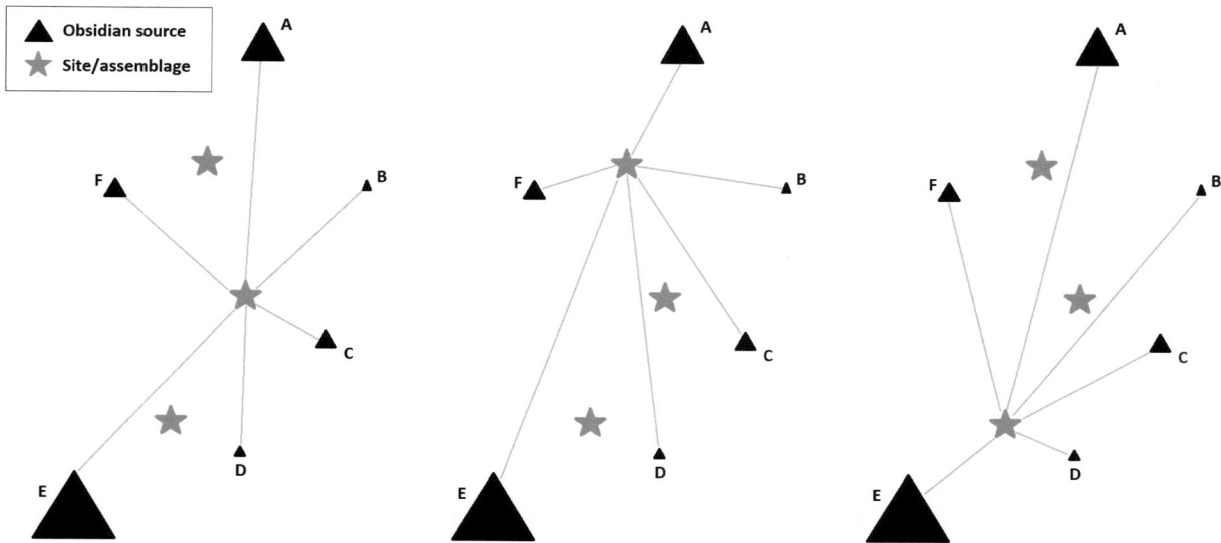

FIGURE 3.2. The *Dlist* for each site is dependent on the relative distances to all lithic sources. This illustration demonstrates the variable distances of regional sources from each of three sites.

statistically to the actual raw material rank-order (*Olist*) of an assemblage. The greater the correlation between the lists, the closer procurement/assemblage creation comes to a random walk on the landscape. Lack of significant correlation with the discoverability rank order list (*Dlist*), then, is behavioral adaptation to the landscape; in this argument such variance represents landscape learning.

ESTIMATING RELATIVE REGIONALIZATION LEVELS

Under this model, I expect to observe a continuum of learning over time and propose that this continuum can be detected. Colonizers will initially utilize easily discoverable lithic resources while potentially retaining exotic (nonlocal) toolstone in their toolkit to reduce risk and uncertainty. During this early phase, their choices should most closely match the baseline, the *Dlist*. As "settling-in" progresses (Fitzhugh, 2004), less discover-

able, but equally usable, patches will be discovered and incorporated into the universe of known lithic sources (this assumption is discussed below). With expanding knowledge, people will have the opportunity to make travel optimization choices when procuring lithic raw material (Beck et al., 2002). As efficiency decisions are made, I expect to observe more sources with lower discoverability values appearing in an assemblage. As regionalization is carried to completion, all available sources will be discovered. As a result, late-stage regionalization should be characterized by assemblages that reflect maximum optimization of less discoverable sources and these "well-settled" sites should exhibit the greatest variation from the baseline (the *Dlist*).

Two confounding issues must be addressed. First, when any two human groups meet on the landscape, issues of territoriality must be considered (Dyson-Hudson & Smith, 1978; Kelly, 1995; Speth et al., 2013). Where present in the Great Basin, obsidian is generally quite abundant (though see Ferguson Wash in Chapter 4 for a notable exception). Dyson-Hudson and Smith observe that if a resource is "so abundant" on the landscape that availability is assured, "then there is no benefit to be gained by its defense and territoriality is not expected to occur" (p. 25). Similarly, in this study, lithic source quality is considered neutral. Beck and Jones (1990, 1997) find that obsidian and fine-grained volcanics (FGV), such as andesite and dacite, appear to have been used interchangeably and as acceptable alternatives when the need arises. This model will operate under these assumptions as regards these resources, but I recognize that all known lithic resources are highly unlikely to be considered equal in terms of quality. In the case of the Old River Bed (ORB) data used in this study, where the available data represents the toolstone people did, in fact, use, poor quality toolstone is self-excluding. Similarly, available material/cobble size is an interesting variable for which we have little data, requiring that this model operates under the assumption that adequate material size is available from all sources. This will become clear in subsequent chapters.

If these expectations and assumptions hold true, then I propose that the "extent" of landscape learning (LL) for an assemblage can be quantified on a scale from 0 to 100% (%LL). The higher the percentage, the greater the extent of landscape learning possessed by the people living there and the greater their residential time on the landscape. This analysis will allow sites to be ordered from lowest %LL to highest %LL, a ranking that should correspond to sites increasingly younger in age. Multiple sites could then be evaluated to gauge the extent of landscape learning and place them in relative chronological order. For this project, the variance from the *Dlist* represents landscape learning, so %LL can be represented by Equation 3.3. Here r_s^2 is the *coefficient of correlation* and the value $(1 - r_s^2)$ is also known as the *coefficient of nondetermination* (Zar, 2010, p. 364), appropriate for gauging the variance from a deterministically derived baseline:

$$\%LL = (1 - r_s^2) * 100 \quad \text{(Eq. 3.3)}$$

Table 3.3 presents a fictional example for the calculation of %LL for the site illustrated in Figure 3.1.

HYPOTHESES AND EXPECTATIONS

The discoverability model allows for several straightforward hypotheses and anticipates the following results:

If colonizing groups entered a new land with little regional experience:

TABLE 3.3. Calculation of %LL.

Source	Expected Proportions (*Dlist*)	Rank	Actual Proportions (*Olist*)	Rank
Source C	53.4%	1	45%	1
Source F	21.2%	2	0%	5.5
Source E	19.5%	3	35%	2
Source A	4.3%	4	10%	4
Source D	1.1%	5	20%	3
Source B	0.6%	6	0%	5.5

Spearman's rank-order correlation (*Dlist/Olist*), r_s:	0.493
Coefficient of correlation (r_s^2):	0.243
%LL = $(1 - r_s^2) * 100\%$:	75.7%

1. For the oldest sites/assemblages, the *Olist* will conform/correlate most closely with its *Dlist*, indicating a more deterministic utilization of the landscape, exhibiting greater exploitation of highly discoverable resources, and less-optimized spatial efficiency.
2. For increasingly younger sites/assemblages, there will be decreasing conformity/correlation between their *Olists* and *Dlists* as landscape learning increases and as factors other than discoverability (e.g., travel optimization) affect toolstone selection.
3. The youngest sites/assemblages will exhibit the lowest conformity/correlation between its *Olists* and *Dlists*, and source discoverability will not factor highly into source selection.
4. Exotic or unknown material (or remote outliers) within the oldest sites/assemblages may occur, consistent with an early regionalization stage. Similarly, if a study region does not reflect a colonizing event, I expect the oldest and youngest sites/assemblages will display a similar lack of correlation between the *Olists* and *Dlists*, indicating that people were familiar with the landscape prior to the occupation of the region, as a result of preexisting shared knowledge and expansive landscape learning. In the opposite way, if all assemblages, across temporal periods, indicate similar correlations between their *Olists* and *Dlists*, landscape learning may take much longer than previously understood.

Of course, the possibility exists that the model described herein is simply flawed and too simplistic to adequately model the confounding behavior of people on a landscape. Specifically, if all assemblages show high correlation between the *Dlist* and *Olist*, the model may simply not properly detect landscape learning, and the model and its assumptions will need to be reexamined.

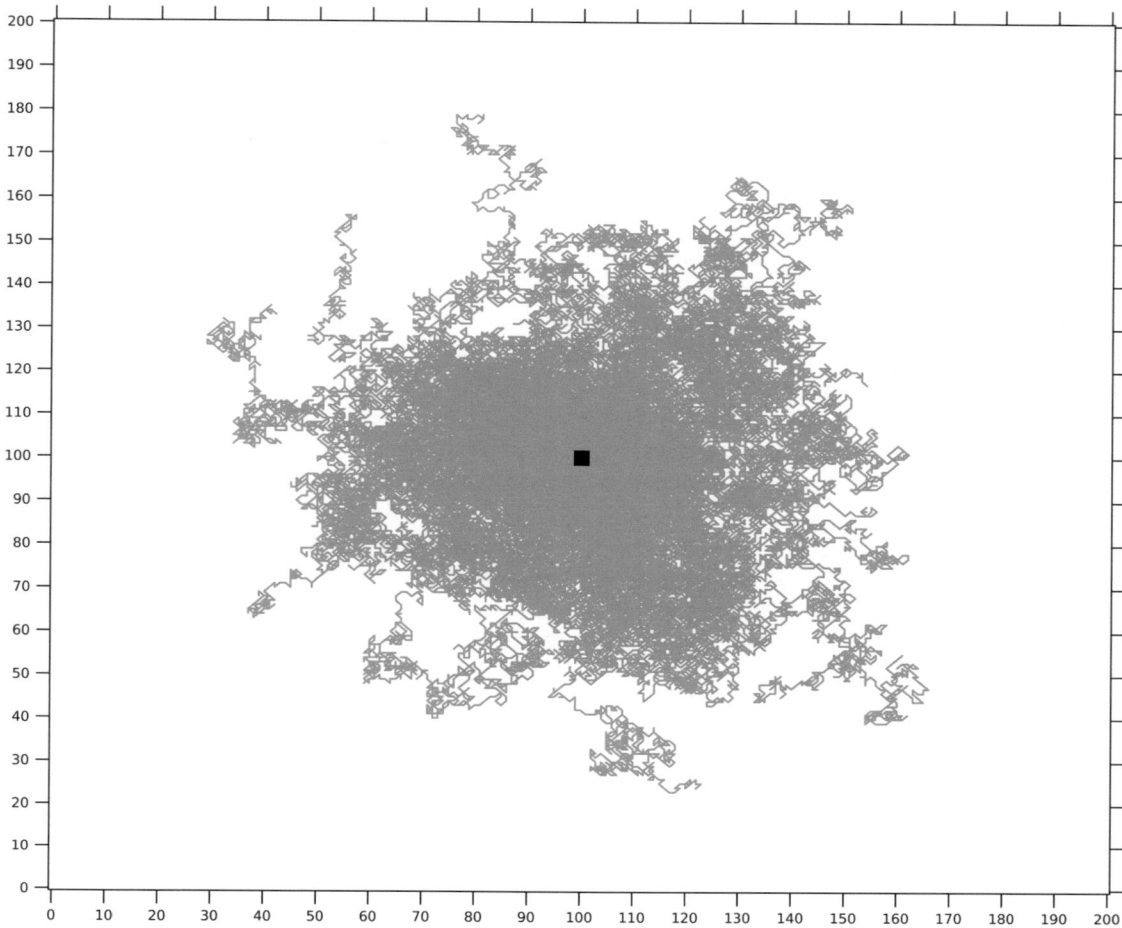

FIGURE 3.3. A simple random walk (100 walks of 1,000 steps each), illustrating Brownian motion and Fickian diffusion, with all walks beginning at a central place, marked by the center square. Here, a correlated random walk (discussed below) with a concentration parameter = 0 is used to mimic a simple random walk.

RANDOM WALKS AND EXPOSURE

The first step in building a methodology of discoverability is verifying the assumptions of my discoverability formulation—essentially, that, on an unbiased landscape, patches of different sizes and distances will be discovered at different rates, presumably with larger patches encountered at higher overall rates than smaller patches. Confirming this assumption provides the empirical warrant required to then build the baseline against which landscape learning will be measured (Chapman & Wylie, 2016). To test this hypothesis, a model based on a random walk simulator was used. While there are numerous permutations of random walk simulators within the broader field of movement ecology, three variations have been used extensively in biological modeling: simple random walks, correlated random walks, and Lévy walks (Codling et al., 2008; Viswanathan et al., 2011).

The most basic of the random walk models is the simple random walk (SRW). In an SRW, step movement is both uncorrelated and unbiased. The walk is uncorrelated in that the direction of each step is independent of the previous step (Codling et al., 2008; Viswanathan et al., 2011). This walk is also unbiased in the sense that there is "no preferred direction" (Codling et al., 2008, p. 813): the walker will just as likely reverse course as continue forward. In two-dimensions, when modeled on a grid, the walker has nine possible moves of equal probability ($p = 1/9$) at each step—to move any of the eight surrounding (nearest neighbor) cells or to just stay in place. The result from a series of such steps is a path across the walking plane that resembles Brownian motion and Fickian diffusion (Bartumeus et al., 2005), as shown in Figure 3.3. This figure also demonstrates the cumulative nature of compounded, independent walks, in this case 100 walks of 1,000 steps, each beginning at the grid center. From this example, we can see that the areas closest to the center are visited more often and with more complete coverage, creating a "gradient of learning" that emanates from the center—those cells closest to the center are far more commonly encountered than those near the outer edge of the learned landscape.

SRWs have been successfully used as first-order approximations of long-term motion and to model the nature of large-scale animal population diffusion (Bartumeus et al., 2005; Benhamou, 2007; Bovet & Benhamou, 1988; Turchin, 2006; Viswanathan et al., 2011). However, they have also been criticized for being "brainless" and failing to model animal motion at lower scales where the animal may be interacting with a stochastic environment, whether it be with the terrain itself or in encounters with mates or prey. SRWs also result in repeat encounters with the same target because of the high tortuosity inherent in their fractal nature (Viswanathan et al., 2011). However, one of the most important critiques, by Patlak (1953), argued that SRWs failed to model directional persistence—"the tendency of animals to continue moving in the same direction" (Bartumeus et al., 2005, p. 3078; Viswanathan et al., 2011).

Correlated random walk models (CRWs) were developed in response to these critiques. Animals tend to move forward more than backwards, what Bovet & Benhamou (1988) refer to as "cephalo-caudal polarization" (p. 419), and with bilateral symmetry, turning equally left or right. To mimic this behavior, CRWs use a symmetrical, unimodal, probabilistic distribution centered on angle zero (representing forward direction). CRWs specifically address the issue of directional persistence by biasing directional selection, utilizing a degree of correlation in the probabilistic selection of successive-step turning angles (Codling et al., 2008; Viswanathan et al., 2011). With these attributes, the turning angle of zero (i.e., no turn) is most heavily biased at the local level, inducing more straight-line sequences of steps (Bartumeus et al., 2005; Benhamou, 2006; Bovet & Benhamou, 1988; Codling et al., 2008; Viswanathan et al., 2011). As a result, a CRW "behaves like linear movement at very small scales…and like Brownian motion at very large scales" (Turchin, 1996, p. 2088). The severity of the walk bias is adjusted by modulating the concentration of the probability density around the mode.

To accomplish this, CRWs make use of "wrapped" distributions—a probabilistic distribution on a line that is wrapped around a unit circle, following Mardia & Jupp (2000, p. 47, Equation 3.5.54). In a wrapped distribution, the variable χ on the linear distribution is transformed to χ_ω lying on the circle, using Equation 3.4:

$$x_\omega = x \,(\text{mod}\, 2\pi) \qquad \text{(Eq. 3.4)}$$

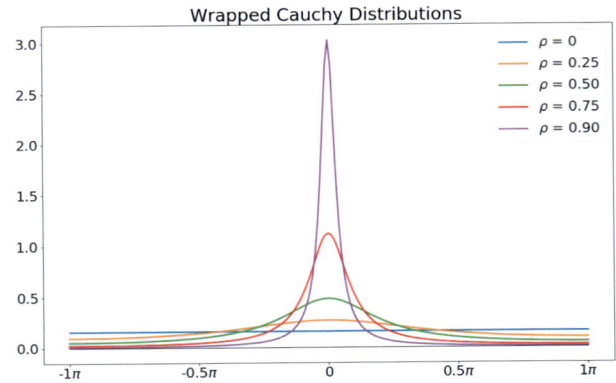

FIGURE 3.4. Linear representation of continuous circular Cauchy distributions at varying concentration levels (ρ).

While a normal or von Mises distribution can be used, the Cauchy distribution is often employed (Figure 3.4) and resembles the Student t distribution with one degree of freedom (Abuzaid et al., 2015; Codling et al., 2008; Fisher, 1993; Lehoczky, 2015; Mardia & Jupp, 2000; Siegrist, 2020). The Cauchy distribution is favored for its "fat tails," which provide more robust handling of outliers. It has also been found to represent animal movement better than Gaussian models (Abuzaid et al., 2015; Bartumeus et al., 2005; Ben-Israel, 2013; Codling et al., 2008; Crist & Haefner, 1994; Jander, 1957; Kareiva & Shigesada, 1983; Siniff, 1967; Viswanathan et al., 2011).

To create a directional distribution, the Cauchy distribution is wrapped around a unit circle using the probability density function shown in Equation 3.5 below (Mardia & Jupp, 2000, p. 51, Eq. 3.5.69):

$$c(\theta;\mu,\rho) = \frac{1}{2\pi}\frac{1-\rho^2}{1+\rho^2-2\rho\cos(\theta-\mu)},$$
$$-\pi \le \theta < \pi,\ \mu < 2\pi,\ 0 \le \rho < 1 \qquad \text{(Eq. 3.5)}$$

Here, two parameters control the distribution: the location parameter (μ), and the concentration parameter or mean resultant length (ρ, *where* $\rho = e^{-\sigma}$; Abuzaid et al., 2015; Batschelet, 1981; Codling et al., 2008; Jammalamadaka & SenGupta, 1996; Kent & Tyler, 1988; Mardia & Jupp, 2000). In the analyses presented here, μ will be zero radians (centered on 0°), representing forward motion. The ρ value modulates the concentration around μ with a range between 0 and 1; the larger the ρ value, the greater the concentration of the distribution moves toward μ, increasing directional persistence. When $\rho = 0$, the distribution around the circle will be uniform, with equal probability of any angle being selected. When $\rho = 1$, the concentration of the distribution is entirely centered at μ, inducing straight-line walks (Abuzaid et al., 2015; Bartumeus et al., 2005;

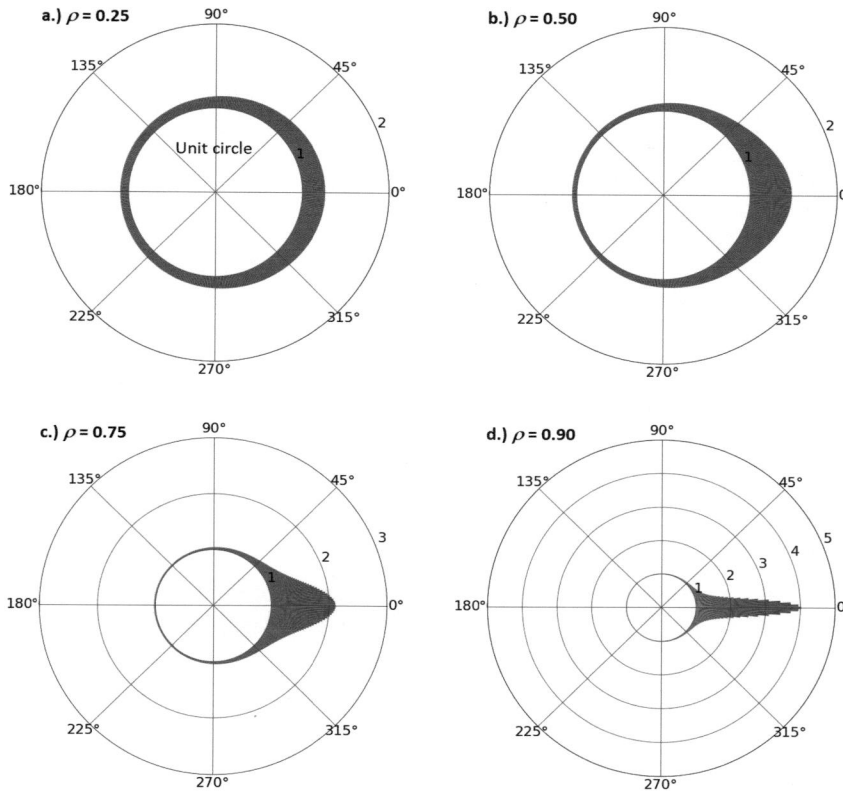

FIGURE 3.5. Polar representations of the wrapped Cauchy distribution with $\mu = 0$ and four different concentration parameters ρ, illustrating the increasing probability concentration centering around μ as ρ increases from 0 to 1 (after Batschelet, 1965, p. 10, Figure 7.3).

Fisher, 1993; Jammalamadaka & SenGupta, 1996; Kato & Jones, 2013). Figure 3.5 illustrates wrapped Cauchy distributions with varying ρ values.

To implement the wrapped Cauchy distribution for this correlated random walk, the circumference of the wrapped circle is divided into octants, representing each of the eight nearest neighbor cells surrounding a cell in a grid (Figure 3.6). The first octant (labelled A) is centered on the mode of the distribution and represents straight-forward motion. The cumulative probabilities represented by these octants are then applied to the selection of successive steps, depending on the concentration parameter chosen for a particular set of test walks. While this strategy necessarily transforms a continuous probability distribution into discrete segments, it will provide the variation needed for this model's approach.

Table 3.4 shows the cumulative probability increases in the A octant (forward motion) as the concentration parameter ρ increases from 0 to 1 ("near 0" and "near 1" shown here since absolute 0 and 1 programmatically result in "divide by zero" and "infinity" results, respectively).

Figure 3.7 demonstrates how the concentration

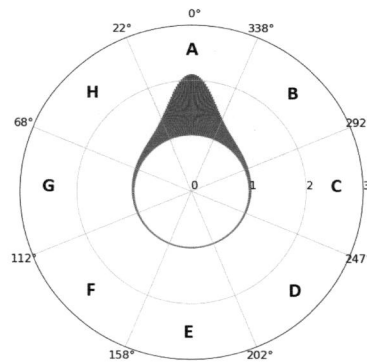

FIGURE 3.6. A wrapped Cauchy distribution ($\rho = 0.75$) divided into 8 "nearest neighbor" octants A–H, with A representing forward motion and E representing reverse direction.

parameter affects the random walk, creating a CRW. The red path ($\rho = 0$) represents a SRW where there is equal likelihood of selecting any of the eight possible directions from step to step. The resultant path is quite tortuous, resulting in high resampling of cells along the way. As ρ increases, tortuosity decreases, and we see increasing stretches of "straight-forward" travel as directional

TABLE 3.4. Probabilities for the Eight Possible Grid Step Directions, Dependent on the Concentration Parameter ρ.

ρ	±s	A	B	C	D	E	F	G	H	Sum
0.01	4.61	12.5%	12.5%	12.5%	12.5%	12.5%	12.5%	12.5%	12.5%	100%
0.10	2.30	15.2%	14.2%	12.3%	10.8%	10.3%	10.8%	12.3%	14.2%	100%
0.25	1.39	20.4%	16.5%	11.2%	8.4%	7.6%	8.4%	11.2%	16.5%	100%
0.50	0.69	34.3%	18.1%	7.8%	4.9%	4.2%	4.9%	7.8%	18.1%	100%
0.75	0.29	60.3%	13.1%	3.7%	2.1%	1.8%	2.1%	3.7%	13.1%	100%
0.90	0.11	83.5%	5.7%	1.4%	0.8%	0.7%	0.8%	1.4%	5.7%	100%
0.99	0.01	98.4%	0.6%	0.1%	0.1%	0.1%	0.1%	0.1%	0.6%	100%

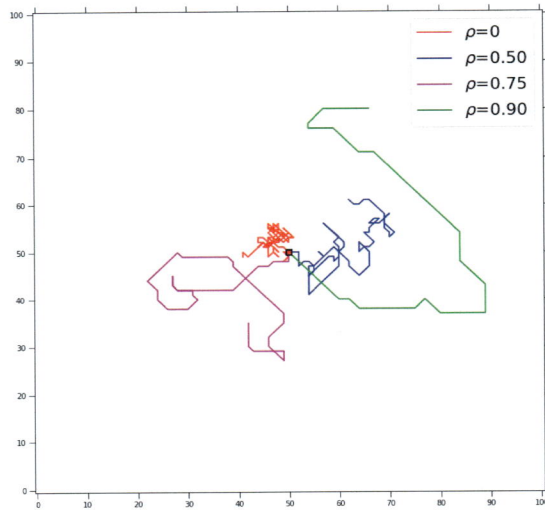

FIGURE 3.7. Four correlated random walks (CRW) of 250 steps, each using different concentration parameters, illustrating increasing directional persistence and diminishing tortuosity as ρ increases.

persistence increases. While not shown, a path where ρ = 1 would simply result in a path that begins at the grid center and moves directly away in a straight line. The range of behavior shown here (0 ≤ ρ < 1) allows the use of a single CRW model to test discovery in various modes, as will be seen below.

For completeness, I mention a third simulation method recently used in movement ecology: Lévy walks or flights. These are a form of random walk where both the turning angle and the step length at each step event are variable. A Lévy walk and a flight differ from each other in that walks encounter any targets between the starting and ending points while flights jump directly to the ending point before continuing foraging (Viswanathan et al., 2011). Flights may be more useful for some models, but since "a Lévy walk allows detection of foraging targets both at the end points of Lévy paths and at intermediate steps between them" (Brantingham,

2006, p. 438), a walk is more useful in a model where the goal is the discoverability of an unknown resource as a byproduct of other foraging activity (encounters versus embedded procurement, *sensu* Binford, 1979).

Lévy walks have found usefulness in modeling foraging mobility in various species, including humans, but are not without issues (Benhamou, 2007; Codling et al., 2008; Pontzer et al., 2014; Viswanathan et al., 2002). Like CRWs, Lévy walks are modulated primarily by a single parameter (μ in this case) that typically ranges between 1 and 3, with values near 1 resulting in extremely long straight paths and values near 3 returning a stepping behavior similar to that of a SRW (Viswanathan et al., 2011). The power law that determines step length also has an extremely long tail, which can result in unrealistically long steps, requiring artificial truncation within the model (Brantingham, 2006).

Fortunately, CRWs appear to mimic Lévy flights and animal paths as ρ approaches 1 (Auger-Méthé et al., 2015; Bartumeus et al., 2005; Benhamou, 2007; Reynolds, 2010). As a result, a single CRW model can be used to replicate foraging mobility patterns from simple random walks using Brownian motion (ρ = 0) to patterns reflecting long, straight journeys (ρ near 1). More importantly, since I am most interested in verifying that patch size impacts encounter rates, and not in the specific form of the path taken by people to achieve the encounter, this analysis can be accomplished using a single CRW model while testing across the full range of 0 ≤ ρ < 1. The implementation of such a model is described below.

CRW TESTS

To test the relationship of exposure, or patch size, to discoverability in a neutral model, a two-dimensional CRW simulator was created using Jupyter Notebook and the Python programming language (*Project Jupyter*, 2021). The simulated landscape is represented by a two-dimensional grid of 200 × 200 cells. Following Brantingham (2003), the landscape is considered neu-

TABLE 3.5. Patch Absolute and Relative Sizes.

Patch Size	Patch Area	Step Size Increase
1×1	1	—
2×2	4	400%
3×3	9	225%
4×4	16	178%
5×5	25	156%
6×6	36	144%
7×7	49	136%
8×8	64	131%
9×9	81	127%

TABLE 3.6. Encounters (Walks with a Patch Encounter) for Each Patch Size ($\rho = 0.25$).

Patch Size	n
1×1	855
2×2	1287
3×3	1490
4×4	1562
5×5	1705
6×6	1751
7×7	1880
8×8	1910
9×9	1932

tral (absent of topography) and uniformly productive (all cells are equally likely to contain target resources), and thus all cells are equally likely destinations during a forager walk. For this experiment, each walk begins at the center of the grid, a central place (Bell, 1990; Bettinger & Eerkens, 2004; Kelly, 1995), referred to here as "Home." For this experiment, walks were run in sets of 100 walks of 10,000 steps each. The direction of the first step in each walk is chosen randomly ($p = \frac{1}{8}$) and all subsequent steps are chosen based on the probability weightings, as described in Table 3.4, according to the concentration parameter for this set of walks. This first random step initially introduces a local directional bias, at a very small scale, which progressively vanishes (Benhamou, 2006; Codling et al., 2008). The walk continues for up to 10,000 steps unless it encounters the test patch or the grid boundary.

The patch is represented by non-zero values in a 200×200 cell array that runs parallel to the grid/step array. As each grid cell is entered, the patch array is tested for the presence of a patch. Walks are terminated when the agent encounters the patch or when the agent encounters the grid boundary (known as an absorbing or non-rebounding border). For walks that encounter a patch, the encounter is tallied, along with the distance of the patch from Home. While this experiment is not focused on traditional questions of central place foraging, such as round-trip energy costs or in-field processing, it does look at the accumulation of resource encounters as walks are repeated from the central place.

To test how patch-size may affect discoverability, a simple test scenario within this program was devised. Single patches of various sizes (1×1 cells, 2×2, 3×3…9×9), as described in Table 3.5, were placed at increasing increments away from Home as shown in Figure 3.8. Only one patch is placed per set of walks.

For each patch size, a single target patch is initially positioned one cell away from Home and 100 walks of 10,000 steps are run. During the 100 walks, each encounter with the target patch is tallied. If a walk encounters the patch, the walk is terminated. This prevents revisits to an already "discovered" patch during a single walk. Similarly, if a walker hits the grid border, the walk is terminated. Following each set of 100 walks, the patch is moved one cell in both the negative x and negative y directions, moving further away from Home. A new set of 100 walks is run on the new patch position, and this operation is repeated until the patch reaches the lower left grid corner.

Figure 3.9 illustrates one set of 100 walks with an 8×8 patch. During the set of 100 walks, the 8×8 cell patch was encountered, at the displayed distance, 19 times. In total, 230,841 steps were taken. Many walks were truncated before reaching 10,000 steps as a result of either encountering the patch or the grid boundary.

Following the procedure described above, the discoverability of variably sized patches (sized 1×1…9×9) was tested using each of the following wrapped Cauchy distribution concentration levels (ρ): 0, 0.25, 0.50, 0.75, 0.90, and 0.95. For programming reasons, 0 was tested using the value 0.0000000001.

RESULTS

Once these experiments were run, the data specific to each concentration parameter were analyzed and graphed. Then, for each patch size, the encounter tally and distance data were segregated for graphing. An example tally set for 100 walks of 10,000 steps using $\rho = 0.25$ is shown in Table 3.6.

For each concentration level and for each patch size, the numbers of encounters were plotted against the distance of the patch from Home and the data points were fitted to a line using the scipy.optimize.curve_fit function within the SciPy 1.6.1 library (Virtanen et al., 2020).

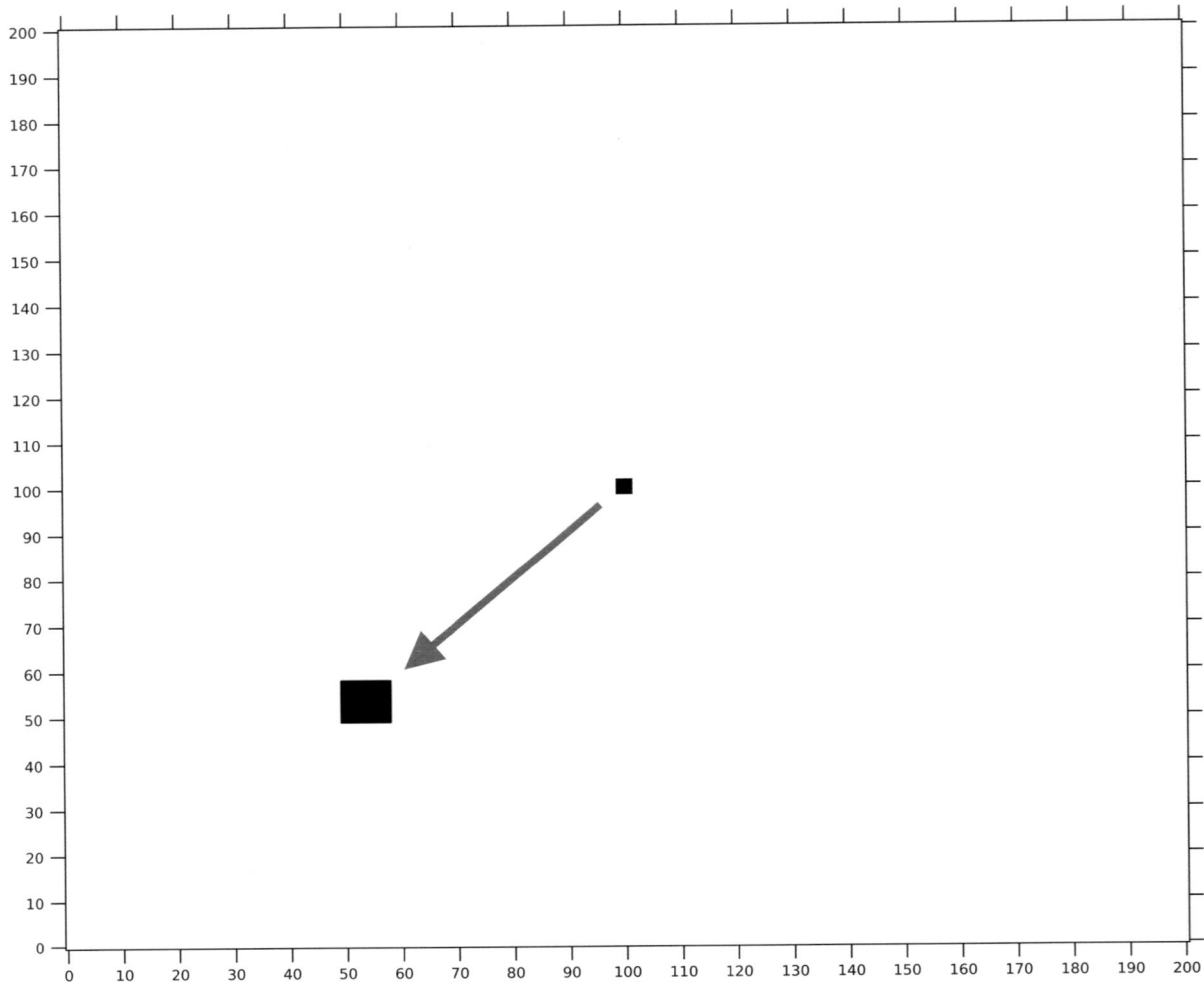

FIGURE 3.8. Demonstrating the placement positions of a single patch size (8×8), at increasing distances from Home. In these tests, only one patch is present in the grid at a time.

Across all concentration levels tested, encounters vs. distance uniformly illustrate an exponential decay in the number of encounters as distance increases. Encounters vs. the natural log of distance produce linear results for all patch sizes. Figures G.1 and G.2 in Appendix G (https://collections.lib.utah.edu/ark:/87278/s6mntfnx) illustrate this exponential decay for the lowest and highest concentration parameters tested against 5 × 5 patches. Similarly, Figures G.3 and G.4 display the linear relationship exhibited in the semi-log graphs of the same data.

When the exponential decay lines for each concentration level are graphed together, the curves present consistently increasing slopes as patch size increases, as shown in Figures G.5 and G.6, which represent the $\rho = 0$ and $\rho = 0.95$ walk results respectively. Figures G.7 and G.8 show these results in semi-log form.

All graphs for all patch sizes at each concentration level, as well as the grouped concentration level graphs, are available in the GitHub repository (See "Repository and Software" section at the end of this chapter).

TESTING THE SLOPES AND INTERCEPTS

For each concentration level, each of the nine semi-log regression lines was tested against the others for significant differences in slope ($\alpha = 0.05$) to ensure they were not estimates of the same population slope, β, using the procedure spelled out in Zar (2010, p. 387). If the null hypothesis (H_0: $\beta_1 = \beta_2$) is rejected, two different regression populations are represented by the regression lines. If the null hypothesis was not rejected, the lines were further tested to determine if their elevations were significantly different, following the procedure for comparing two elevations in Zar (2010, p. 391). The results of the tests follow in Figures G.9 and G.10.

In almost all cases, the regression line comparisons reject the null hypothesis (Table 3.7). It is notable that

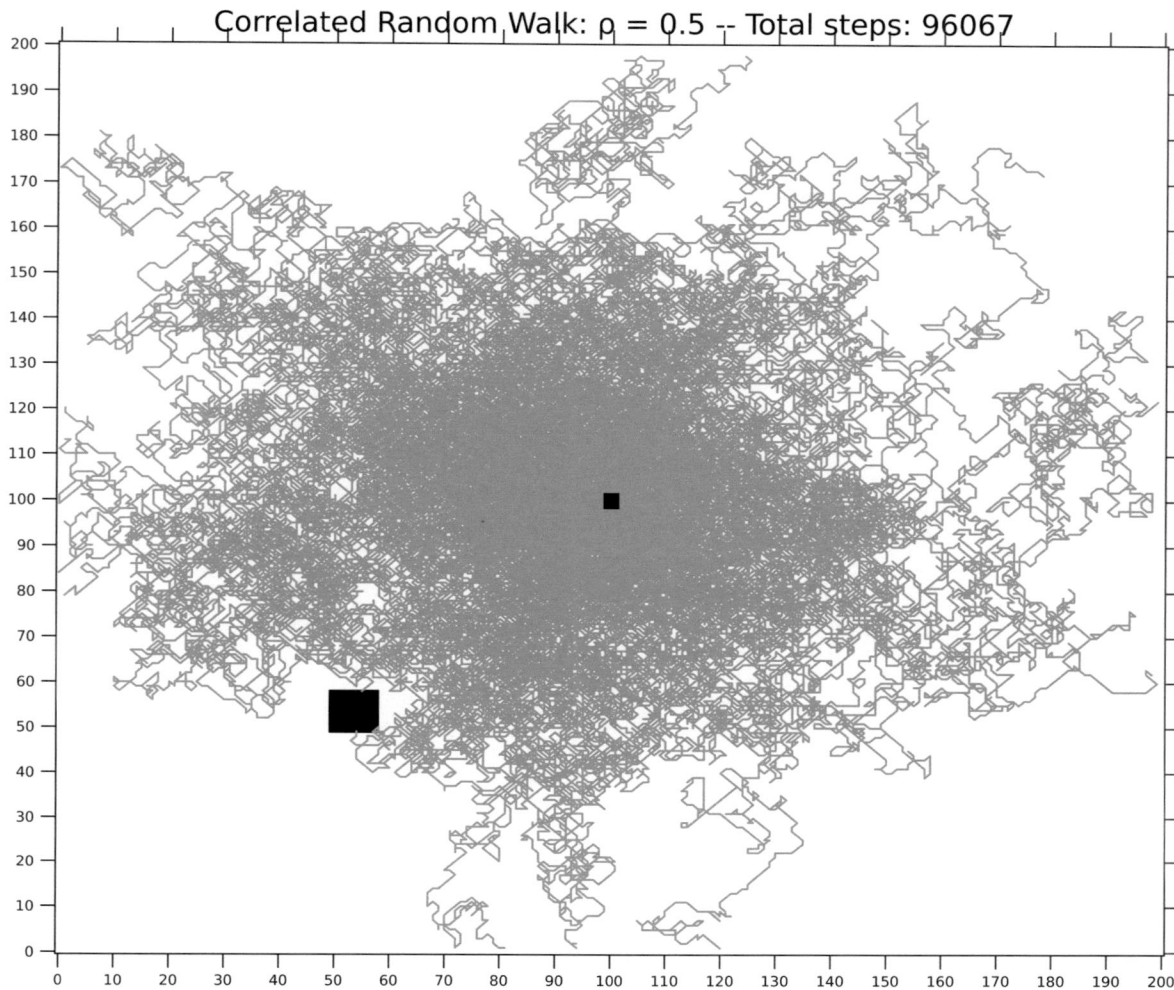

FIGURE 3.9. Full set of 100 walks searching for one 8×8 patch ($\rho = 0.5$).

TABLE 3.7. Linear Regression Line Comparisons.

ρ	H_0 Rejected (n)	H_0 Not Rejected (n)	% Rejected
0.01	31	5	86%
0.25	32	4	89%
0.50	32	4	89%
0.75	33	3	92%
0.90	35	1	97%
0.95	35	1	97%

the comparisons increasingly fail as directional persistence (ρ) increases.

CONCLUSION

In this chapter, I developed a model to predict the order in which patchy resources would be found on a neutral landscape dependent only on patch size and distance. This work drew from Brantingham's (2003) neutral model of raw material procurement and expanded it by

varying patch size. The results of this model should predict the rank-order discoverability of resource patches on an unlearned landscape.

To test this model, a CRW simulator was built specifically for this purpose. The simulator allowed me to systematically test how encounter rates change as patch size and distance vary. The simulator tracked encounters of correlated random walkers and their encounter rates with patches varying in size from 1×1 cells to 9×9 cells on a 200×200 cell grid. CRWs with concentration parameters from $0 \leq \rho < 1$ were tested and consistently returned size-dependent linear regression results.

Nearly all the resultant regression lines differ significantly from one another in terms of slope and/or elevation, and thus represent different sample populations. For a few cases at the higher patch sizes where the relative size change between patches is not as great (for example, 8×8 patches vs. 9×9 patches), the results did not differ significantly. That outcome is to be expected in a random walk process in which patch sizes closely approach one another. A remarkable observation from the results is that as directional persistence (ρ) increases, the cases where the null hypothesis could not be rejected diminish considerably.

The results overwhelmingly support the hypothesis that patch size affects discoverability. With this empirical warrant in hand, toolstone sources can now be ranked by their relative discoverability and be used to set the baseline of an "unknown landscape" against which to measure landscape learning over time (see Chapter 6).

REPOSITORY AND SOFTWARE

The following software tools were used to create the programs described in this chapter:

Anaconda Navigator, v. 1.9.12 (Anaconda Software Distribution, 2021). The versions of all installs and libraries encapsulated in this aggregation are listed in the environment.yml file in the repository referenced below.

Jupyter Notebook, v. 6.0.3 (*Project Jupyter*, 2021). Three notebooks were created to run the CRW simulation, graph and analyze the resultant data, and to replicate various figures that appear in this chapter.

Python v. 3.7.6 (64-bit) (Python Software Foundation, 2021). The CRWutils.py file was written using this Python version.

GitHub repository (*GitHub*, 2021). All notebooks, code, data (.csv files), and graphical output are available in this GitHub repository assigned DOI: 10.5281/zenodo.6544114. Also available directly at GitHub: https://github.com/davehuntoo/dhuntoo_dissertation.

4

A Method for Predicting the Discoverability of Obsidian Sources

INTRODUCTION

Testing the discoverability model, as outlined in Chapter 3, requires a means to quantify the areal extent, or discoverable signal, of obsidian sources on the landscape. In this chapter, a method for predicting this signal is tested, starting with known primary source exposures, using these as upslope catchments, and then applying hydrographic computational algorithms to predict the downslope distribution of obsidian sediments. Five obsidian toolstone sources, used by people occupying the Old River Bed (ORB) delta (see Appendix A, Table A.42, https://collections.lib.utah.edu/ark:/87278 /s6mntfnx), were predicted at varying levels of digital elevation model (DEM) smoothing, field tested, and evaluated for precision. The results provide a gauge of the level of smoothing required to operationalize this method of predicting the secondary distribution of sediments and the scale factor of that extent.

REGIONAL GEOLOGY

The Great Basin resides within the Basin and Range Province, a region of north–south oriented, horst and graben mountain ranges and valleys, within the western United States (R. L. Christiansen & Lipman, 1972; Grayson, 2011; Hunt, 1967). The province emerged around 60 million years ago (Ma) as the result of tectonic events in the early Cenozoic and, over time, resulted in a "rugged erosional topography with towering pinnacles rising above narrow usually dry valleys" (Lipman et al., 1978, p. 134). In the late Cenozoic (beginning ~20 Ma), this region entered an age of rhyolitic volcanism that extended to

at least the middle Pleistocene (as recently as 0.5 Ma) and remains seismically active today (E. H. Christiansen et al., 1986; Crecraft et al., 1981; Lipman et al., 1978). During this geologically recent period of volcanism, the primary sources of obsidian (a glassy form of rhyolite) in this region were formed, mostly along existing fault lines (Crecraft et al., 1981; Rowley et al., 2002).

Obsidian forms as the result of various eruptive mechanisms (Hughes & Smith, 1993). In the Great Basin and the surrounding region, including the Snake River Plain to the north, the two most common mechanisms are rhyolitic lava flows and pyroclastic ash-flow tuffs (Armstrong, 1970; E. H. Christiansen et al., 1984; Crecraft et al., 1981; Lindsey, 1979; Lipman et al., 1978; Rowley et al., 2002; Williams et al., 1997). In the first case, obsidian deposits form when highly viscous silicic-rich magma is extruded during an eruption and the basal members of these flows cool quickly against the surrounding environment, forming bands, or veins, of glass. These deposits comprise the most chemically homogenous glass. Obsidian may also be formed during pyroclastic eruptions of ash-flow sheets, or tuff, resulting in obsidian nodules forming in situ (Ellis et al., 2012; Hughes & Smith, 1993; Monnereau et al., 2021). The Great Basin, and particularly the nearby Snake River Plain, were subjected to massive ash-flow eruptions covering hundreds of square kilometers. These flows are variously welded, dependent on temperature, and may produce obsidian nodules large enough for tools.

The following five regional sources were used to test the methodology described in this chapter (Table 4.1).

TABLE 4.1. Ages (Millions of Years) of Obsidian Sources Being Investigated.

Obsidian Source	Age	Reference
Black Rock Area	2.2–2.6 Ma	Crecraft et al., 1981; Hintze et al., 2003
Ferguson Wash	unknown, poorly studied	Armstrong, 1970; Jackson et al., 2009
Mineral Mountains	0.79 Ma	Evans et al., 1978; Lipman et al., 1978
Panaca Summit/Modena	11–13 Ma	Rowley et al., 2002; Williams et al., 1997
Topaz Mountain	6–7 Ma	E. H. Christiansen et al., 1984; Lindsey, 1979, 1982

In the time since their formations, alluvial and colluvial forces have transported obsidian sediments—their secondary distribution—from uphill locations to the valley bottoms (Lipman et al., 1978; Miller & Juilleret, 2020; Rowley et al., 2002). This form of erosion, described by Hunt (1967, p. 340), repeats itself throughout the Great Basin:

> A typical basin in the Basin and Range Province consists of two kinds of ground. At the center is a playa or alluvial flat of clayey or silty ground, with or without a crust of salts, and surrounding this are gravel fans that rise from the flats to the foot of the bordering mountains. Many of the fans are several miles long and more than a thousand feet high. They consist of coarse debris, mostly gravel and sand deposited at the mouths of canyons by streams flowing from the mountains.

That the first people known to have moved into and lived in the Great Basin discovered and made extensive use of these primary obsidian sources for tools is clear (Beck & Jones, 1990; Grayson, 2011; Jenkins et al., 2012; Jones et al., 2003; Madsen, Schmitt, et al., 2015). Further, due to the unique geochemical signature of each obsidian flow, the primary locations of almost all obsidian sources utilized by early peoples are known today, at least in the general sense of tens of square kilometers (Jackson et al., 2009; Madsen, Schmitt, et al., 2015; see also Skinner 2021 and Appendix D, Table D.2, https://collections.lib.utah.edu/ark:/87278/s6mntfnx). What is less well-known, and which forms a central aspect of this research, is how the secondary distributions, the downslope alluvial and colluvial flows of obsidian sediments, may have created a noisy "signal" on the valley bottoms where early inhabitants of the Great Basin made their living (Grayson, 2011). These signals, up to

several orders of magnitude larger than the primary sources themselves, consist of obsidian granules and pebbles (2–64 mm, per the Wentworth scale) within the greater alluvial package and would effectively inform alert hunter-gatherers that tool-grade lithic sources were close at hand (Wentworth, 1922).

THE DISCOVERABILITY MODEL OVERVIEW

The goal for this portion of the project was to develop and test a method for reliably estimating the size or surface area exposure of these secondary signals. Modern geographical information systems (GIS) provide numerous tools and algorithms to analyze drainage networks and downslope flow patterns as a means for understanding hydrographic processes and to simulate sediment erosion (Fairfield & Leymarie, 1991; Freeman, 1991; O'Callaghan & Mark, 1984; Quinn et al., 1991; Tarboton, 1997). Alluvial flows in particular have been the subject of recent research using these tools (Argialas & Tzotsos, 2006; Miliaresis & Argialas, 2000; Nangia, 2010; Norini et al., 2016). Each methodology shares similar processes for calculating the downslope flow of material (water or sediments):

1. Determine the location of the primary source exposure.
2. Acquire a suitable regional digital elevation model (DEM) raster.
3. Condition the DEM for hydrographic analysis.
   a. Fill artificial sinks.
   b. Smooth the raster to eliminate dams and flat spots which might hinder a flow calculation.
4. Establish a catchment region. This can be the upslope area from an alluvial fan apex or an artificial "starting point" for downslope analysis. In this model, I describe the use of a weighted raster representing the obsidian primary sources that simulate the starting points for downslope erosional flow, as well as the use of "proxy sources" when primary sources are poorly defined.
5. Perform the downslope analysis or simulation that disperses hydrographic and erosional action to lower elevations within the regional raster. Various algorithms are available to define downslope drainage networks and disperse flows downslope. In this model, the multiple flow direction method is used (described below).

While there are inherent limitations in any attempt to model what is ultimately an infinitely dynamic process, recent hydrographic algorithms provide useful tools for modeling erosional processes. Specific limitations will be discussed in situ as the general steps are described.

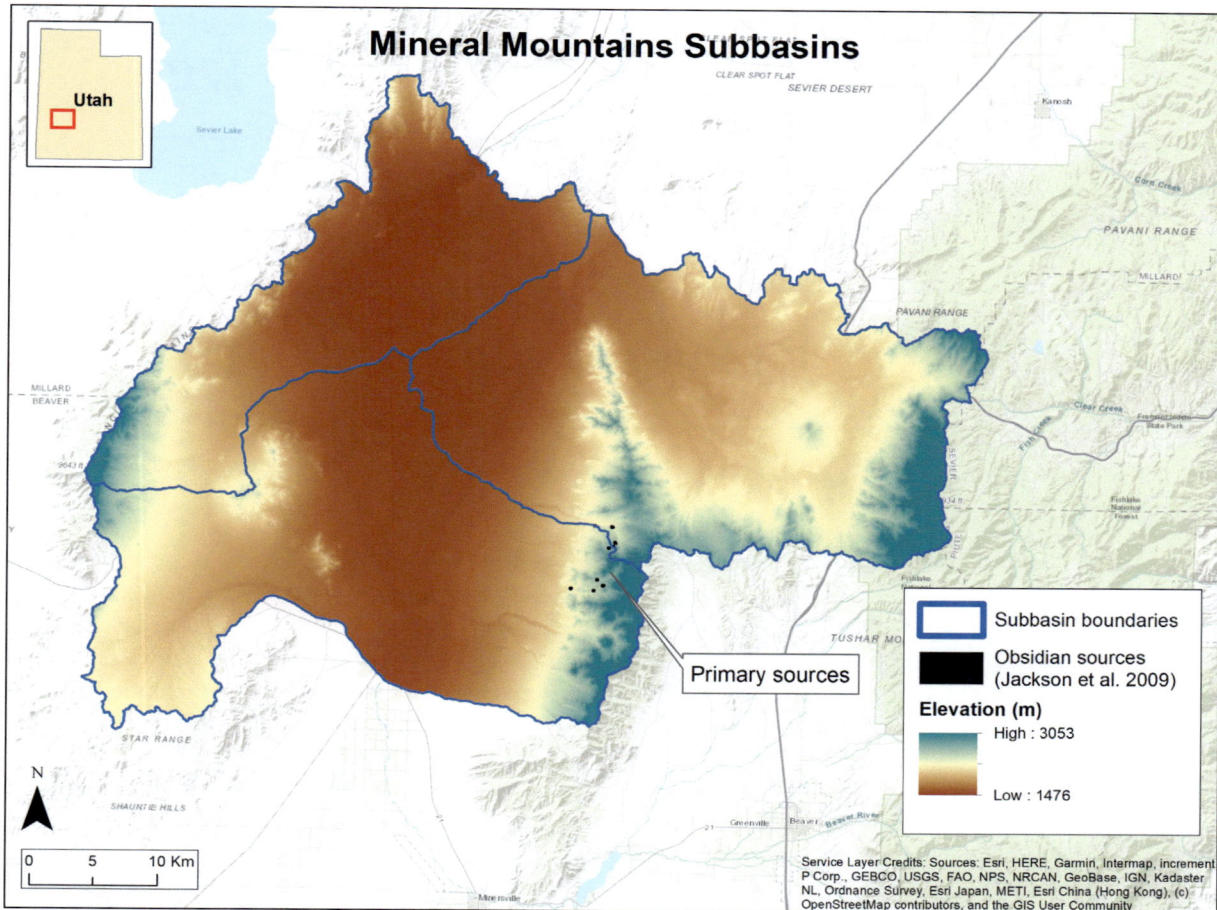

FIGURE 4.1. Example of a digital elevation model (DEM) showing the subbasins in the vicinity of the Mineral Mountains primary obsidian sources.

Determine Primary Source Location

In this method, the primary source location acts as the seed for downslope flow calculations. For these test cases, obsidian sources with primary exposures that are generally well described in the literature were used (Hull, 1994; Jackson et al., 2009; Talbot et al., 2015). In the Panaca Summit/Modena section of this chapter and in Chapter 5, I offer strategies for creating a proxy source when only sample points are available and the primary source is unknown or no longer exists.

Acquire Suitable Regional DEMs

For each study region, U.S. Geological Survey (USGS) ⅓ arc-second DEMs were acquired using The National Map Viewer tools (Archuleta et al., 2017; U.S. Geological Survey, 2020c). The 1/3 arc-second DEMs provide resolution of approximately 10 m per cell (U.S. Geological Survey, 2020a). Due to the remote locations of the obsidian sources researched here, which have both low human population densities and generally low economic use, no higher resolution DEMs (such as LiDAR) are available.

Also acquired were GIS shapefiles for regional Watershed Boundary Datasets (WBD; U.S. Geological Survey, 2020b). The WBD datasets describe the surface drainage for a region at various scales. These provide useful limiting boundaries and a means to reduce the overall computational load, by clipping large DEMs down to regions within hydrographic subbasins that capture any downslope flow of water and sediment.

For each obsidian source (Black Rock Area, Ferguson Wash, Mineral Mountains, Panaca Summit/Modena, and Topaz Mountain), a seamless, clipped DEM encompassing the source's local subbasin or subbasins was created using the ArcMap GIS program (Esri, 2021a). Figure 4.1 is an example from the Mineral Mountains region. The primary obsidian source locations for the Mineral Mountains are well-researched and shown as black polygons (Jackson et al., 2009). They are positioned at high altitude, but below the range crest or eastern hydrographic boundary, and downslope flow will likely run west into the lower subbasin floors.

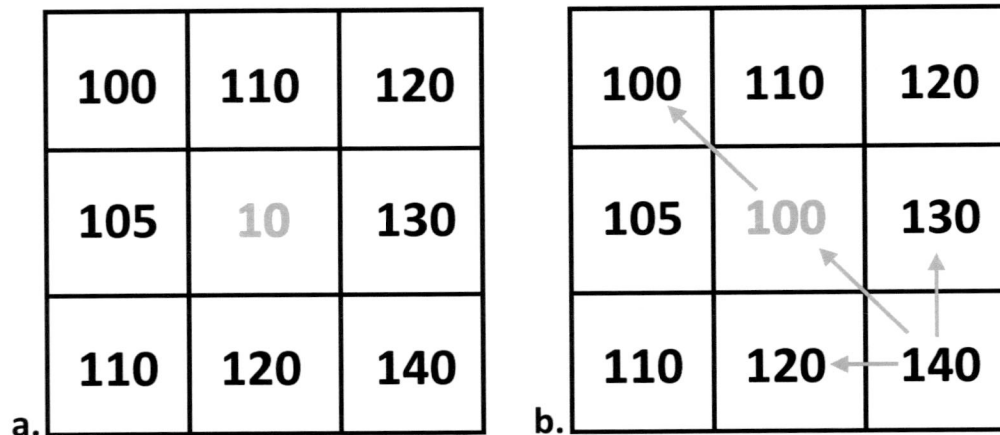

FIGURE 4.2. A sink in a digital elevation model (DEM), before (*a*) and after (*b*) Fill function, arrows indicate possible new flow paths.

Condition the DEM

A DEM is a discrete, gridded representation of a continuous topology. As such, it needs to be prepared, or "conditioned" (Jenson & Domingue, 1988), so that hydrographic flow can be simulated over the topology it represents.

Fill artificial sinks: DEMs are subject to errors, called pits or sinks, where a cell (or cells) contain(s) an elevation value lower than its eight nearest neighbors (Figure 4.2a). Sinks greater than 10 m wide are extremely rare in the natural environment but common in DEMs (Mark, 1988). Sinks in DEMs are typically the result of errors in surface interpolation (continuous to discrete), rounding errors (real numbers rounded to integer values), or satellite photographic classification errors, for example confusing treetops with the ground surface (Costa-Cabral & Burges, 1994; Esri, 2021d; Jenson & Domingue, 1988; Mark, 1988). These artificial pits need to be removed as they cause hydrographic flow algorithms to terminate unnaturally at these low spots.

The process for sink removal is straightforward. The ArcMap 10.0 Fill function (Esri, 2021b) is an iterative tool that locates each sink, evaluates the eight neighboring cells, and assigns the sink cell to the same value as the neighboring "pour point" value (the neighboring cell with the lowest elevation). The end result is a depressionless DEM where every cell will "be part of at least one monotonically decreasing path of cells leading to an edge of the data set" (Jenson & Domingue, 1988, p. 1594), allowing continuous flow through the erroneous cell (Figure 4.2b).

Smooth the raster: Along with sinks, raised ridges or "dams," both natural and artificial, and flat areas can stymie hydrographic flow algorithms. Like sinks, dams can be the result of interpolation or rounding errors,

except in a "positive" direction, creating a ridge through which flow algorithms cannot pass (Fairfield & Leymarie, 1991; O'Callaghan & Mark, 1984; Quinn et al., 1991). Recent anthropogenic barriers on the landscape, such as raised railway beds, highways, and pipelines, also appear in DEMs and may block computed flow patterns. In very flat areas, such as basin bottoms, these linear structures can be particularly problematic, rising several meters above and transecting natural valley bottoms or very gently sloping areas (see discussion in the Panaca Summit/Modena section of this chapter for a particularly vexing issue and workaround). Finally, in a DEM represented by integer elevation values, large "flat" blocks of cells containing the same value—resulting either from rounding in the interpolation of very gentle natural slopes, or from the computational filling in of large sinks as described above—can also create artificial flow termination points or pools.

To predict millennia of hydrographic flow and erosion at a regional scale, it is necessary to eliminate such obstructions by smoothing the DEM. The amount of smoothing to apply to the model during this predictive stage is somewhat subjective and the product of trial and error which must be evaluated against results from the field. However, in this study, this process is not entirely subjective due to known observation and/or collection data points from previous workers (Hull, 1994; Jackson et al., 2009; Talbot et al., 2015; also Skinner 2021 and Appendix D, Table D.2) and my own fieldwork (Appendix B, Table B.6, https://collections.lib.utah.edu/ark:/87278/s6mntfnx). One can expect that the flow must extend at least to these points (see the source-specific results below).

The ArcMap 10.0 Focal Statistics function (Esri, 2021c) takes a filled DEM and creates a new raster that

100	110	120
105	100	130
110	120	140

3x3 Neighborhood Mean

→

	116.875	

FIGURE 4.3. The 3×3 neighborhood mean for a single cell produced by the Focal Statistics function.

sets each cell value to a statistical value based on the values of the neighboring cells. In this case, the Mean value was used with neighborhoods of increasing sizes (3×3, 5×5, 7×7, 11×11, and 21×21 cells). This function creates increasingly smoothed surfaces as the averages are spread out and is especially useful when "smoothing" large flat areas as the fractional averages will give the flat area a gentle slope. The smoothed DEMs, now grids of averaged real numbers or floating-point values, provide a continuously sloped gradient for water and sediment to "flow" across (Figure 4.3).

Establish a Catchment Region

In hydrology, the catchment area is the uphill region that feeds into drainage channels (Freeman, 1991; O'Callaghan & Mark, 1984; Tarboton, 1997). While the size of the catchment region is important when calculating aspects like the volume of water in a channel, for this project I only need to know how material will flow downhill from specific points or areas—a "top down" approach. As my interest is in the flow of obsidian sediment from its primary exposure to its extended and diffuse secondary distribution, I need to know the upslope topographical locations of each primary source or sources. For this project, these primary sources will act as the catchment region.

For the five study areas (see Table 4.1), the primary source locations are illustrated in maps from previous work (Jackson et al., 2009; Talbot et al., 2015). From these, polygons and weighted rasters were created which were then used in the flow direction and accumulation calculations. Figure 4.4 demonstrates the weighted raster for the Mineral Mountains. In this raster, the raster cells representing the primary sources are set to 1 and the cells representing the remainder of the region are set to zero.

Perform the Downslope Analysis/Simulation

The final step of predicting downslope flow using a DEM is calculating the direction and accumulation of the flow as it moves from one cell to the next in a grid. This problem has been addressed by multiple researchers and algorithms (Costa-Cabral & Burges, 1994; Fairfield & Leymarie, 1991; Freeman, 1991; O'Callaghan & Mark, 1984; Qin et al., 2011; Quinn et al., 1991; Seibert & McGlynn, 2007; Tarboton, 1997; Tarboton et al., 1991). As the goal here is to predict the extent of flows, not drainage channels or volumes, the multiple flow direction (MFD) method was chosen (Freeman, 1991; Quinn et al., 1991). Freeman's algorithm has weaknesses in flat regions and sinks, but both issues are addressed by earlier steps in my process and the MFD algorithm works well with the sort of divergent alluvial flows being explored here (O'Callaghan & Mark, 1984).

The MFD method assumes that outflow from any given cell will be divergently dispersed to all its lower neighboring cells. The flow is fractionally allocated based on the slopes between the sending cell and the receiving cells (see Equation 4.1, after Freeman, 1991, p. 415, where best results were achieved using the constant $p = 1.1$):

$$\int_i = \frac{Max\left(0, Slope_i^p\right)}{\sum_{j=1}^{8}\left(Max\left(0, Slope_j^p\right)\right)} \qquad \text{(Eq. 4.1)}$$

Figure 4.5 provides a simple example of a single cell (center) and the allocation of flow to three downslope cells. In execution, the MFD algorithm is recursive, as many cells will have multiple cells flowing into them. The recursive nature of the algorithm captures the full accumulation of flow into each downslope cell.

The System for Automated Geoscientific Analyses (SAGA) is a specialized, open-source GIS system

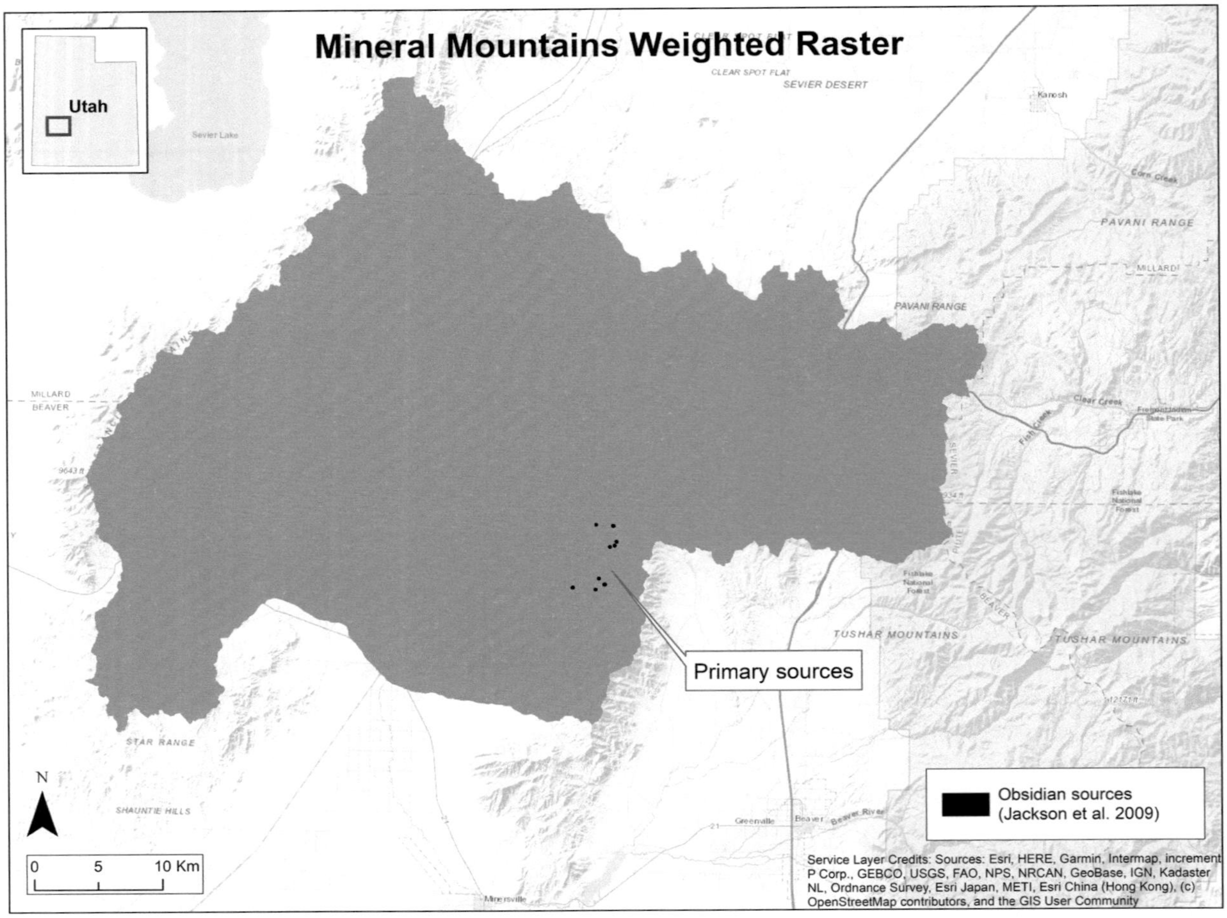

FIGURE 4.4. The primary source weighted raster for the Mineral Mountains subbasins.

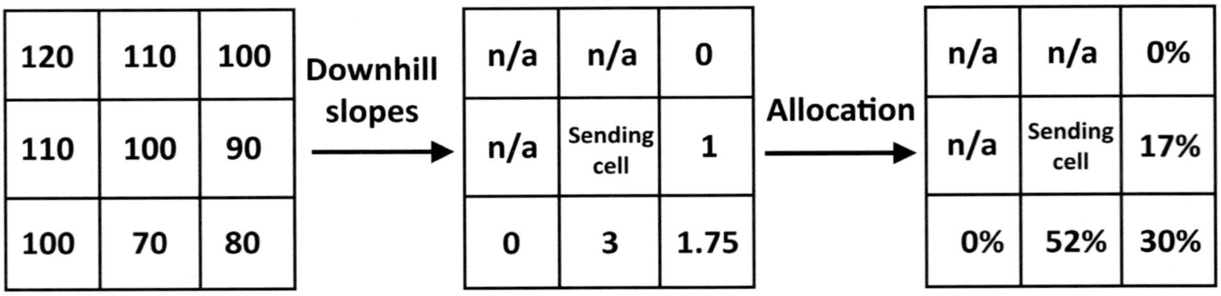

FIGURE 4.5. Multiple flow direction (MFD) allocation of flow based on downhill slopes (elevations in meters, 10 m cell size).

tailored to geoscientific methods (Conrad et al., 2015). SAGA v. 7.5.0 and its flow accumulation (Top Down) functionality (based on the ta_hydrology module) were used to model downslope flow. This function accepts an elevation model and a weighted DEM representing the catchment region; in this case, the filled and smoothed regional DEM and the weighted DEM of the primary source locations, respectively. The function allows the user to select one of several different accumulation algo-

rithms (cited above), including Freeman's (1991) MFD algorithm.

Flow accumulation rasters were created for each of the smoothed DEMS (3×3, 5×5, 7×7, 11×11, and 21×21 nearest neighbors) using SAGA. These DEMs were then imported into ArcMap and various ArcMap functions were used to convert the flow accumulation rasters into polygons and outlines that could be used to create maps and inform fieldwork. The 11×11 flow accumulation in

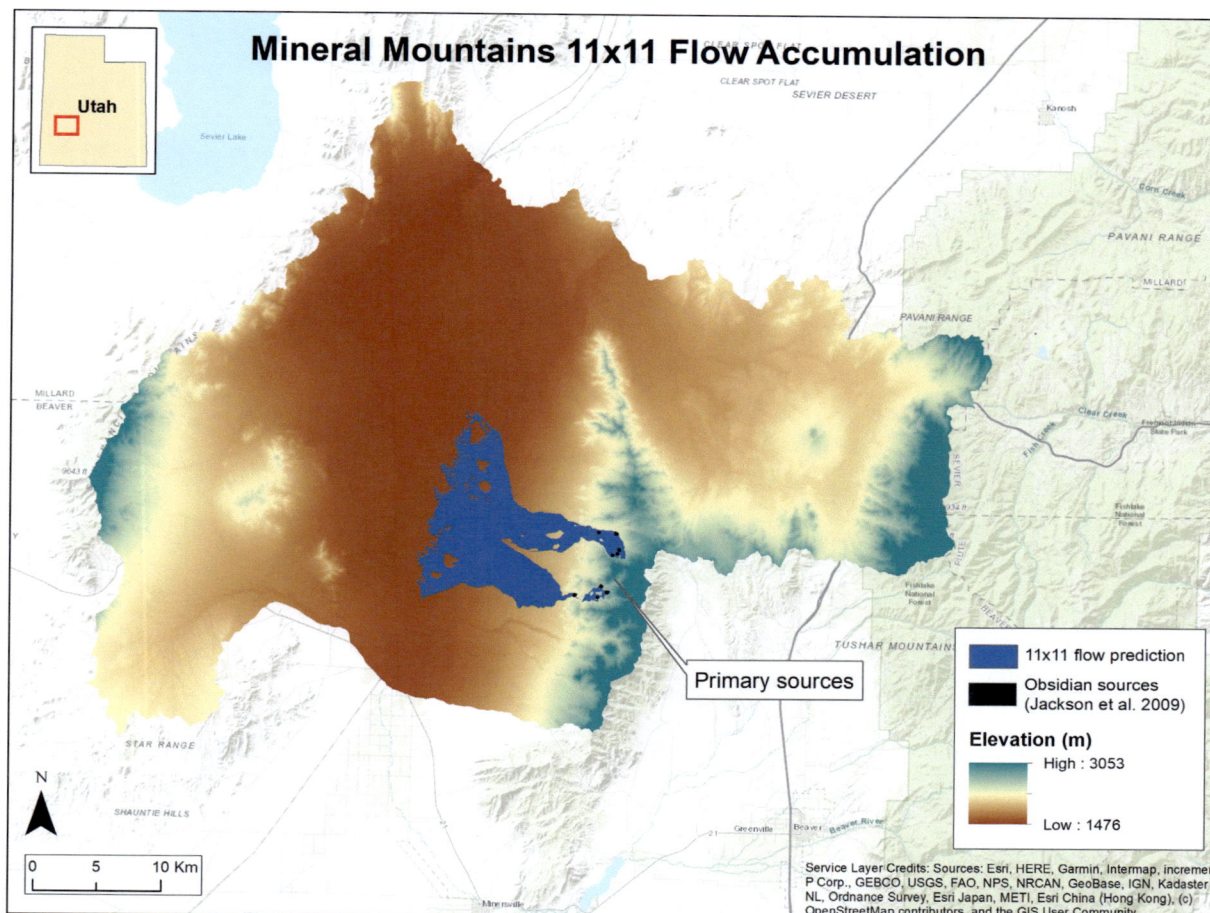

FIGURE 4.6. Mineral Mountains 11×11 flow accumulation (blue, moving east to west) calculated using the multiple flow direction (MFD) algorithm on an 11×11 smoothed digital elevation model (DEM).

context of the Mineral Mountains hydrographic sub-basin is shown in Figure 4.6.

All five flow accumulations (3×3 to 21×21 nearest neighbors) can then be "stacked" to show the areas with the highest likelihood to contain secondary obsidian deposits downslope from the primary sources (Figure 4.7).

Preparing for Survey Field Work

The final step of analysis is creating the maps that were used for fieldwork. Using ArcMap, outline perimeters were created for each flow. As can be seen in Figure 4.7, most of the flow variation occurs at the distal ends (the left north-south running edge in this diagram), the lowest energy extents of the flows. The "sides" of the flow (in this case the east–west running edges) are quite uniform regardless of the level of smoothing. The "islands" or voids that can be seen in Figure 4.7 within the flows are of no concern here as they are interior to the general flow; a hunter-gatherer would encounter the flow signal regardless of the interior void. Rather, the outline of the

flow—the interface between the secondary deposit and a person walking across the landscape is most important. Figure 4.8 shows this outline along with transects placed at 1 km spacing. From this map, the UTM coordinates for the intersections between the outline and the transects were generated, as well as the angle of the transect used during the fieldwork to test the accuracy of the models.

SURVEY METHODOLOGY

Survey fieldwork was carried out, by myself and an assistant, during the summers of 2020 and 2021.

For each of the five survey areas, the regional flow prediction that best fit the known samples or previous observation points was used, and survey transect maps and lists of survey starting points were prepared, as described above. The process of running the transects involved locating the starting point and observing whether obsidian was present in the sediment around that predicted flow edge. If obsidian sediment was

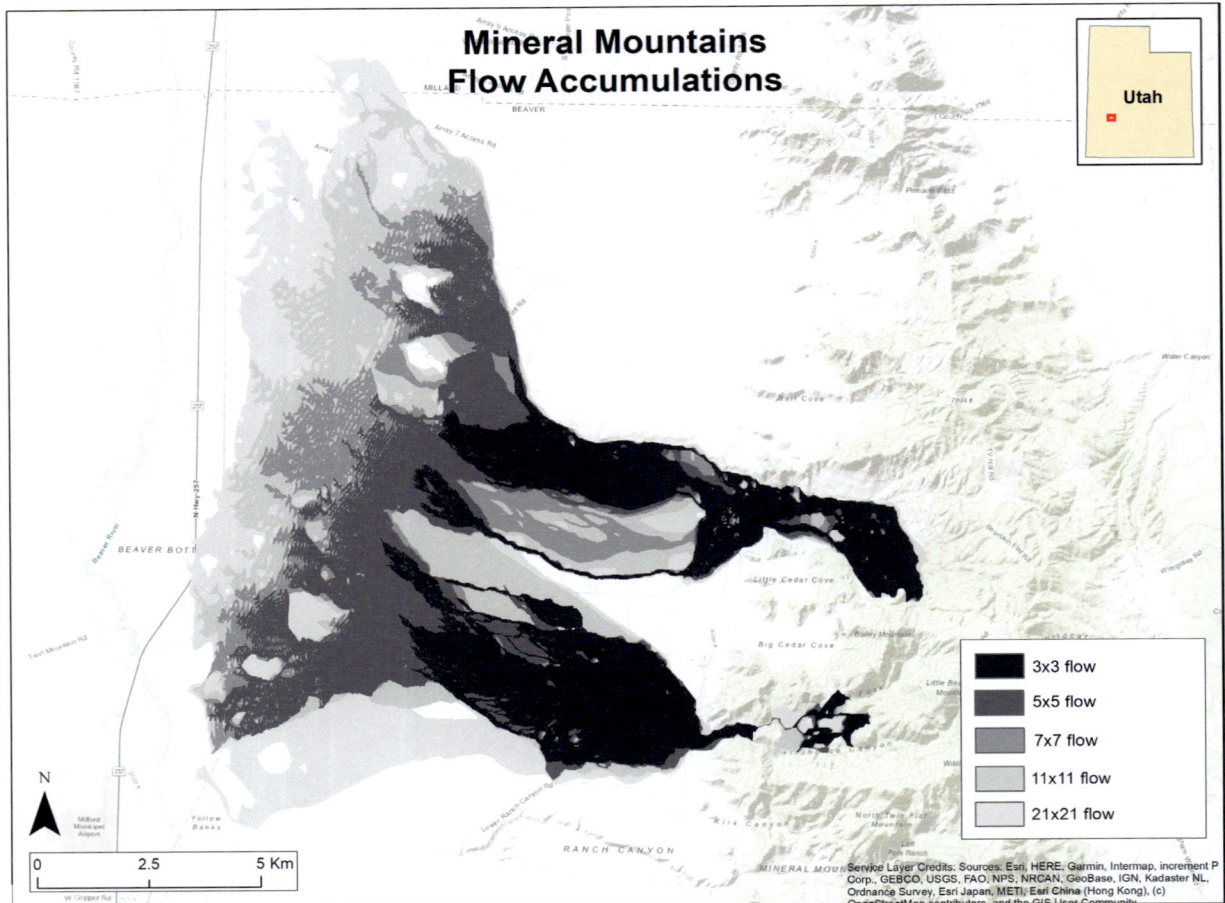

FIGURE 4.7. Stacked flow accumulation digital elevation models for varying levels of elevation smoothing (darkest is lowest nearest neighbor smoothing starting at 3×3, lightest is highest smoothing, at 21×21).

present, the surveyor moved "outward" from the flow, on the transect bearing, looking for the most exterior edge of the flow. This edge was considered "found" when no further presence of obsidian sediment was observed after 100 m from the last observation point. If no obsidian was observed near the starting point, then the bearing was reversed, and the surveyor moved "inward" until the flow edge was identified. A natural (non-artifactual) obsidian sample was taken at the most external edge of the flow.

The survey transects generated by these processes (as in Figure 4.8) are idealized in that not all transects can or need to be run. Various restrictions occur in the field, such as impassable terrain, private property, livestock, and other access limitations. Also, in some cases, the survey flow prediction was incorrect (extended too far or not far enough), requiring abandonment of some transects or the ad hoc creation of new transects in the field. In these cases, we worked "from the known to the

unknown," using the last known observation points and knowledge of the hydrographic basin to close the sides of the flow polygon.

In addition, the size of obsidian sediment varies significantly over the course of a secondary flow. Close to the primary source, large tool-sized nodules may appear, but these nodules naturally diminish in size the farther the secondary distribution expands outward. At the most distal ends of an alluvial flow, flow energy is dissipating, and the sediment package transitions to extremely fine-grained sediments and silt. Obsidian pebbles similarly diminish in size, making the distal edge of the secondary flow the hardest to define as obsidian grains move below 2 mm in size. These grains can still be recognized at this low end, and I suggest that hunter-gatherers did make this connection, but below 2 mm visual limitations emerge. Similarly, as will be discussed below, the flow predictions are most unreliable at the distal ends where this transition occurs due to

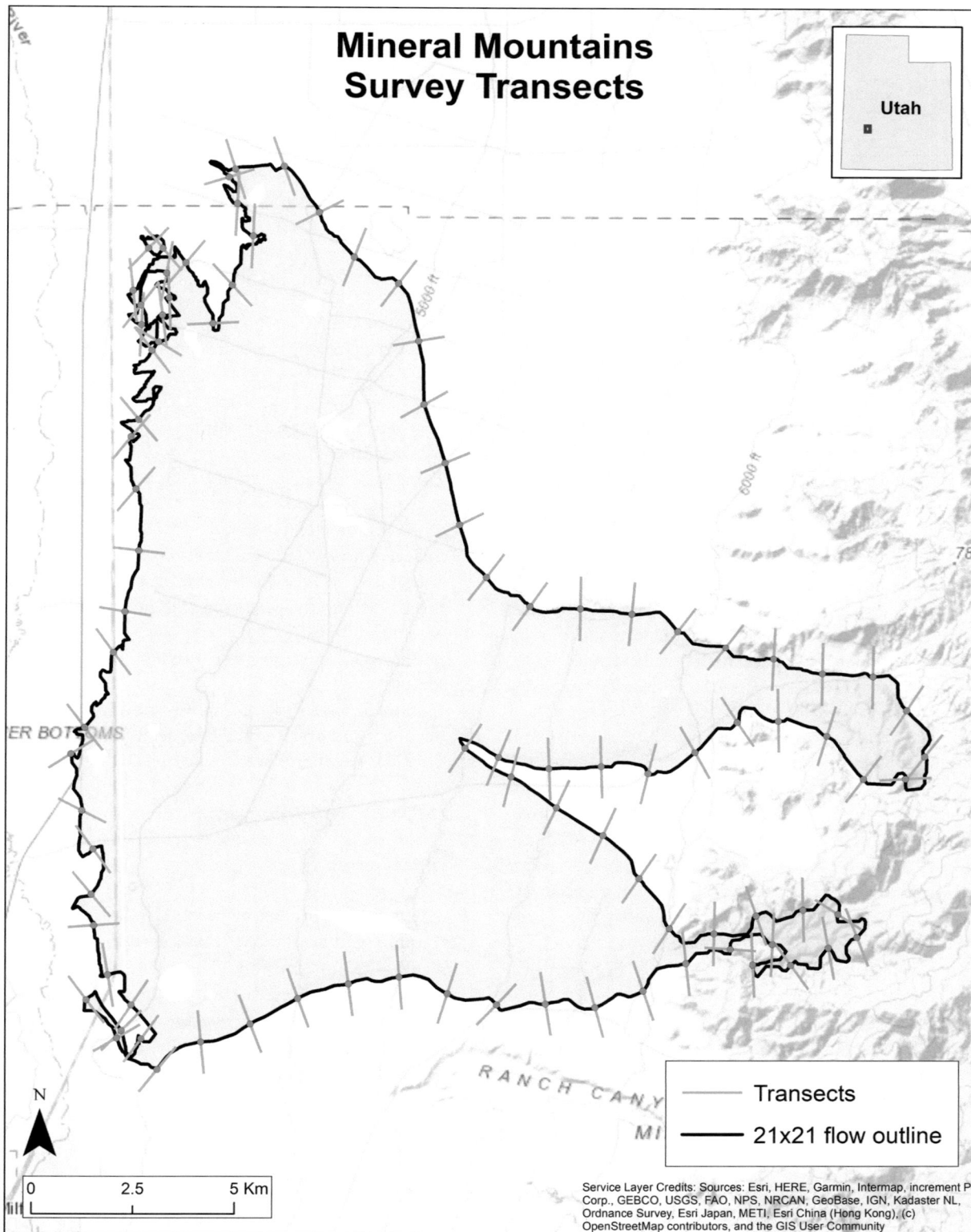

FIGURE 4.8. Outline of the 21×21 flow and survey transects.

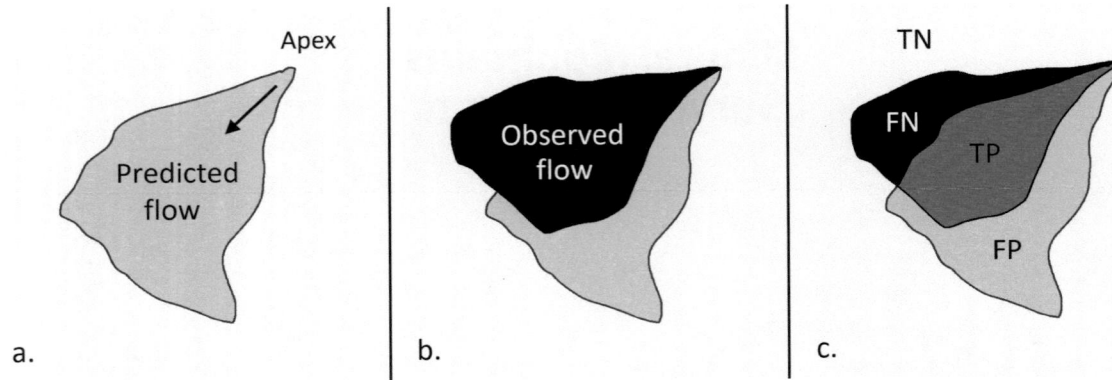

FIGURE 4.9. Mapping flow predictions to actuals using a modified confusion matrix: (*a*) the flow predicted by one smoothing level of the model, (*b*) the observed surveyed flow, (*c*) the overlapping and non-overlapping regions mapped to confusion matrix nomenclature.

TABLE 4.2. Confusion Matrix Classification.

		Predicted Flow	
		Negative	Positive
Observed Flow	Negative	TN	FP
	Positive	FN	TP

limitations in the accuracy of DEM elevations and the extremely gentle slopes typical of most basin bottoms. Together, these factors compound the level of imprecision at the distal ends of these surveyed extents.

ANALYZING SURVEY RESULTS

The overarching goal of this process is to determine if this methodology can be used to accurately predict the extent and scale of the secondary distribution of obsidian when only the primary source location is known. Five known primary sources were used to predict secondary flows and then surveyed to determine the actual flows. Following survey data collection, these observed secondary extents were mapped as polygons. These were then compared against the original predicted flows using a modified confusion matrix (Bruce & Bruce, 2017; Kulkarni et al., 2020; Marcos Llobera, personal communication, April 2, 2021).

A confusion matrix is a tool used to test the predictive performance of a classification model. In this case, the confusion matrix was used to test how well my model classified, or predicted, the area that would contain secondary flows versus what was observed during the survey.

This binary classification test can be illustrated by a simple 2 × 2 matrix (Table 4.2) and the following definitions:

- *True Positive (TP)* is the area that was correctly classified, or predicted, to contain secondary flow.
- *False Positive (FP)* is the area predicted to contain

flow but did not (was classified as positive when it was negative).
- *False Negative (FN)* is the observed flow area that is outside the prediction (area classified as negative when it should be positive).
- *True Negative (TN)* is the area accurately classified as containing no flow. In this case, this is the area that is outside both the predicted and the observed flow.

These classifications are further illustrated in Figure 4.9.

Confusion matrices are typically used to determine the accuracy and precision of a model using the following formulas (Kulkarni et al., 2020):

$$\text{Accuracy} = \frac{TN + TP}{TN + FP + FN + TP} \qquad \text{(Eq. 4.2)}$$

$$\text{Precision} = \frac{TP}{TP + FP} \qquad \text{(Eq. 4.3)}$$

In the case of predicting secondary flows, two factors require modification to the typical confusion matrix application. First, my model involves progressively smoothing the flow prediction, for example, starting with a 3 × 3 nearest neighbor average and progressing to a 21 × 21 nearest neighbor average. If taken to extremes, increasing the nearest neighbor value would eventually smooth the entire DEM to a single regional average, or a flat surface. Such extreme smoothing would not provide a useful predictive model. Second, in this model, TN is essentially equal to infinity, as it represents all of the world where the flow is not. This eliminates the usefulness of the standard confusion matrix accuracy calculation.

In this modified use, I want to find the smoothing level that provides a balance between correct classification and excessive smoothing. Therefore, to find the best fit, the ratio of the correctly predicted flow (TP) to the observed flow is used and then that value is penalized using the ratio of the incorrectly predicted flow (FP) to the observed flow:

$$\text{Best Fit} = \frac{TP}{Observed} - \frac{FP}{Observed} + \frac{TP - FP}{Observed} \quad \text{(Eq. 4.4)}$$

Table 4.3 illustrates these calculations using the Black Rock Area (BRA) data, applying increasing smoothing levels (3×3 to 21×21 in increments of two). As can be clearly seen, as smoothing increases, the "% survey predicted" increases and will increase eventually to 100 percent with sufficient smoothing. At the same time, the predictions inside and outside the actual surveyed flow (353 km^2 at BRA) are at odds with each other. As smoothing increases, the "% prediction inside observed" decreases while "% prediction outside observed" increases. To find the optimal smoothing level, the highest TP offset by the least FP, these values are balanced, using the "% prediction inside observed" and then penalized with the "% prediction outside observed" (after Equation 4.4). This value is seen in the "(TP/FP)/observed" column, revealing that the 13×13 smoothing level provides the "best fit" and optimal predictive value for the BRA. This method was repeated for each of the five survey areas to determine if there is an average smoothing level that is best for predicting secondary obsidian flows from known primary sources (more below).

REGIONAL SITE CONSIDERATIONS AND OBSIDIAN FLOW PREDICTIONS

Black Rock Area

Location: Millard County, Utah
Alternative Names: None
Hull (1994) Sample Points: $n = 7$ (Appendix D, Table D.1)
Skinner Sample Points: $n = 10$ (Appendix D, Table D.2)
Hunt 2019 Observation Points: $n = 17$ (Appendix B, Table B.6)
ORB Paleoindian Artifacts: $n = 10$ (Appendix A, Table A.37)

The Black Rock Area (BRA) is an expansive region with multiple primary obsidian source exposures (Figure 4.10) in Millard County, Utah, east of the Cricket Range and north of the Mineral Mountains (Figure 4.11). Hull (1994, p. 10) suggested that the area is one of the largest primary sources of obsidian in Utah, measuring in at 50 km². However, based on just the primary outcrops documented in Jackson et al. (2009), an outline of the area covers at least three times the area estimated by

Hull. This knowledge set early expectations that the secondary obsidian distributions emanating from the BRA would likely cover several hundred square kilometers.

BRA Geology

While the region experienced volcanism beginning about 20 Ma and continuing to about 0.97 Ma, Crecraft et al. (1981) state that silicic volcanism occurred in a tight range between 2.6 to 2.2 Ma in the BRA. During this time regional primary obsidian sources were formed from quickly-cooling rhyolitic flows containing at least 76 percent silica (Crecraft et al., 1981).

Hintze et al. (2003) mapped and named the local rhyolite flow the "Cudahy Mine rhyolite" (*Tcr*, Figure 4.11). This area produces a black obsidian as well as a "snowflake" obsidian that contains phenocrysts (embedded crystals) that do not knap well (Jackson et al., 2009). The largest Cudahy Mine rhyolite flow manifests as the Coyote Hills, where Jackson et al. (2009) reported over 37 separate obsidian exposures, although several smaller rhyolite exposures also occur to the east (Figure 4.11).

More recently, about 18,000 cal BP, much of the region, including some BRA primary sources, was inundated by Pleistocene Lake Bonneville at its height (Chen & Maloof, 2017b; Oviatt & Jewell, 2016; Utah Geospatial Reference Center, 2017), reaching about 1552 m above sea level at this location (Figure 4.12). After Lake Bonneville receded, the areas below the remnant shoreline were covered in lacustrine fine silt, sandy loam, and pebble fields, which remain today.

The Coyote Hills, as well as the South Twin Peaks, Black Point, and Dee's Ridge to the east, are topographically moderate hills, with almost all areas rising less than 300 m above the basin floor.

BRA Archaeology

The archaeological significance of the BRA is well appreciated in Utah state prehistory and the region has been subject to numerous archaeological surveys (Hull, 1994; Jackson et al., 2009; Mullins et al., 2009). More than 2000 sites, both prehistoric and historic, have been reported within the local subbasins (Utah Division of State History, 2020). Most of the prehistoric sites are obsidian lithic scatters of varying sizes although Jackson et al. (2009) report at least five prehistoric quarries, three in the Coyote Hills (42Md1089, 42Md1090, and 42Md1091) and two at Black Point (42Md871 and 42Md872). However, the detection of prehistoric quarrying is confounded by historic and contemporary obsidian and pumice mining. Many of the large obsidian exposures in the Coyote Hills show deep pitting that is

FIGURE 4.10. Black Rock Area: typical primary source exposure in the Coyote Hills.

likely the result of mechanized excavation. On the west side of the Coyote Hills, the Cudahy Mine destroyed a significant portion of the hillside in the process of mining pumice for household cleansers in the early 20th century (Everts, 1991). On the south end of the Coyote Hills, modern surface mining for jewelry-grade obsidian continues today.

BRA Past Work

Our understanding of the scope and extent of the BRA primary and secondary obsidian extents has changed significantly in the last 30 years and is illustrated in Figure 4.13. The earliest X-ray fluorescence (XRF) testing at this locality by Nelson & Holmes (1979) and Nelson (1984) provide insufficient locational data to be helpful here, as it is only detailed to township-range sections or quarter sections. Hull (1994) provides a useful early dataset of XRF tests on seven samples from the region. These samples appear to be centered on primary sources, though the township and range quarter-quarter-quarter descriptions can still be several hundred

meters off when compared to modern GPS coordinates. Skinner (2021; Appendix D, Table D.2) has aggregated an extensive dataset of Intermountain West XRF test results, including 10 XRF samples from the BRA, and these capture the southeast extent of BRA obsidian. In 2019, I conducted a pilot survey and observed obsidian (Appendix B, Table B.6, $n = 17$) at various points around the BRA. While these are not XRF test points, they provide a useful indication that obsidian is distributed on the southwest slope of the Coyote Hills. The work by Jackson et al. (2009), however, provides the best resource of primary obsidian sources throughout the region and suggests a secondary distribution as well.

All this information was used in selecting the best flow prediction for the BRA obsidian.

BRA Flow Prediction

Using the process described earlier in this chapter, five flow distributions were created.

The starting requirement for all flow prediction is the location of the primary sources, illustrated for

BRA in Figure 4.11. Using these primary source starting points (Jackson et al., 2009), the downslope flows were predicted for 3×3, 5×5, 7×7, 11×11, and 21×21 nearest neighbor smoothed DEMs. These are presented in "stacked" form in Figure 4.14, with the 3×3 nearest neighborhood flow represented by the darkest shade and the 21×21 flow represented by the lightest shade.

A comparison to the known sample points by Hull (1994; Appendix D, Table D.1), Skinner (2021; Appendix D, Table D.2), and my own pilot project (Appendix B, Table B.6) revealed some anomalies (Figure 4.15). Hull targeted primary sources, and her samples find good concordance with the flow predictions. However, three of Skinner's sample points, particularly SO-65-1352 and SO-65-1353, appear to be well out of range of the predictions. Finally, a cluster of my observation points in the southwest, near the active quarry, are problematic. These points appear to be on the other side of the highest Coyote Hills ridge and the subbasin boundary. In this case, I suspect that Jackson et al. (2009) chose not to consider the active quarry as a prehistoric exposure simply because the natural exposure has been completely destroyed.

In preparation for fieldwork, a polygon shapefile was created to represent the location of the active quarry as a primary source. The flow generation steps were then replicated to recreate the five flows while including this primary source on the south slope of Coyote Hills. The result was a large dispersal prediction, which is shown in context of the original northern flows in Figure 4.16, ensuring that I was prepared to run the appropriate survey transects if a secondary distribution appeared south of the ridge. There were still problematic sample points, particularly BRA07 and SO-65-1352, but the flow prediction covered more of these anomalous points. The final 21×21 prediction outline and transects for both north and south flows are shown in Figure G.11.

BRA Survey Results

The Black Rock Area secondary distribution of obsidian was surveyed during the summer of 2020, and the observed extent is illustrated in Figure 4.17. As suspected, the BRA secondary distribution is expansive, covering more than 353 km² with a perimeter of ~193 km. During the survey, 233 observation points were recorded, and 164 natural obsidian samples were collected (Appendix B, Table B.1). Of these collected samples, 32 were submitted to Northwest Research Obsidian Studies Laboratory (NWROSL) for X-ray fluorescence (XRF) testing (Appendix C, Table C.1, and Appendix E, https://collections.lib.utah.edu/ark:/87278/s6mntfnx) and were

confirmed as "Black Rock Area" obsidian (triangles in Figure 4.17).

The surveyed flow encompasses almost all previous sample points recorded by Hull (1994; Appendix D, Table D.1), Skinner (2021; Appendix D, Table D.2), and myself (Appendix B, Table B.6), with minor exceptions (no previously recorded points are more than 150 m outside the surveyed extent). However, the predictions did not account for large areas of secondary (or tertiary) distribution to the west and south of the Coyote Hills (annotated as A and B in Figure 4.18). Given the impact on the area by the rise and fall of Lake Bonneville, I suspect that obsidian was transported into these areas as the result of longshore movement and thousands of years of wave action on the west side of the obsidian-bearing hills. The Beaver River also flows south along the west side of these hills and may have entrained some sediments south, particularly in the area parallel to the Antelope Mountains, towards the town of Milford. Black Rock Area obsidian sediments also intermingled with those of the Mineral Mountains to the south, which is discussed below. Undiscovered, or now fully eroded, obsidian sources may also have occupied the west side of the hills, accounting for the extensive secondary distribution in regions A and B.

Aside from these anomalies, the predicted flows provided a generally accurate guide for the secondary distribution extents. Following the modified confusion matrix methodology described in the "Analyzing Survey Results" section of this chapter, the optimal smoothing level for the BRA occurs at the 13×13 nearest neighbor average (Table 4.3). At this level, 64 percent of the actual survey region was predicted by the 13×13 model.

Ferguson Wash

Location: Elko County, Nevada and Tooele County, Utah
Alternative Names: Dead Cedar Wash, Ferguson Flat
Skinner Sample Points: n = 4 (Appendix D, Table D.2)
Hunt 2019 Observation Points: n = 36 (Appendix B, Table B.6)
ORB Paleoindian Artifacts: n = 1 (Appendix A, Table A.37)

Ferguson Wash (FW) is a small primary obsidian source originating in Elko County, Nevada, with a secondary alluvial flow (Figure 4.19) into Tooele County, Utah (Jackson et al., 2009). The source is located near the state border, about 35 km south of Wendover, on unnamed phenorhyolitic hills south of the Lead Mine

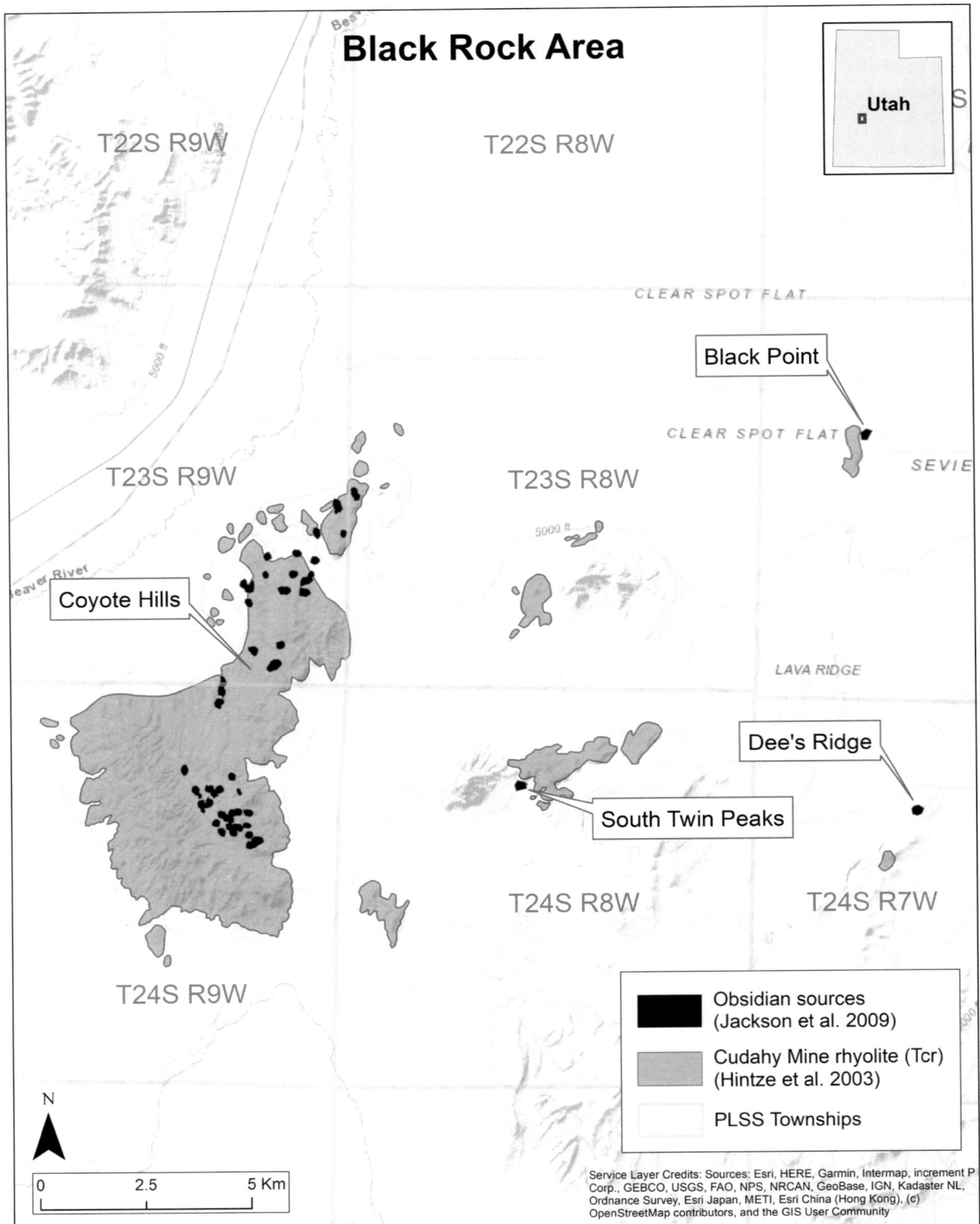

Black Rock Area

Utah

T22S R9W

T22S R8W

CLEAR SPOT FLAT

Black Point

CLEAR SPOT FLAT

T23S R9W

T23S R8W

SEVIE

5000 ft

LAVA RIDGE

Coyote Hills

Dee's Ridge

South Twin Peaks

T24S R8W

T24S R7W

T24S R9W

Obsidian sources
(Jackson et al. 2009)

Cudahy Mine rhyolite (Tcr)
(Hintze et al. 2003)

PLSS Townships

N

0   2.5   5 Km

FIGURE 4.11. Black Rock Area regional view.

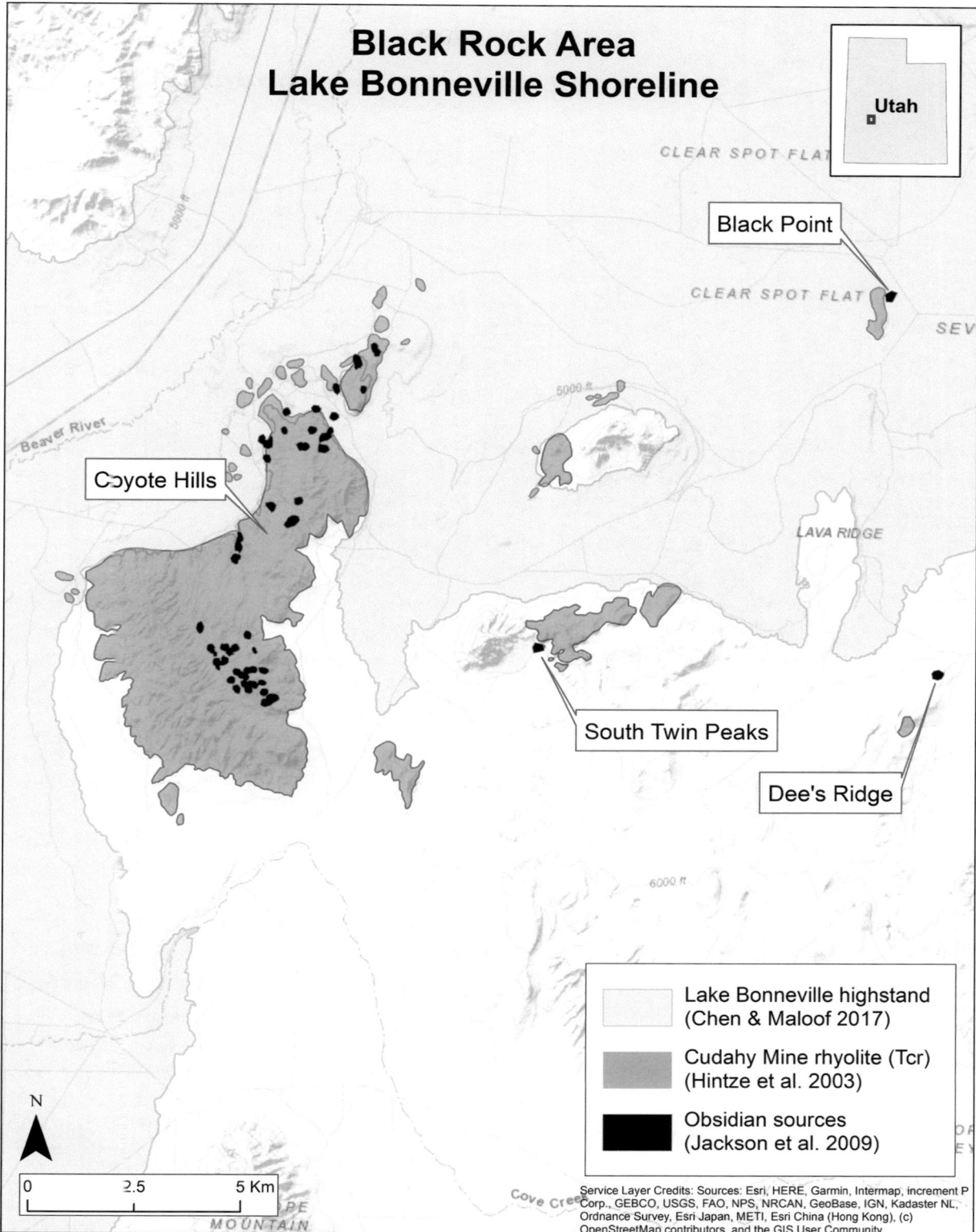

FIGURE 4.12. Black Rock Area primary sources in relation to the Lake Bonneville highstand.

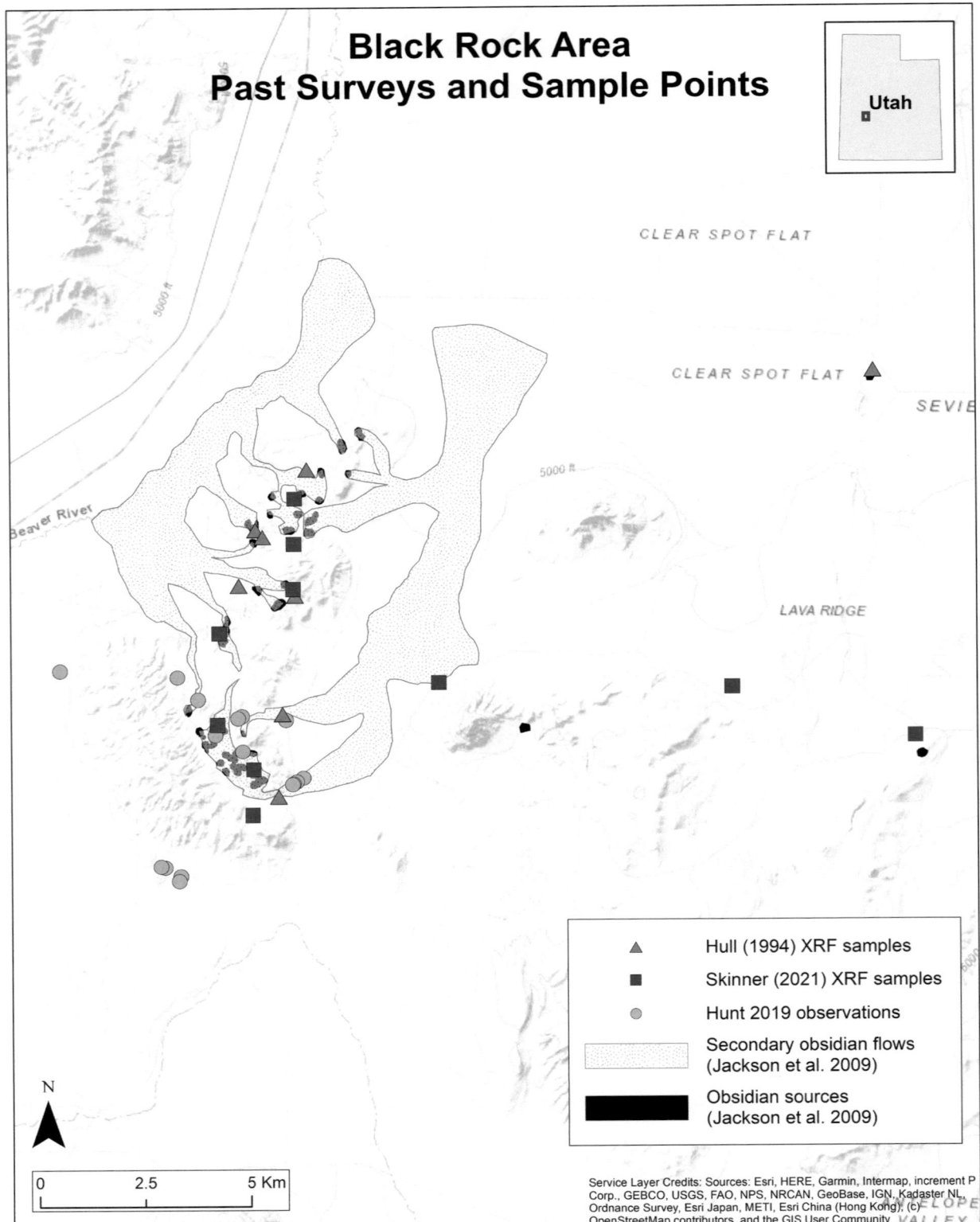

FIGURE 4.13. Black Rock Area past surveys and sample points.

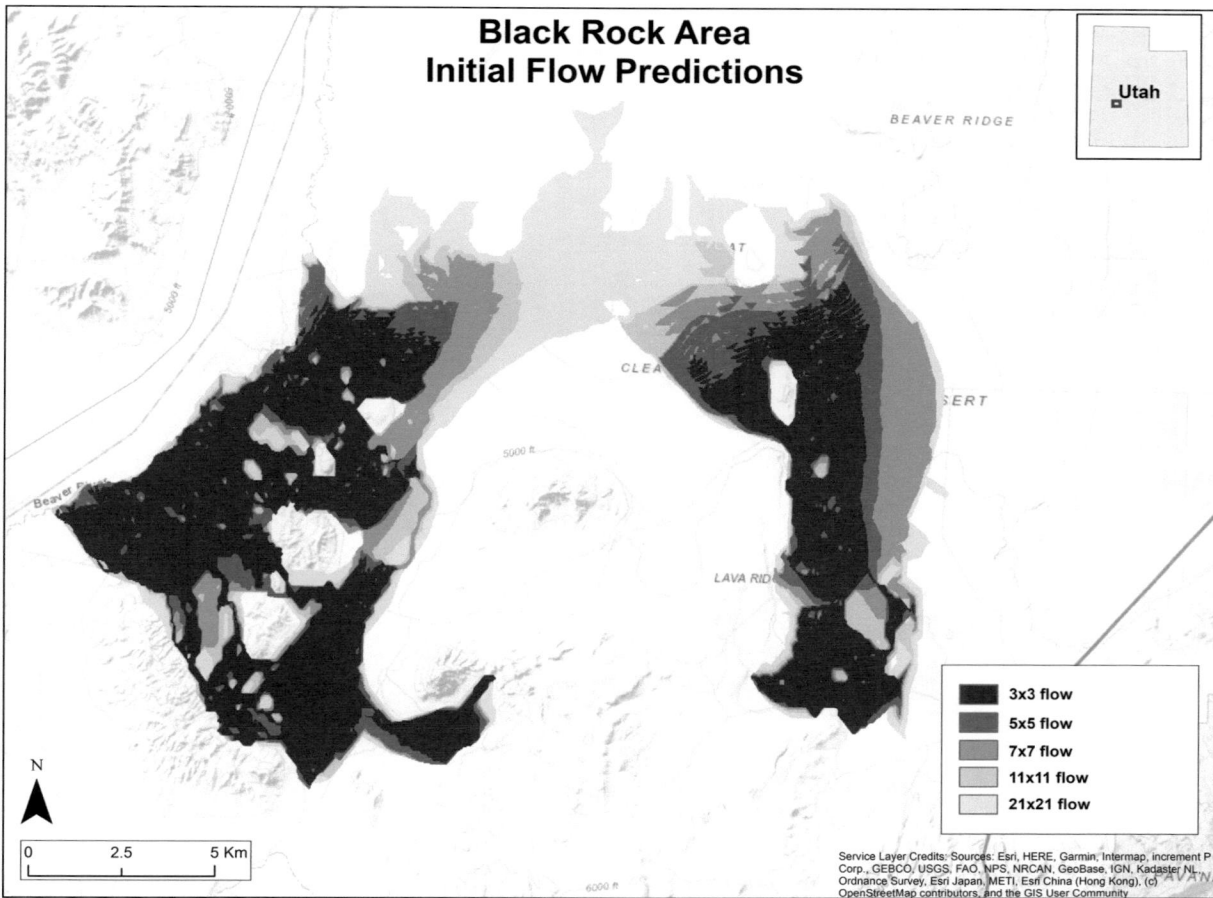

FIGURE 4.14. Black Rock Area initial flow predictions.

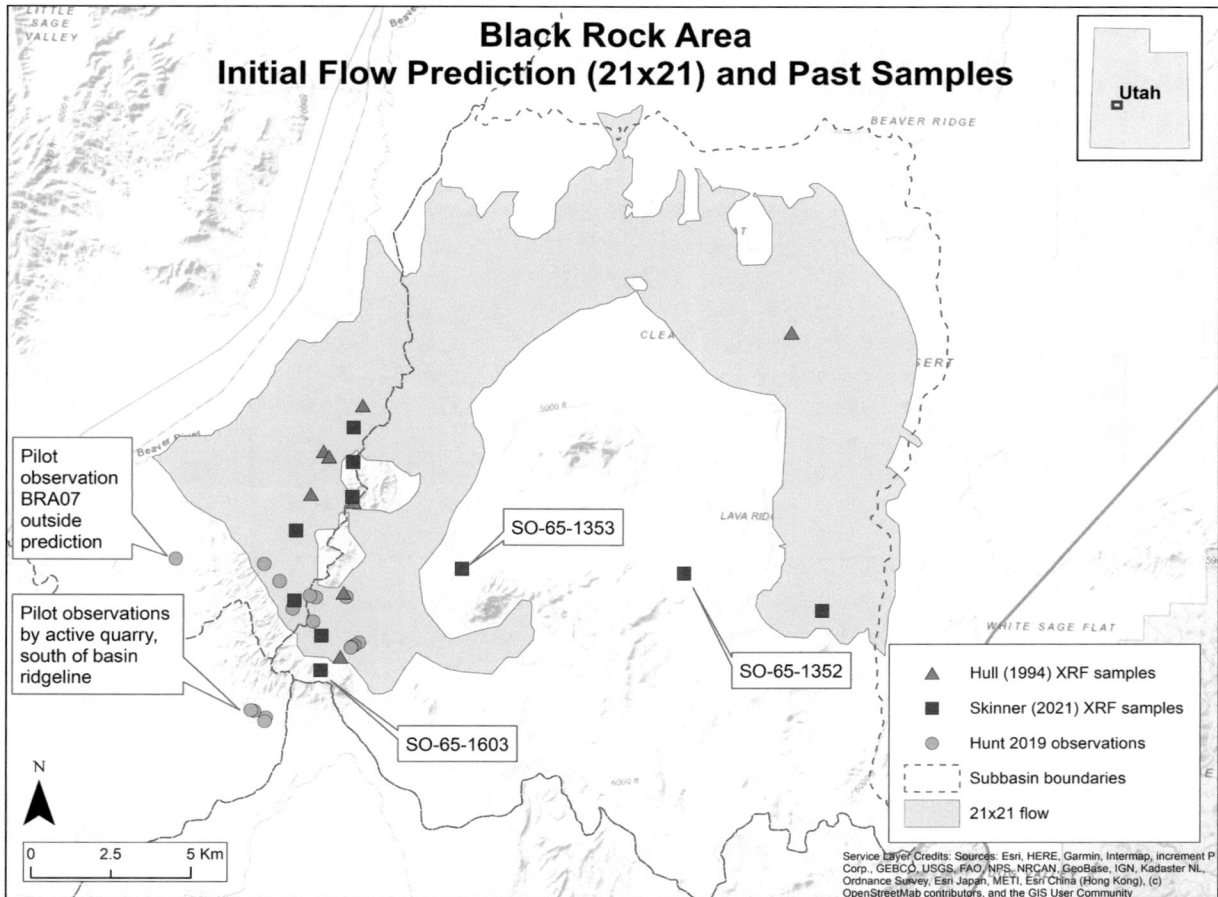

FIGURE 4.15. Black Rock Area initial 21×21 flow prediction in comparison with past sampling.

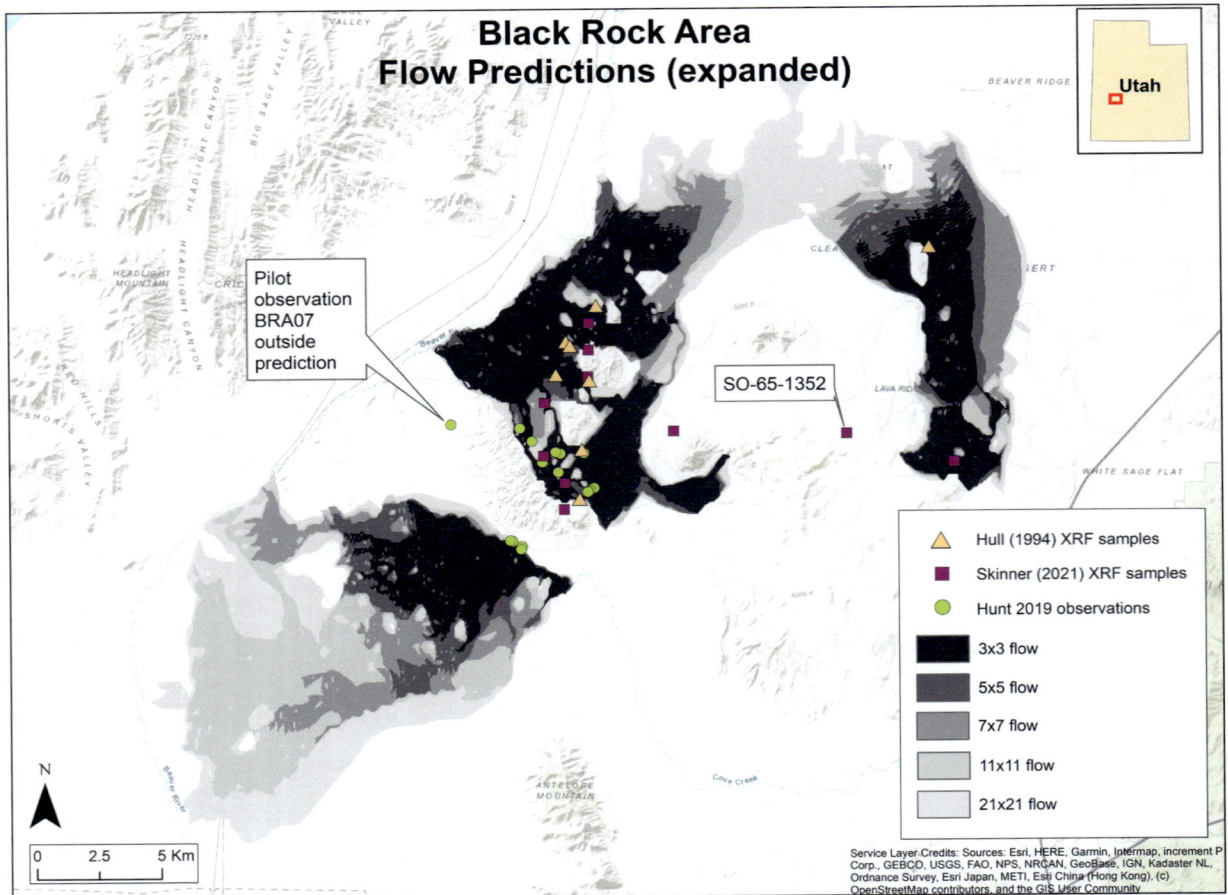

FIGURE 4.16. Black Rock Area flow predictions including expanded southern region.

TABLE 4.3. Confusion Matrix Results for the Black Rock Area.

Smoothing	Predicted Flow Area (km²)	TP	FP	% Survey Predicted	% Prediction Inside Observed	% Prediction Outside Observed	TP/ Observed	FP/ Observed	(TP-FP)/ Observed
3×3	116.2	110.5	5.7	31%	95%	5%	31%	2%	29.7%
5×5	144.3	130.8	13.5	37%	91%	9%	37%	4%	33.3%
7×7	194.3	168.6	25.7	48%	87%	13%	48%	7%	40.5%
9×9	225.1	187.7	37.4	53%	83%	17%	53%	11%	42.6%
11×11	259.0	212.1	46.9	60%	82%	18%	60%	13%	46.8%
13×13	**287.9**	**226.9**	**61.1**	**64%**	**79%**	**21%**	**64%**	**17%**	**47.0%**
15×15	302.6	233.5	69.1	66%	77%	23%	66%	20%	46.6%
17×17	312.8	237.9	75.0	67%	76%	24%	67%	21%	46.2%
19×19	324.5	241.6	82.9	68%	74%	26%	68%	24%	45.0%
21×21	330.6	242.0	88.6	69%	73%	27%	69%	25%	43.5%

Hills, east of the Goshute Mountains (and the smaller Ferguson Mountain), and west of the expansive mud flats that make up the western edge of the Great Salt Lake Desert. The source is less than 3 km south from the restricted Utah Test and Training Range South military zone (Figure 4.22).

Ainsworth (email communication, 2001) and Hockett (B. Hockett to C. Skinner, P. Ainsworth, & T. Goebel, email communication, November 3, 2001) make the case that the name "Ferguson Wash" is a misnomer, in that there is no actual place named "Ferguson Wash," rather that the nearest geographical features are Dead Cedar

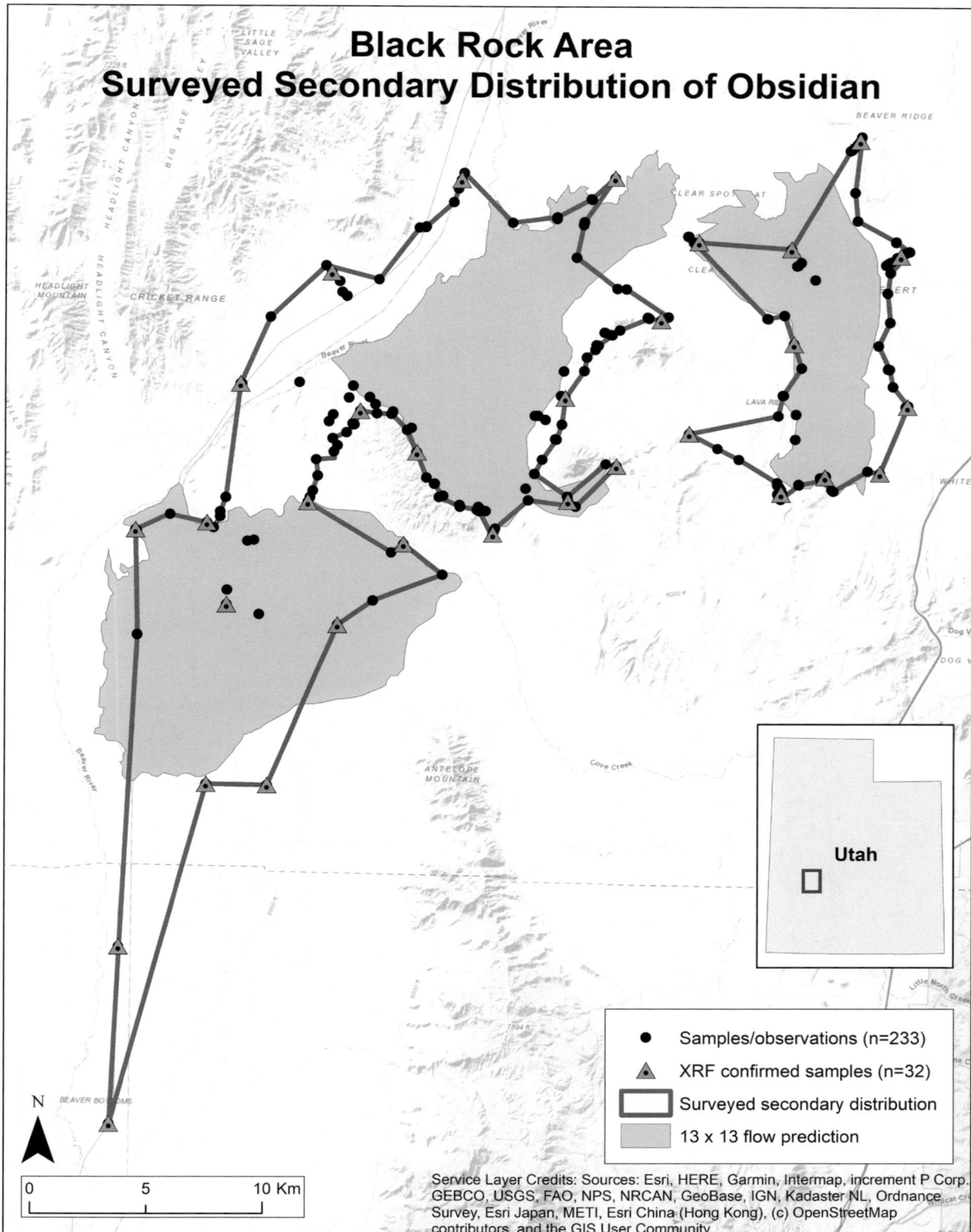

Black Rock Area Surveyed Secondary Distribution of Obsidian

Utah

Samples/observations (n=233)

XRF confirmed samples (n=32)

Surveyed secondary distribution

13 x 13 flow prediction

N

0   5   10 Km

Service Layer Credits: Sources: Esri, HERE, Garmin, Intermap, increment P Corp.
GEBCO, USGS, FAO, NPS, NRCAN, GeoBase, IGN, Kadaster NL, Ordnance
Survey, Esri Japan, METI, Esri China (Hong Kong), (c) OpenStreetMap
contributors, and the GIS User Community

FIGURE 4.17. Black Rock Area surveyed secondary distribution of obsidian in comparison to 13 × 13 flow prediction.

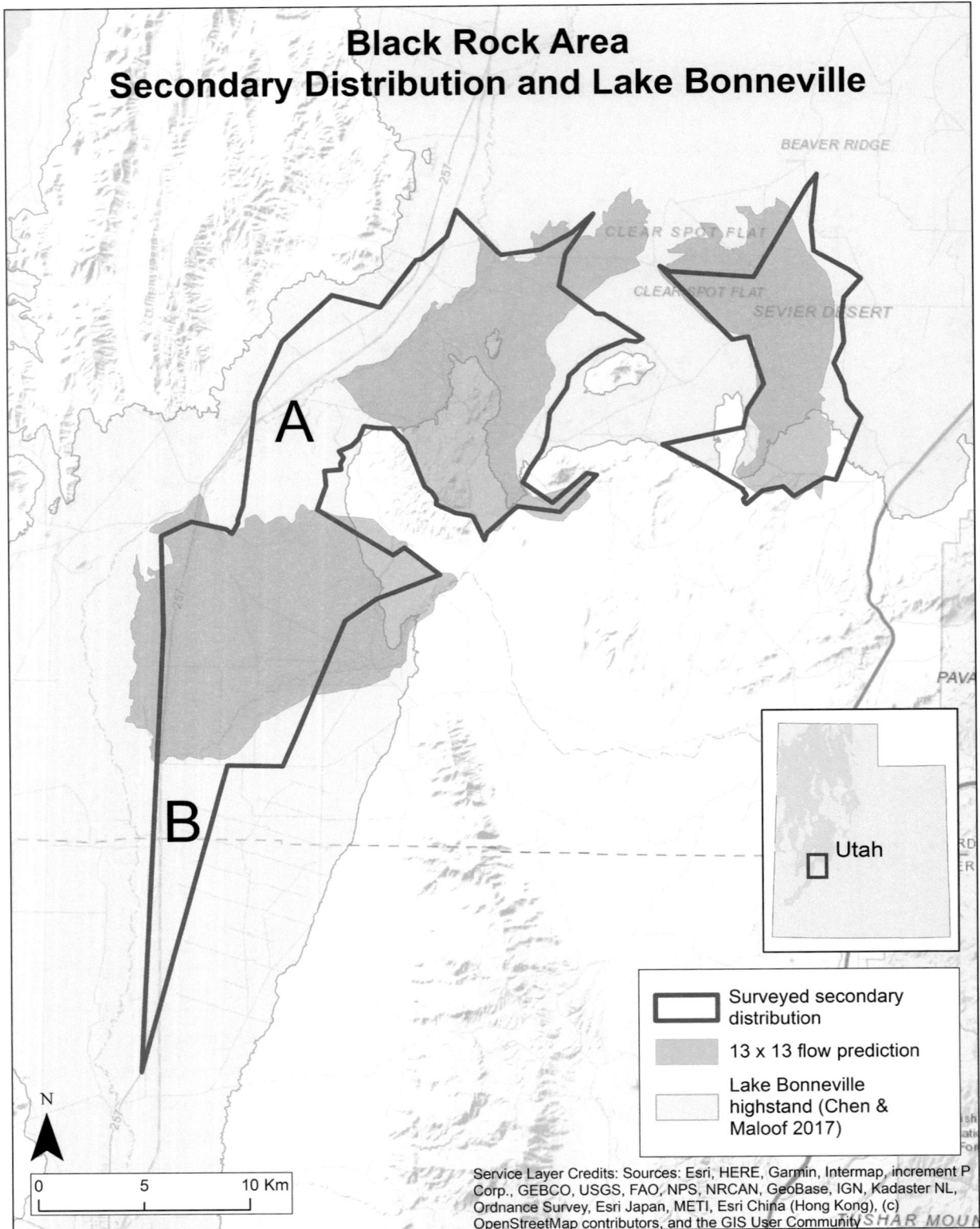

FIGURE 4.18. Black Rock Area surveyed secondary distribution in relation to the Lake Bonneville shore. Obsidian observed in areas A and B, extending well beyond the regions predicted by hydrographic movement, suggest sediment movement by Lake Bonneville wave action.

FIGURE 4.19. Ferguson Wash flowing south from the primary source area [near 11S 750183 4476826].

Wash, to which some secondary deposits are near, and Ferguson Flat, which is more to the west. Regardless, the name has stuck, though in some reports, the source may appear as "Dead Cedar Wash" or "Ferguson Flat."

FW Geology

The age of Elko County volcanism is not well researched, but several studies (Coats, 1987; Crafford, 2007; Regnier, 1960; Smith Jr. & Ketner, 1976) describe similar phenorhyolitic flows and domes across Nevada. A K-Ar date of 15.0 ± 1.0 Ma for the Palisade rhyolite in Eureka County is offered by Armstrong, who notes the "consistent regional pattern" (1970, pp. 212–213) of volcanic activity shifting from the west/central area of the Great Basin and bringing volcanic activity to the eastern edge around the Miocene (~23 Ma). This finding is consistent with the broad range of regional volcanism suggested by Crecraft et al. (1981), beginning about 20 Ma (discussed above).

Phenorhyolitic flows and domes were mapped by Crafford (2007) on the Nevada side of the state border (as *Tr3*) and by Hintze et al. (2000) on the Utah side (as *Tmr*). The FW primary source, as mapped by Jackson et al. (2009) is shown in context of these geological structures in Figure 4.22.

At present, this location appears to have only one primary area of exposure, about 300 m long (Freund et al., 2021; B. Hockett to C. Skinner, P. Ainsworth, & T. Goebel, email communication, November 1, 2001; Jackson et al., 2009). Hockett (email communication, November 3, 2001) describes this location as a "mas-

sive exposure of several beds of welded tuff, capped by rhyolite" with two distinctly-colored beds. One is a "pinkish-orange tuff" bed (Figure 4.20), loosely welded, and the other a "greyish tuff" bed, more tightly welded (Figure 4.21). Phenorhyolitic flows differ from rhyolitic flows in that obsidian forms not as a layer but directly within the tuffs as nodules (as in Figure 4.21). These nodules then erode from the beds directly as pebbles, rarely exceeding 4 cm in diameter at this locality. Hockett (email communication, November 3, 2001) questions whether the full extent of the exposure has been discovered based on similar nodules found 4 miles to the north.

The Ferguson Wash area was completely inundated by Pleistocene Lake Bonneville at its height, around 18,000 cal BP, as illustrated in Figure 4.23 (Chen & Maloof, 2017b; O'Connor, 2016; Oviatt & Jewell, 2016; Oviatt & Shroder, 2016; Utah Geospatial Reference Center, 2017). As noted earlier, Lake Bonneville reached its highstand at approximately 1552 masl. A catastrophic failure of the north basin wall and subsequent regional warming reduced the lake to the Provo shoreline level at roughly 1450 masl, around 14,500 cal BP. The lake continued receding, arriving at the Gilbert shoreline level (1290 masl) around 13,000 cal BP before settling into its current levels as the Great Salt Lake (~1275 masl; Oviatt & Shroder, 2016). This prehistory and Figure 4.23 suggest that the Ferguson Wash area was subjected to wave action for millennia, even before its subsequent exposure to erosion and alluvial forces. Possibly Lake Bonneville longshore currents are responsible for the far-flung

FIGURE 4.20. Ferguson Wash "pinkish-orange" welded tuff [11T 750346 4477032].

FIGURE 4.21. Ferguson Wash "greyish tuff" with in situ obsidian nodules [11T 750266 4477077].

northward distribution of cobbles noted by Hockett (email communication, November 3, 2001).

After Lake Bonneville receded, the area was covered in lacustrine fine silt, sandy loam, and pebble fields, which remain today.

FW Archaeology

Several dozen prehistoric sites are recorded surrounding the Ferguson Wash area (Utah Department of Heritage and Arts, 2020; Utah Division of State History, 2020; Wallace, 2017, 2018). These are almost exclusively lithic scatters, occasionally with diagnostic artifacts present. The sites range in classification from "Paleoindian" to Fremont, representing activity in the region over a great deal of time. Also present are recent historical sites as the hillside was used as a target site for World War II munitions practice.

Use of FW obsidian is known from multiple archaeological sites, predominantly during the Archaic. Madsen and Schmitt (2005) associated a Rosegate corner-notched point found at the Buzz-cut Dune site with FW obsidian. Similarly, Page and Skinner (2008) sourced 21 Danger Cave artifacts back to FW (Jackson et al., 2009). At the Bonneville Estates rockshelter, less than 10 km to the north, Goebel et al. (2018) reported that a majority (52 percent) of the Archaic and none of the Paleoindian artifacts at that site were manufactured using FW obsidian. However, from the Old River Bed XRF data (see Appendix A), there are only eight FW-sourced artifacts, spanning types from Silver Lake ($n = 4$) to Rosegate (Page, 2015a). Of these, only one is included in the final, cleaned Paleoindian dataset (Appendix A, Table A.37) associated with a dated ORB delta channel. So, while the available material size may have limited the use of FW obsidian for larger Paleoindian points, it does appear that it was utilized during the Paleoindian period.

FW Past Work

Our understanding of the FW primary, secondary, and tertiary obsidian extents relies on relatively recent work, in comparison to other sources explored here, and is illustrated in Figure 4.24. Ainsworth (P. Ainsworth to C. Skinner & T. Goebel, email communication, November 1, 2001) provides the earliest description of the primary source location and the flow of secondary alluvium into the lake flats. Ainsworth also describes a tertiary extent, reworked by the neighboring Dead Cedar Wash alluvial fan. Jackson et al. (2009) provide a more extensive description of the primary source and secondary flow, extending it quite a bit farther east. Skinner (2021; Appendix D, Table D.2) provides three unique XRF sample locations, which include samples by Hockett (email communication, November 1, 2001).

In 2019, I conducted a pilot survey and observed the primary sources (photos above) and the secondary distributions of obsidian at various points around the primary source (Appendix B, Table B.6, $n = 36$). While these samples are not XRF-tested, these observations provided a useful indicator of how obsidian is flowing out of the FW source into the flats in preparation for fieldwork.

FW Flow Prediction

Using the process described in the beginning of this chapter, five flow distributions were created.

The starting requirement for all flow prediction is the location of the primary source, illustrated for FW in Figure 4.22. The outline provided by Jackson et al. (2009) was used, rather than Ainsworth (email communication, November 1, 2001) as it was larger and fit more closely with my own 2019 observations of the source. Using this primary source as the starting point, the downslope flows were predicted for 3×3, 5×5, 7×7, 11×11, and 21×21 nearest neighbor smoothed DEMs. These are presented in "stacked" form in Figure 4.25, with the 3×3 nearest neighborhood flow represented by the darkest shade and the 21×21 flow represented by the lightest shade.

During preparation for fieldwork, the comparison to the known sample points by Skinner (2021; Appendix D, Table D.2), and my own pilot project observations (Appendix B, Table B.6) showed good concordance with the 21×21 flow prediction, with one exception, sample SO-65-896 (Figure 4.26). It seemed likely this exception was the result of rounding in a conversion "round-trip," as the original location was reported in UTM, converted to decimal degrees (with only one decimal point of precision), and then back to UTM. A point was added to the figure based on the original UTM value report by Hockett (email communication, November 3, 2001). This moved the point from ~530 m away from the 21×21 flow to ~390 m away. The area was investigated during fieldwork to verify the location and ensure there is no obsidian flowing down Dead Cedar Wash or alternative unknown primary sources (see below).

The final 21×21 prediction outline and transects are shown in Figure G.12. An important consideration here was that the distal ends of most of the FW flow predictions (3×3 is the only exception) appear to extend into the restricted military zone to the north. This boundary is at the UTM northing of 4479648 m and is preceded by a dirt road about 30 m south of the boundary. Knowing that during fieldwork we would need to stay well below the southern boundary of the installation, a survey track was included that cut across the predicted flows to help assess if the flows really extended that far

TABLE 4.4. Confusion Matrix Results for Ferguson Wash.

Smoothing	Predicted Flow Area (km²)	TP	FP	% Survey Predicted	% Prediction Inside Observed	% Prediction Outside Observed	TP/ Observed	FP/ Observed	(TP-FP)/ Observed
3×3	0.1	0.0	0.1	0%	21%	79%	0.5%	1.8%	−1.3%
5×5	16.4	3.9	12.5	99%	24%	76%	99.1%	313%	−214%
7×7	20.0	3.9	16.1	99%	20%	80%	99.1%	404%	−305%

north and east before working near the military zone. The extent of the secondary flow mapped by Jackson et al. (2009) suggested it would not flow that far.

FW Survey Results

The Ferguson Wash secondary distribution was surveyed during summer 2020, and the observed extent is illustrated in Figure 4.27. FW is the smallest of the secondary distributions surveyed, with an area of only ~4 km² and a perimeter of ~14 km. During the survey, 118 observation points were recorded, and 37 natural obsidian samples were collected (Appendix B, Table B.2). Of these collected samples, 13 were submitted to NWROSL for XRF testing (Appendix C, Table C.2) and were confirmed as "Ferguson Wash" obsidian (triangles in Figure 4.27).

As an aside, I note that the original XRF lab report, Appendix E, classified these samples as "Ferguson Wash, Type B," which is "a newly identified subtype of Ferguson Wash obsidian, distinguished by elevated strontium (Sr) and yttrium (Y) levels relative to the well-characterized Ferguson Wash source" (Alex Nyers, personal communication, November 12, 2021). Given that the sample area is relatively small, these results raised questions and the samples were retested on new spectrometers. In the end, the samples were confirmed to be "Ferguson Wash" samples, as shown in Appendix F. The error was attributed to equipment issues, and all survey samples were confirmed as secondary outflow from the FW primary source.

Skinner (2021; Appendix D, Table D.2) reported three FW samples taken by Hockett (email communication, November 1, 2001). Two of these points (Figure 4.24) are within 300 m of the observed flow, and it is reasonable that conditions on the ground have changed in the last 20 years. However, sample SO-65-896 was clearly out of scope (Figure 4.26), positioned more than 800 m from the observed flow edge and at an elevated position. I surveyed this sample location and observed only large basaltic boulders, no obsidian, and geology out of character with the primary and secondary source areas. I also surveyed the mouth of Dead Cedar Wash, just before it empties into the flat, and no obsidian is evident in this wash. This sample point may have a recor-

dation error. Aside from this point, the surveyed flow encompasses almost all previous sample/observation points recorded by Skinner (2021; Appendix D, Table D.2) and me, with minor exceptions.

As the secondary distribution flows south and east into the lake flat, the survey found good concordance with the secondary distribution illustrated in Jackson et al. (2009, Figure 10-2). However, the observed eastern flow is truncated even when compared to the 5×5 predicted flow (Figure 4.28). As can be seen in Table 4.4, even very low smoothing levels (5×5 and 7×7) result in a "blow out" or "flooding" of the region with regard to flow prediction and the confusion matrix results provide no meaningful information.

The failure of the model in this case is attributed to two factors. First, Ferguson Wash is unusual in that the primary and secondary source areas were entirely submerged during the Lake Bonneville highstand (Chen & Maloof, 2017b; O'Connor, 2016; Oviatt & Jewell, 2016; Oviatt & Shroder, 2016). During this period, longshore transport may account for the movement of obsidian to the north of the primary source area, but the receding shorelines may have also covered the eastward movement of this FW obsidian with lacustrine sediments. Similar results have been observed in other survey regions as flows move into the very flat basin bottoms affected by Lake Bonneville (see the discussion of the Fish Springs Flat in the Topaz Mountain section). In these cases, I believe the discernable grains of obsidian (< 2mm) have been sorted into lacustrine silts and out of sight.

Second, FW is unique in that the primary source and the proximal end of the secondary flow are at very low elevations when compared to the distal end in the basin bottom. In this case, the primary source is only about 25 m above the point where it erodes into a wash. The apex of that wash, at about 1400 masl, is only about 100 m above the distal end of the 5×5 flow prediction (at about 1300 masl), which is more than 5.5 km away. In these low slope regions, my model treats the sediment like water, allowing the flow to disperse without regard to particle size.

The effect of this dynamic shoreline environment on the primary source and its past erosional history, as

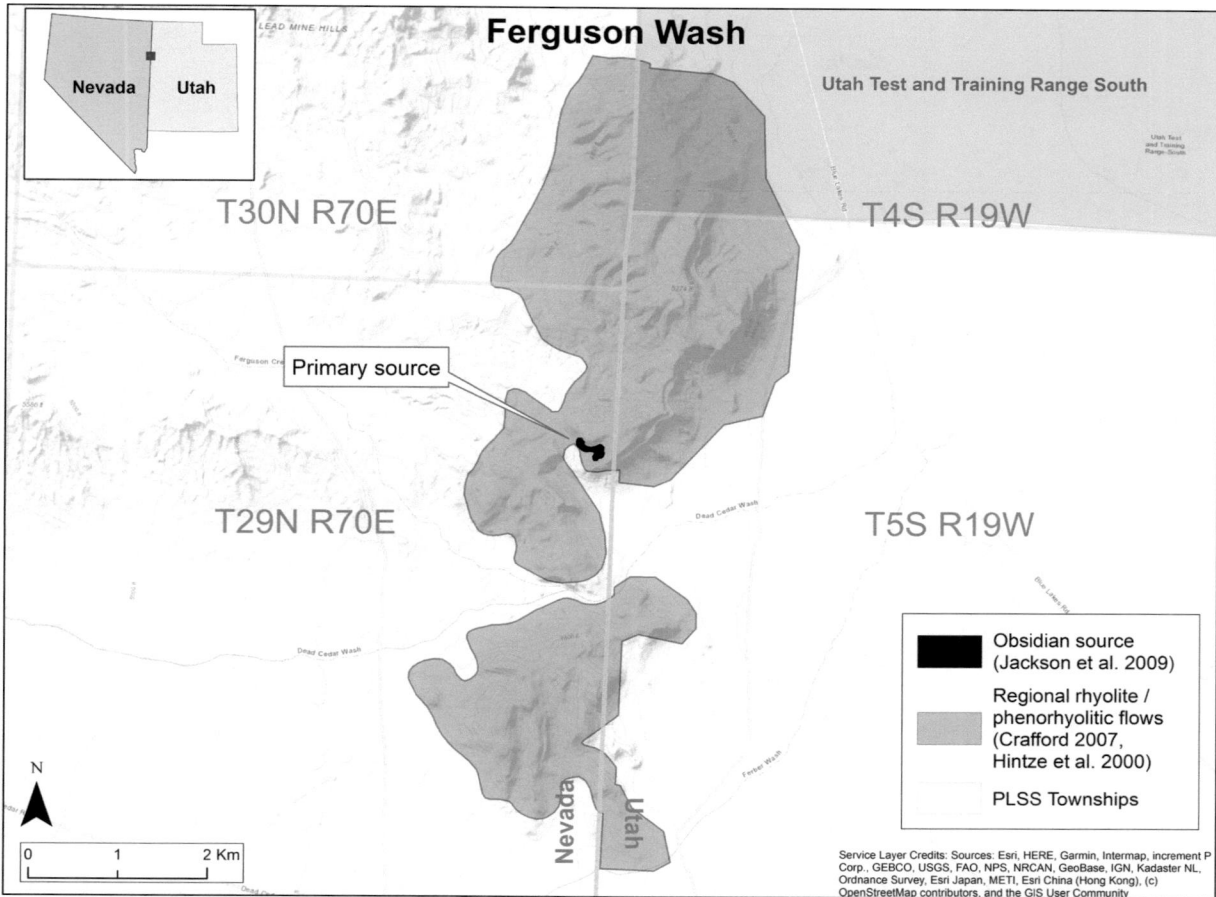

FIGURE 4.22. Ferguson Wash regional view.

well as the very low-slope basin bottom, appear to have resulted in an excessive flow prediction with the model used here. As a result of these issues, the predictions at FW are considered to have failed.

Mineral Mountains

Location: Beaver County, Utah

Alternative Names: Wildhorse Canyon, Wild Horse Canyon, Bailey Ridge, Negro Mag Wash

Hull (1994) Sample Points: n = 22 (Appendix D, Table D.1)

Skinner Sample Points: n = 8 (Appendix D, Table D.2)

Hunt 2019 Observation Points: n = 20 (Appendix B, Table B.6)

ORB Paleoindian Artifacts: n = 9 (Appendix A, Table A.37)

The Mineral Mountains (MM) are a horst and graben range in Beaver County, Utah, about 15 km east of the town of Milford and directly south of the Black Rock Area previously described (Figure 4.31). The rhyolitic flows in the MM are geologically relatively recent and the area is still geothermally active. A commercial

geothermal plant operates only a few kilometers from the two main primary obsidian source locations: the Wildhorse Canyon and Bailey Ridge sources (Lipman et al., 1978). The Pumice Hole Mine source is also found near these sources and is discussed in Chapter 5. Two additional obsidian sources a few kilometers south in the range, Kirk Canyon and Pumice Hole Mine B, are known and likely the result of later eruptions. These latter sources contain abundant phenocrysts, making them unsuitable for knapping (Hull, 1994; Jackson et al., 2009). This project focused on mapping the secondary distributions of the Wildhorse Canyon and Bailey Ridge obsidian (Figure 4.29).

MM Geology

The Mineral Mountains (MM) were formed from a granitic batholith approximately 9–15 Ma and rise about 1 km above the basin floor (Evans, Jr. et al., 1978). Around 0.79 ± 0.08 Ma, two highly-fluid, silicic rhyolitic flows erupted (Evans, Jr. et al., 1978; Lipman et al., 1978).

These flows, up to 100 m thick, emerged in the north end of the range at Bailey Ridge, including flow into Negro Mag Wash, and in the central region at

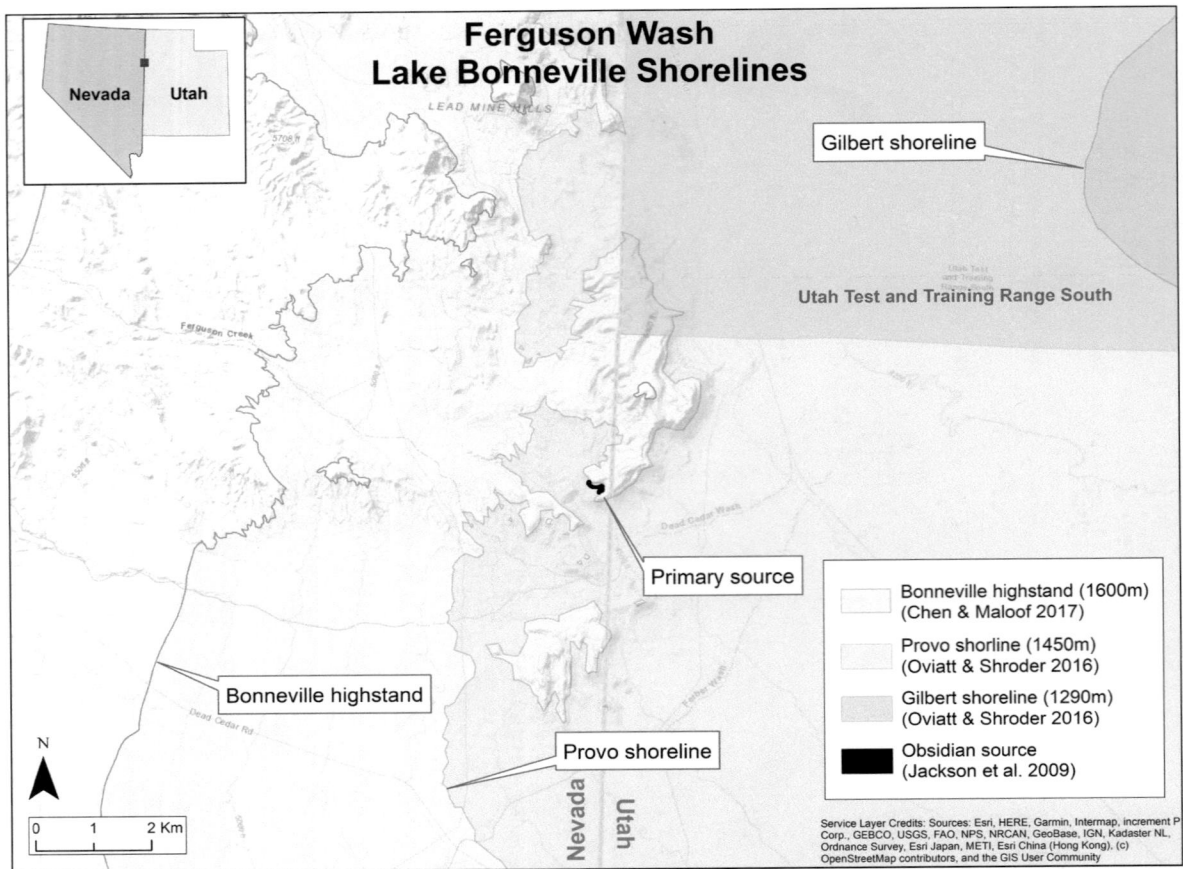

FIGURE 4.23. Ferguson Wash primary sources in relation to the Lake Bonneville highstand and subsequent receding shorelines.

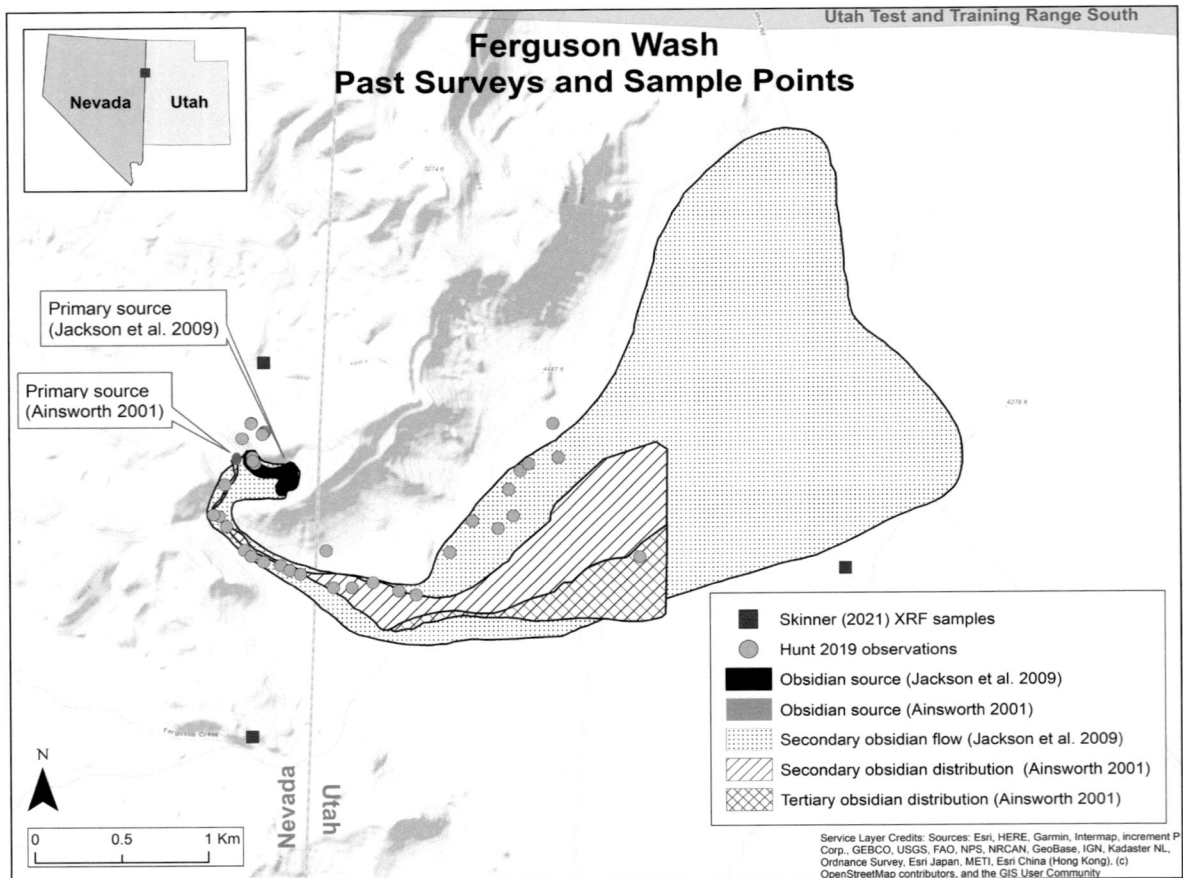

FIGURE 4.24. Ferguson Wash past surveys and sample points.

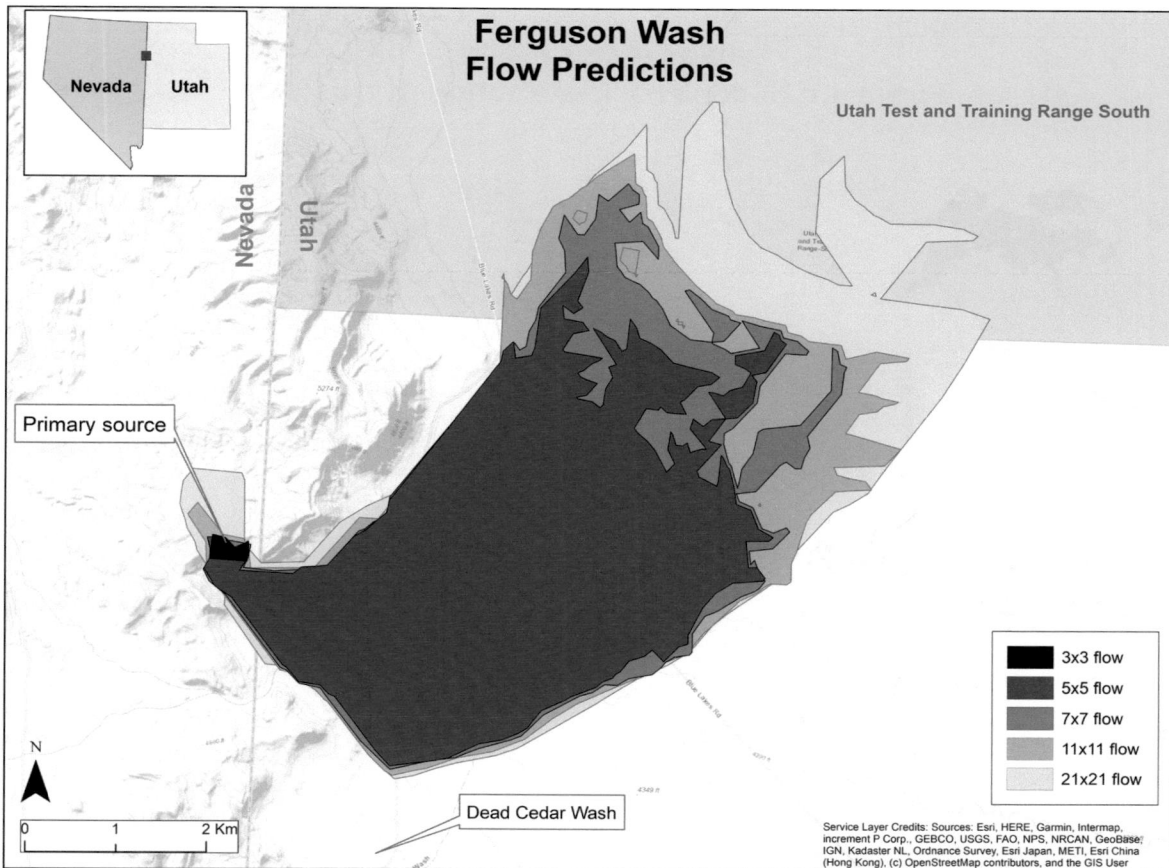

FIGURE 4.25. Ferguson Wash flow predictions.

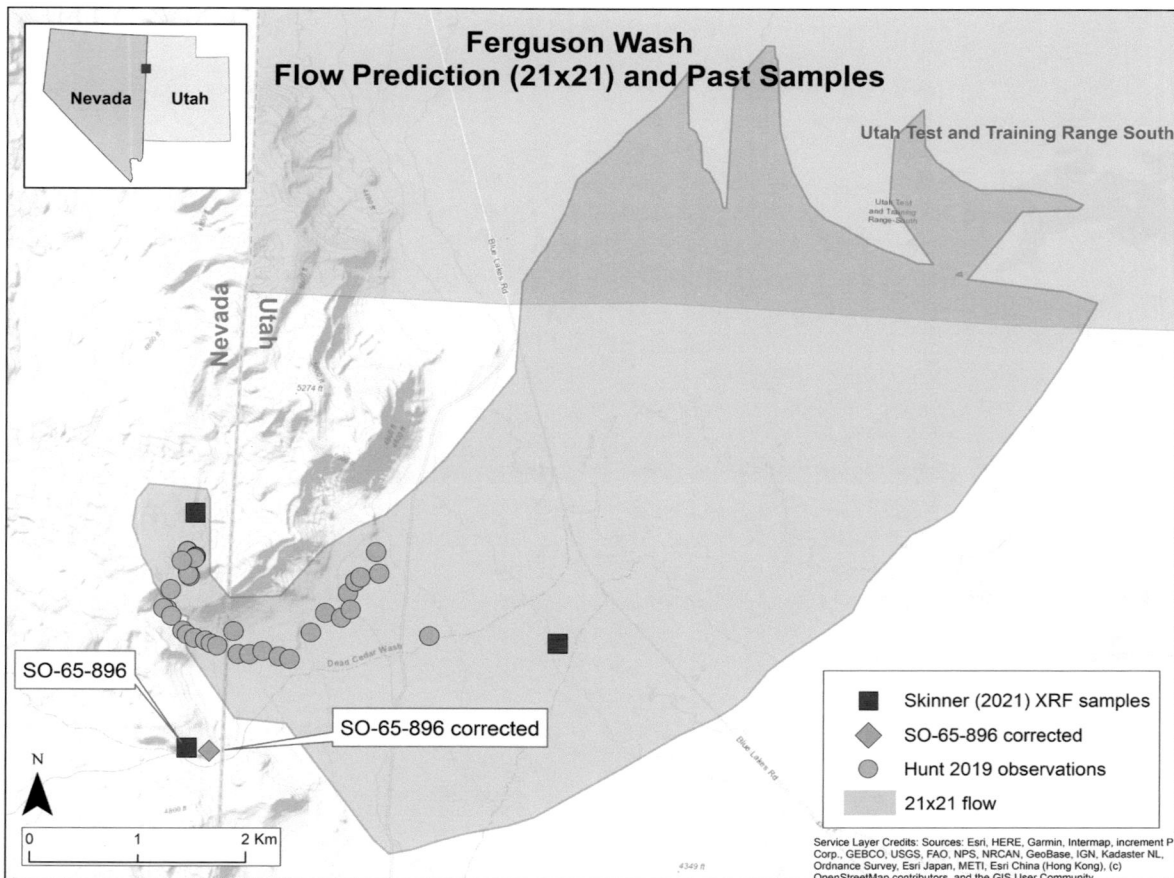

FIGURE 4.26. Ferguson Wash 21×21 flow prediction in comparison with past sampling.

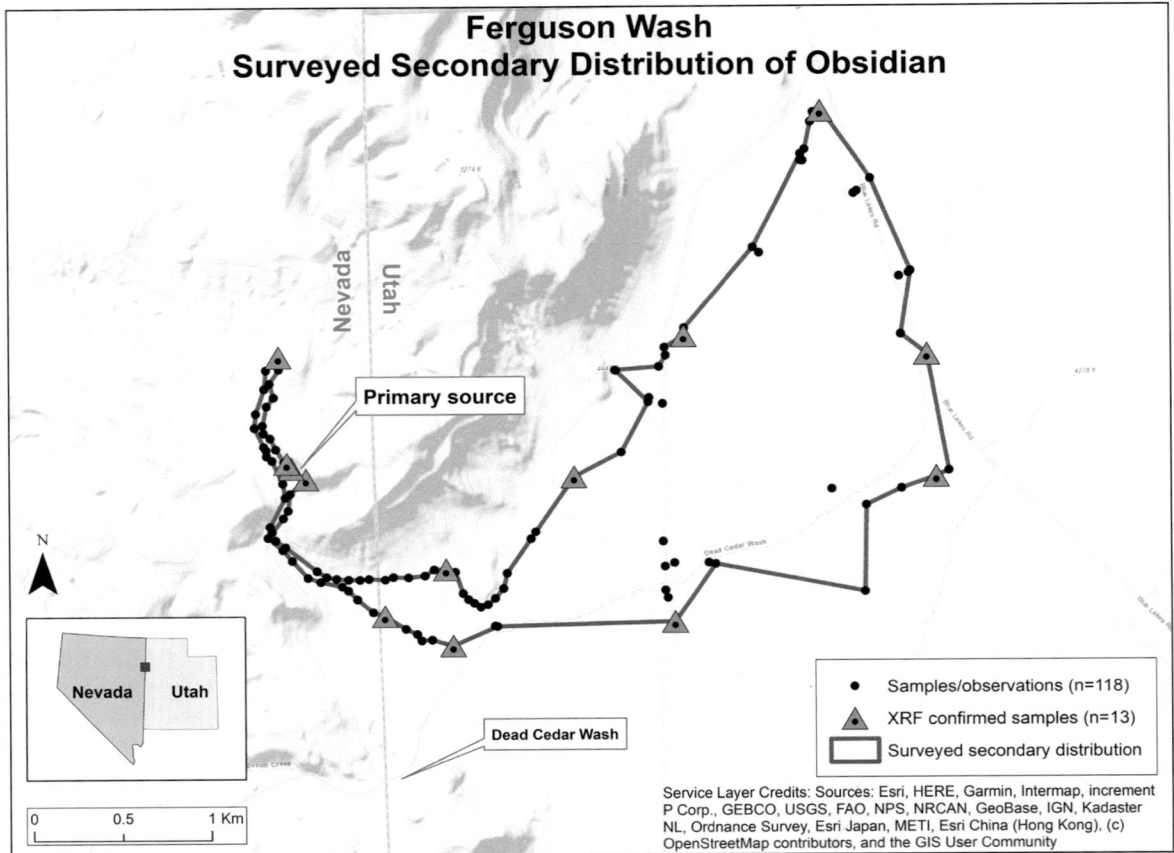

FIGURE 4.27. Ferguson Wash surveyed secondary distribution of obsidian.

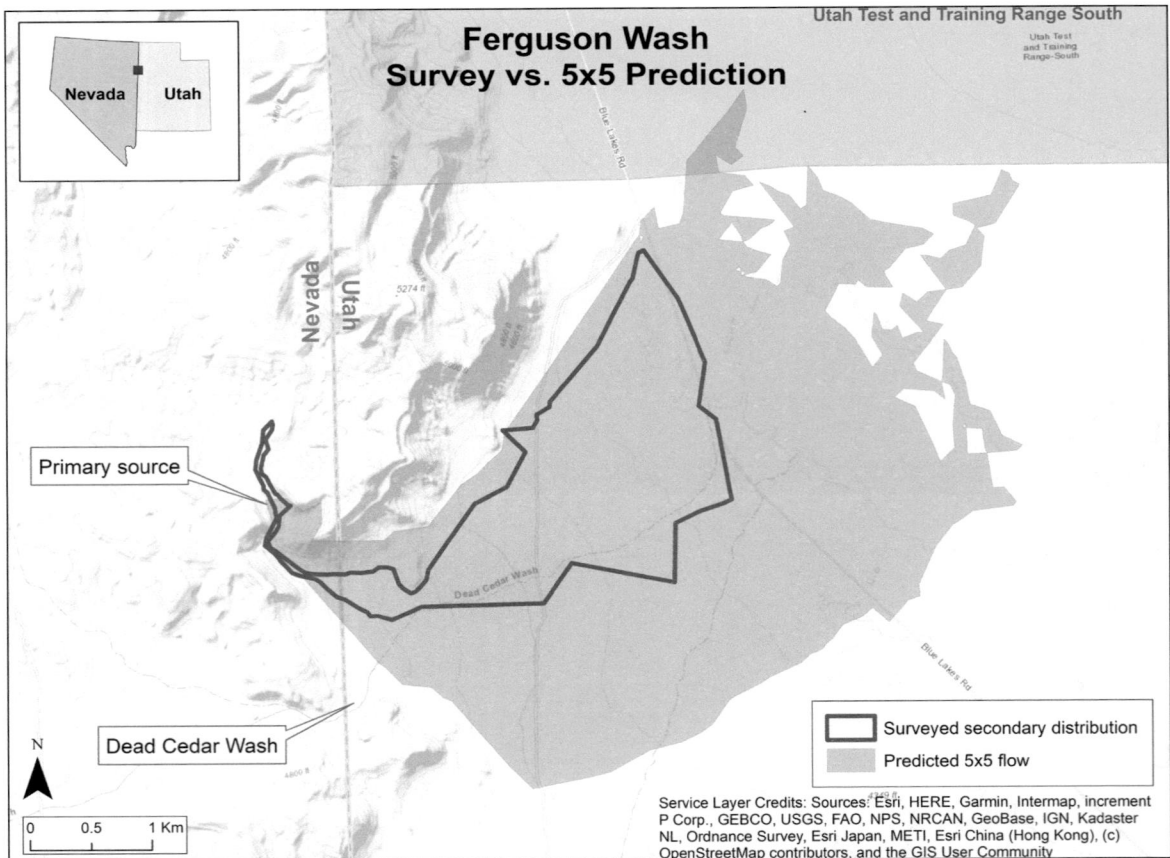

FIGURE 4.28. Ferguson Wash surveyed secondary distribution in relation to the 5×5 flow prediction.

FIGURE 4.29. Obsidian exposure at the mouth of Wildhorse Canyon, 2019.

Wildhorse Canyon, as illustrated in Figure 4.31 (Rowley et al., 2005). The flows are highly silicic (76.5% SiO2) and nonporphyritic with "less than 0.5 percent total phenocrysts" (Lipman et al., 1978, p. 137), resulting in an obsidian that knaps exceptionally well (Hull, 1994). The two flows are also highly laminar, indicating flows of low viscosity, and are geochemically similar, to the point of being indistinguishable from each other by XRF testing (Evans, Jr. et al., 1978; Hull, 1994; Lipman et al., 1978). In the literature, the source is known predominantly as Wildhorse Canyon (or Wild Horse Canyon) obsidian.

Figure 4.32 illustrates the relationship of the MM to the Lake Bonneville highstand shoreline (Chen & Maloof, 2017b; Oviatt & Jewell, 2016; Utah Geospatial Reference Center, 2017). The MM are located on the southernmost arm of Lake Bonneville. While the primary sources were not affected by the highstand, the secondary distribution likely was as it flowed westward (as will be shown below). This southern arm of the lake was completely drained as the lake receded to the Provo shoreline. After Lake Bonneville receded, the areas below the remnant shoreline were covered in lacustrine fine silt, sandy loam, and pebble fields, which remain today.

Most recently, the Milford Flat Fire of 2007 stripped the mouth of Wildhorse Canyon of vegetation, which has not returned. This calamity was followed by a flash flood in 2008, significantly impacting the canyon and downslope area, covering up to 40 percent of the alluvial fan (Jackson et al., 2009). These environmental events may have impacted survey results.

MM Archaeology

The archaeological sites at Wildhorse Canyon and Bailey Ridge have been extensively studied and surveyed in recent decades. The Wildhorse Canyon site (42Be52) was first recorded in 1964 when it was recognized as an intensive quarry site (Weide, 1964). Similarly, the Bailey Ridge site was first recorded as an undisturbed quarry and "chipping" site in 1974 (Fike, 1974). Since then, numerous surveys of the downslope secondary distributions and local lithic scatters, consisting of thousands of artifacts and millions of flakes, have been merged under the 42Be52 trinomial. The full extent of the combined sites exceeds 54 km² (Jackson et al., 2009; Utah Department of Heritage and Arts, 2020). The alluvial flows are so rich with material that at least three quarries (42Be236, 42Be248, and 42Be270) have been recorded within the fans themselves, each extending more than 1000 m across (Jackson et al., 2009; Utah Department of Heritage and Arts, 2020). Hundreds of smaller sites, primarily lithic scatters, surround the Mineral Mountains primary obsidian sources.

Bailey Ridge and Wildhorse Canyon have been subjected to contemporary disturbances. Both sites were mined in the 1950s for perlite, a form of hydrated volcanic glass with industrial uses, such as thermal and

FIGURE 4.30. Abandoned bulldozer at Wildhorse Canyon, 2019.

acoustic insulation (Tripp, 2000). The remnants of this activity are evident today in the form of abandoned equipment and trenches from mechanical excavation (Figure 4.30). Wildhorse Canyon is still frequented by obsidian collectors and knappers; during my pilot project I witnessed a family fill the back of their minivan with obsidian from Wildhorse Canyon to use for knapping.

MM Past Work

Our understanding of the scope and extent of the MM primary and secondary obsidian extents is illustrated in Figure 4.33. Hull (1994) provides an early dataset of XRF testing on 22 samples from Bailey Ridge (labeled as Negro Mag Wash in her report) and Wildhorse Canyon (Appendix D, Table D.1). These samples appear to be centered on primary sources, though the township and range descriptions can be several hundred meters off when compared to modern GPS coordinates. Skinner (2021: Appendix D, Table D.2) provides an additional eight sample locations. In 2019, I conducted a pilot survey and observed obsidian at various points around the MM primary sources (Appendix B, Table B.6, n = 20). The work by Jackson et al. (2009), however, provides the best resource of primary obsidian sources at the MM, as well as an excellent secondary distribution survey, illustrating the alluvial fan emanating from the two primary sources.

All this information was used in selecting the best flow prediction for the MM obsidian.

MM Flow Prediction

Using the process described in the beginning of this chapter, five flow distributions were created.

The starting requirement for all flow prediction is the location of the primary sources and is illustrated for MM in Figure 4.31, which were derived from Jackson et al. (2009). Using these primary sources as the starting points, the downslope flows were predicted for 3×3, 5×5, 7×7, 11×11, and 21×21 nearest neighbor smoothed DEMs. These are presented in "stacked" form, in Figure 4.34, with the 3×3 nearest neighborhood flow represented by the darkest shade and the 21×21 flow represented by the lightest shade.

A comparison to the known sample points by Hull (1994; Appendix D, Table D.1), Skinner (2021; Appendix D, Table D.2), and my own pilot project (Appendix B, Table B.6) shows good concordance with, at least, the top of the predicted flows (Figure 4.35), though a few samples around the apex of the fans fall outside the projected flows. These outliers suggest the primary source extents may be greater than known, allowing some alluvial flow into smaller neighboring canyons and Big Cedar Cove that lies between Bailey Ridge and Wildhorse Canyon. A comparison of the secondary flow—recorded by Jackson et al. (2009), as seen in Figure

4.33—with the 21 × 21 flow illustrated in Figure 4.34 shows a remarkable similarity and suggests a positive correlation with the predicted flow.

The final 21 × 21 prediction outline and transects are shown in Figure G.13.

MM Survey Results

The Mineral Mountains secondary distribution was surveyed during summer 2020, and the observed extent is illustrated in Figure 4.36. The MM extent covers an area of ~160 km² with a perimeter of ~77 km. During the survey, 70 observation points were recorded, and 54 natural obsidian samples were collected (Appendix B, Table B.3). Of these collected samples, 22 were submitted to NWROSL for XRF testing (Appendix C, Table C.3) and were confirmed as "Wildhorse Canyon" obsidian (triangles in Figure 4.36).

The surveyed flow encompasses almost all previous sample points recorded by Hull (1994; Appendix D, Table D.1), Skinner (2021; Appendix D, Table D.2), and myself (Appendix B, Table B.6), with minor exceptions. In the primary source regions, a few previously recorded points are up to ~700 m outside the surveyed extent. This region is extremely rugged and overgrown, making it easy to miss specimens; however, the placement of these points would not significantly affect the predicted secondary distributions.

Survey access in the predicted secondary flow areas was significantly restricted by private property (Figure G.13). The valley is used extensively by the wind, solar, and geothermal energy industries as well as for hog farming. Almost 50 percent of the land within the final survey outline is private property. The bottom of the flow also spills into a heavily modified basin bottom where a railway and a highway skirt the basin bottom and parallel the distal end of the predicted flows.

Despite these limitations, the predicted flows provided an exceptionally accurate guide for the secondary distribution extents. Following the modified confusion matrix methodology described in the "Analyzing Survey Results" section of this chapter, the optimal smoothing level for the MM occurs at the 23 × 23 nearest neighbor average (Table 4.5). At this level, 82 percent of the observed secondary extent was predicted by the model.

In addition, the MM results provide an excellent example of the impact of Lake Bonneville on the secondary distribution beyond the hydrographic flow predictions. Figure 4.37 illustrates the relationship between the 13 × 13 and 23 × 23 flow predictions and the Lake Bonneville highstand shoreline (Chen & Maloof, 2017b). Above the shoreline (to the east), we can see tight conformance between both flow predictions, even though the difference in smoothing levels is quite large.

East of the shoreline, the 13 × 13 and 23 × 23 predictions provide almost identical fits. Below the shoreline, which is still 5 to 8 km upslope from the basin bottom, the observed secondary distribution is more spread out than predicted. The north shoreline (annotated by "A") appears to show the sharp impact of longshore transport to the north. This eventually results in spreading out the distribution, leading to a broader base by the time the flow hits the basin bottom. This additional impact will be discussed further when deciding on a "universal" nearest neighbor averaging scheme for other obsidian sources (see below).

Panaca Summit/Modena

Location: Lincoln County, Nevada and Iron County, Utah

Alternative Names: Modena, Panaca Summit, Panaca Summit/Modena area (PS/MA) (Hull 1994)

Hull (1994) Sample Points: *n* = 10 (Appendix D, Table D.1)

Skinner Sample Points: *n* = 8 (Appendix D, Table D.2)

Talbot (2015) Sample Points: *n* = 65 (Appendix D, Table D.3)

Hunt 2019 Observation Points: *n* = 14 (Appendix B, Table B.6)

ORB Paleoindian Artifacts: *n* = 1 (Appendix A, Table A.37)

The Panaca Summit/Modena (PS/M) obsidian originates in the hills of eastern Lincoln County, Nevada. The primary source erodes both eastward and westward from this hilltop area. To the east it flows more than 35 km, across Prohibition Flat and down Gold Springs Wash (Figure 4.38) into and around the town of Modena in Iron County, Utah, as well as into the nearby basin bottom and playa on the western edge of the Escalante Desert (Figure 4.45). To the west, it flows through Gleason Canyon Wash and Flatnose Wash and then more than 20 km farther out to Dry Valley, near Echo Canyon State Park.

The source appears in the literature as "Panaca Summit" or "Modena" obsidian; however, both are misnomers. Panaca Summit lies more than 13 km to the southwest and has no association with either the primary or secondary sources while the town of Modena is 15 km to the east and is simply the downslope recipient of secondary distribution nodules. The combination name "Panaca Summit/Modena" is the current best-practice appellation in the literature, though Talbot et al. (2015) suggest Prohibition Spring or Prohibition Flat better describes the source geographically. The misnaming is the result of XRF testing in the 1970s and 1980s on samples from the surrounding area before the

TABLE 4.5. Confusion Matrix Results for the Mineral Mountains.

Smoothing	Predicted Flow Area (km²)	TP	FP	% Survey Predicted	% Prediction Inside Observed	% Prediction Outside Observed	TP/ Observed	FP/ Observed	(TP-FP)/ Observed
3×3	35.1	32.1	3.0	20%	91%	9%	20%	2%	18.1%
5×5	70.0	66.3	3.7	41%	95%	5%	41%	2%	39.1%
7×7	82.1	78.5	3.6	49%	96%	4%	49%	2%	46.8%
9×9	98.1	94.1	4.0	59%	96%	4%	59%	3%	56.2%
11×11	106.5	102.3	4.3	64%	96%	4%	64%	3%	61.2%
13×13	122.4	116.4	6.0	73%	95%	5%	73%	4%	68.9%
15×15	127.6	121.0	6.6	75%	95%	5%	75%	4%	71.3%
17×17	119.5	114.9	4.6	72%	96%	4%	72%	3%	68.9%
19×19	131.8	125.2	6.6	78%	95%	5%	78%	4%	74.1%
21×21	134.6	126.5	8.0	79%	94%	6%	79%	5%	73.9%
23×23	**142.0**	**131.0**	**11.0**	**82%**	**92%**	**8%**	**82%**	**7%**	**74.9%**
25×25	144.7	132.1	12.5	82%	91%	9%	82%	8%	74.6%
27×27	146.9	133.4	13.5	83%	91%	9%	83%	8%	74.8%
29×29	149.9	134.8	15.0	84%	90%	10%	84%	9%	74.8%
31×31	152.6	136.0	16.6	85%	89%	11%	85%	10%	74.5%

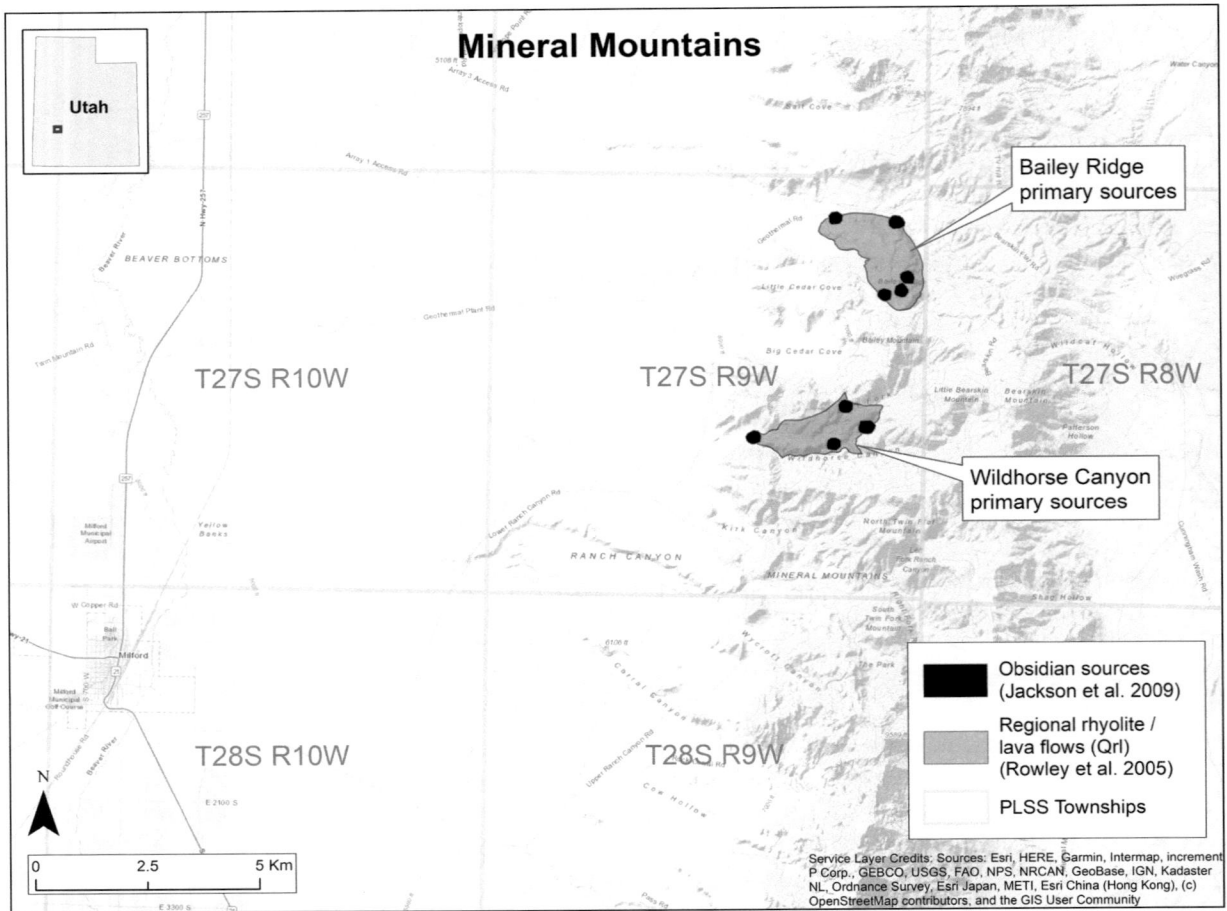

FIGURE 4.31. Mineral Mountains regional view.

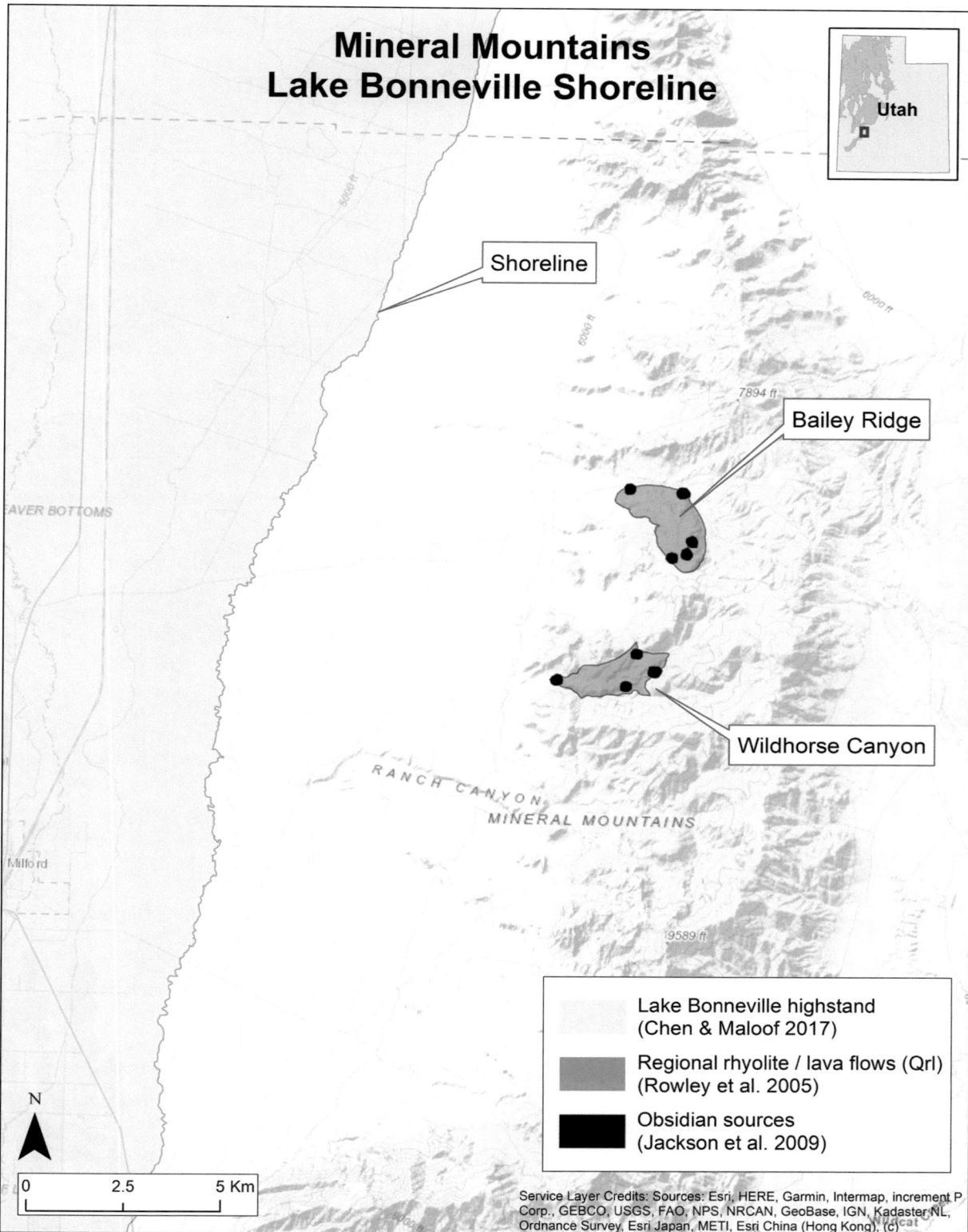

FIGURE 4.32. Mineral Mountains primary sources in relation to the Lake Bonneville highstand.

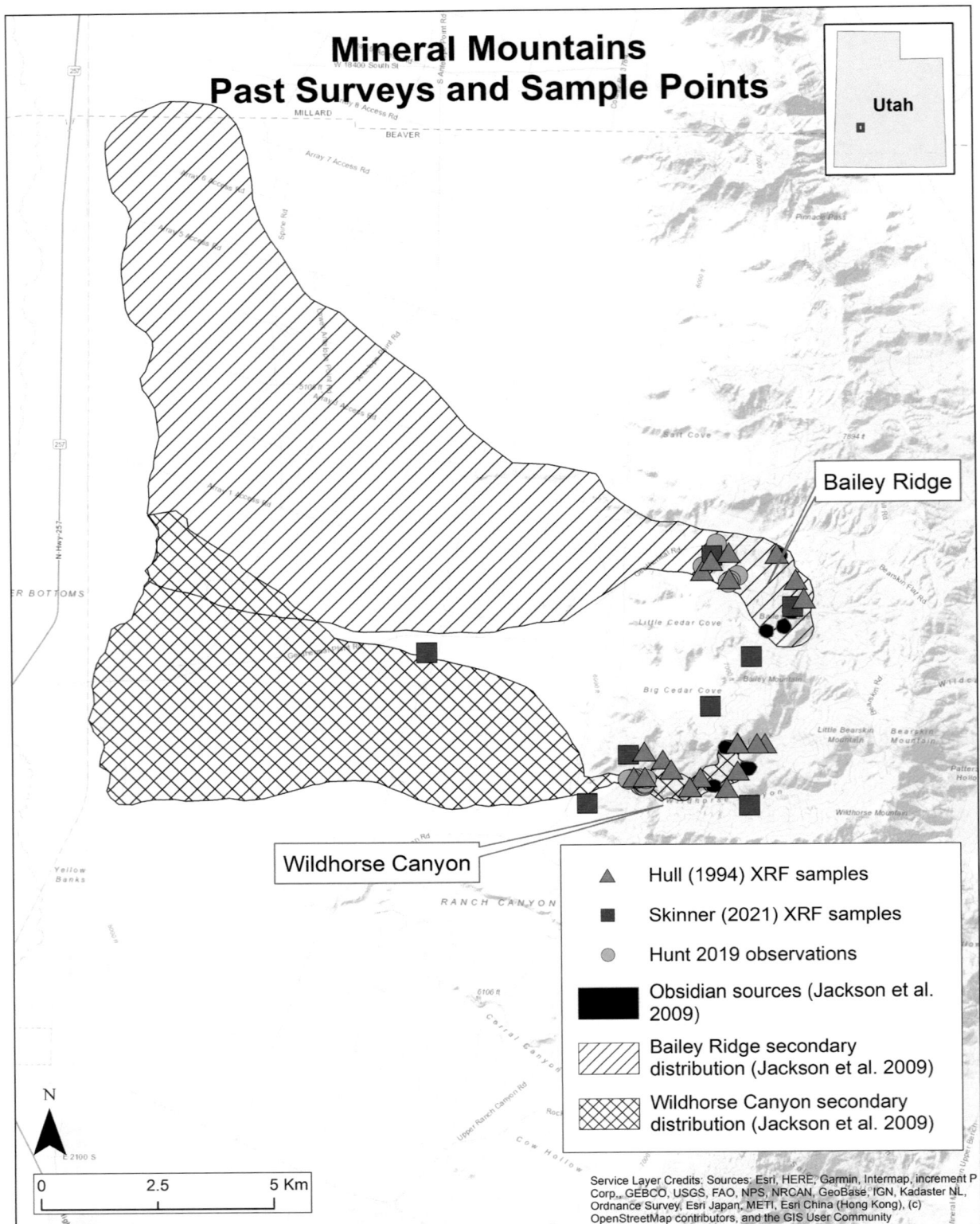

FIGURE 4.33. Mineral Mountains past surveys and sample points.

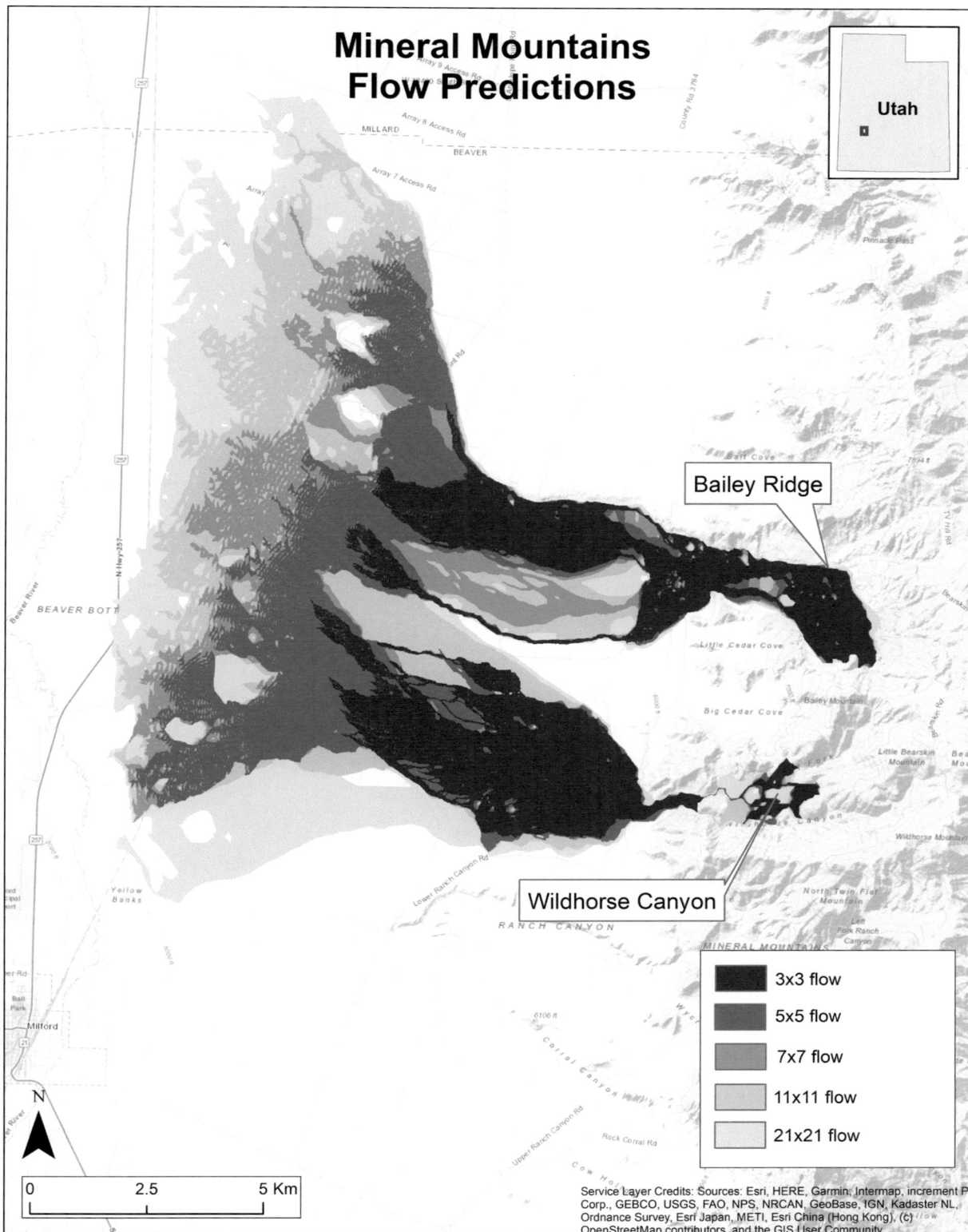

Mineral Mountains Flow Predictions

Utah

Bailey Ridge

Wildhorse Canyon

■	3x3 flow
■	5x5 flow
■	7x7 flow
■	11x11 flow
■	21x21 flow

0   2.5   5 Km

N

FIGURE 4.34. Mineral Mountains flow predictions.

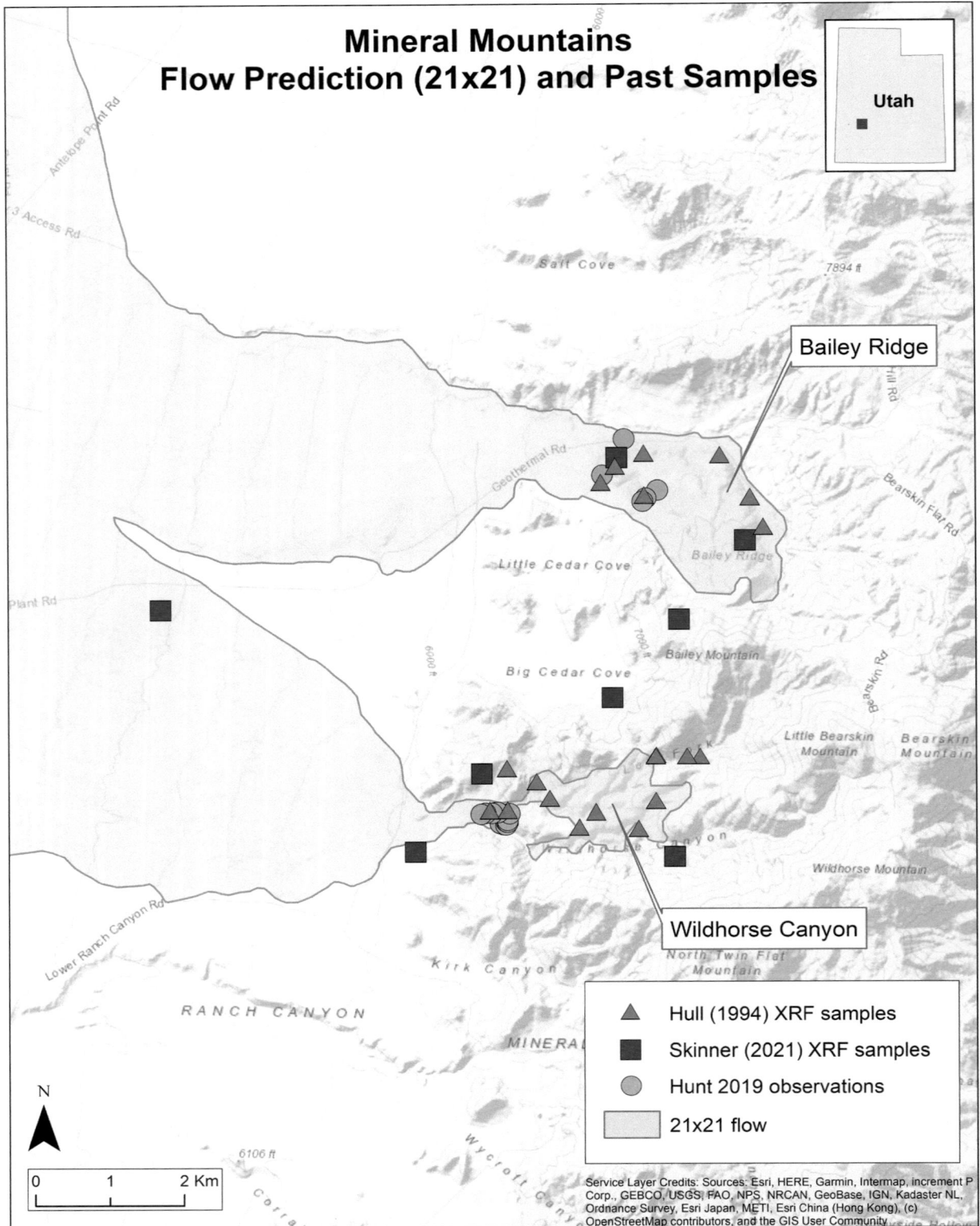

**Mineral Mountains
Flow Prediction (21x21) and Past Samples**

Utah

Bailey Ridge

Wildhorse Canyon

▲	Hull (1994) XRF samples
■	Skinner (2021) XRF samples
●	Hunt 2019 observations
	21x21 flow

N

0   1   2 Km

Service Layer Credits: Sources: Esri, HERE, Garmin, Intermap, increment P Corp., GEBCO, USGS, FAO, NPS, NRCAN, GeoBase, IGN, Kadaster NL, Ordnance Survey, Esri Japan, METI, Esri China (Hong Kong), (c) OpenStreetMap contributors, and the GIS User Community

FIGURE 4.35. Mineral Mountains 21×21 flow prediction in comparison with past sampling.

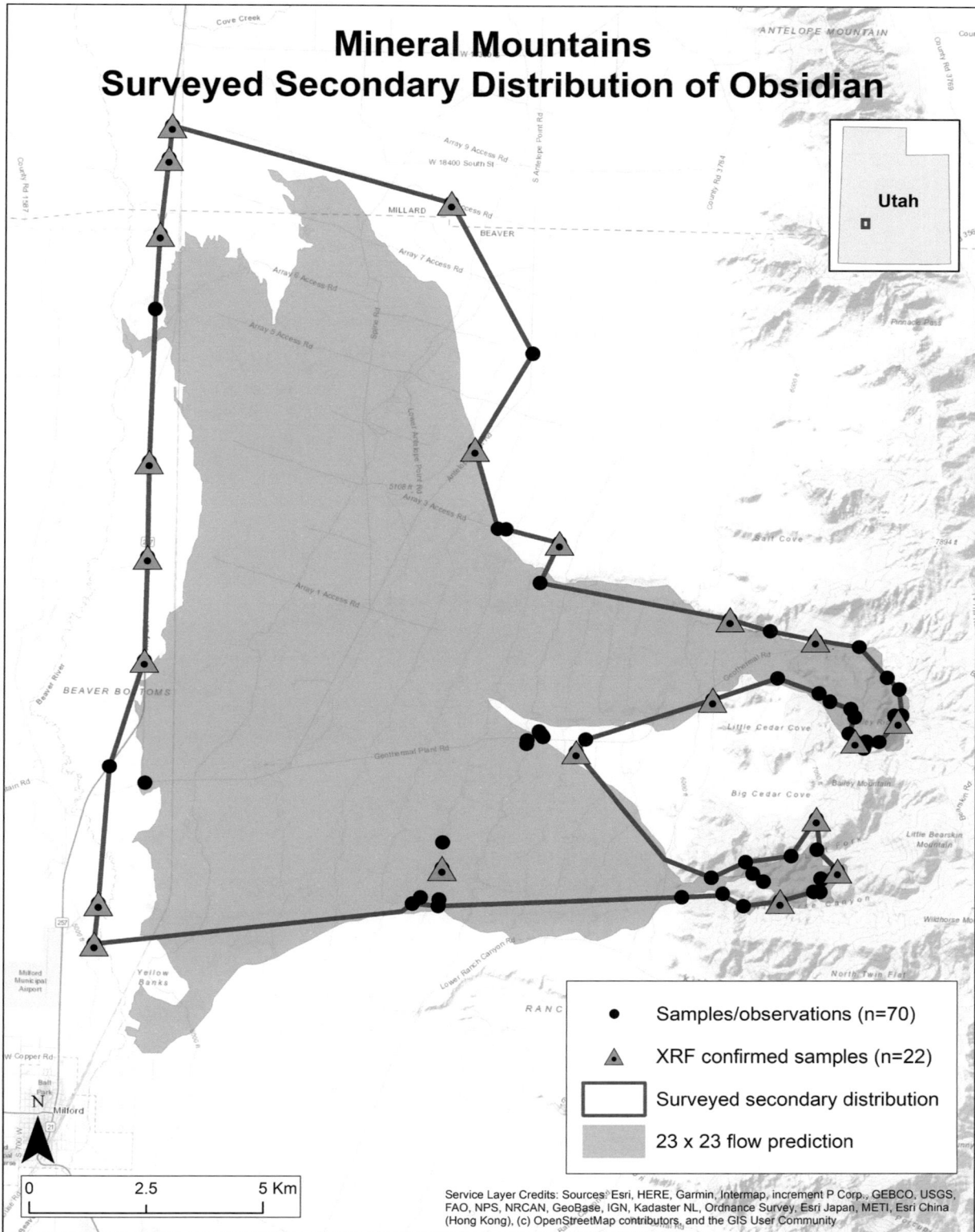

FIGURE 4.36. Mineral Mountains surveyed secondary distribution of obsidian.

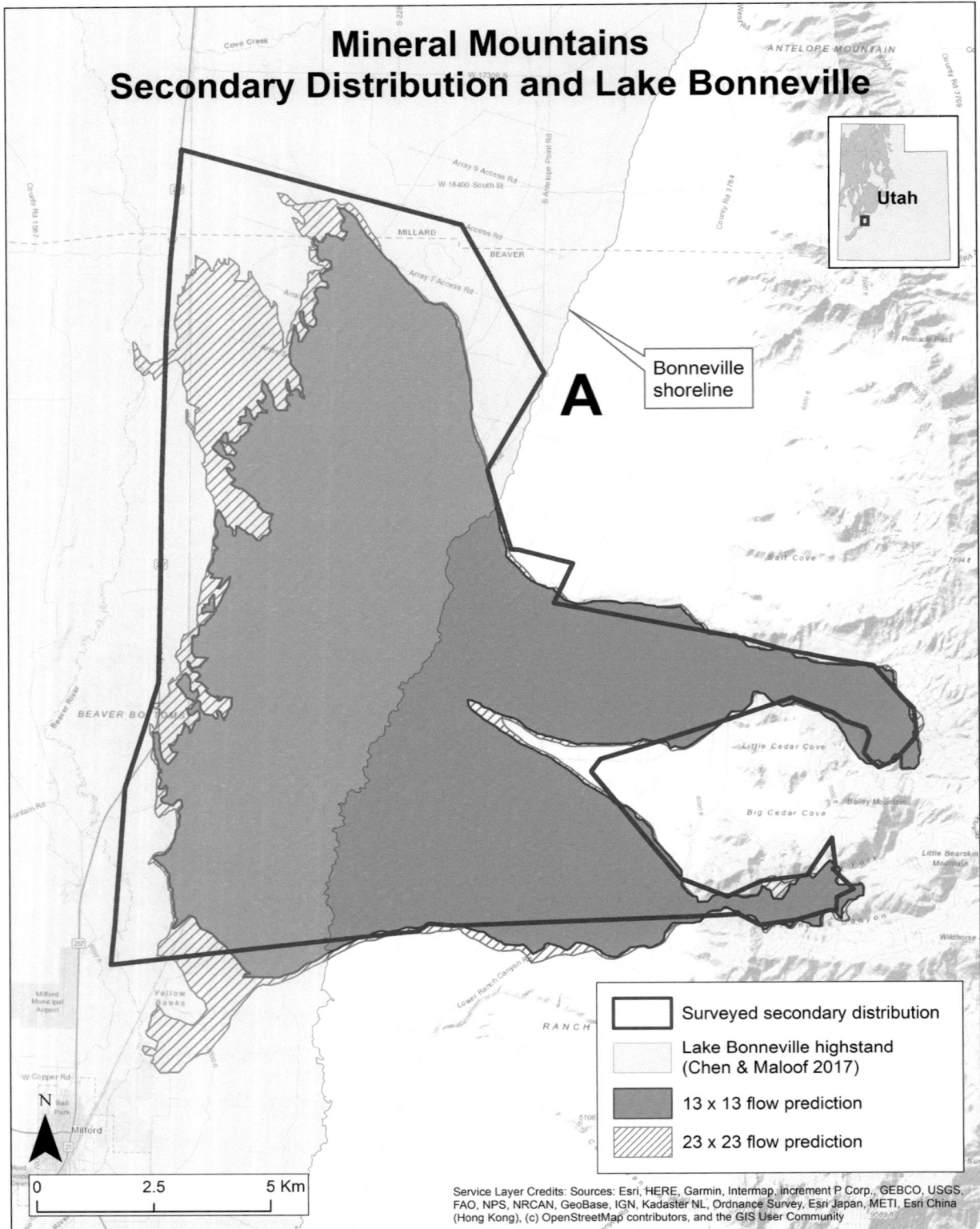

FIGURE 4.37. Mineral Mountains surveyed secondary distribution in relation to Lake Bonneville. The survey profile at label "A" suggests influence on the secondary distribution by the highstand shoreline.

FIGURE 4.38. Looking east across Gold Springs Wash [near 11S 762137 4187156].

actual primary source location was recorded in 1998 (Jackson et al., 2009; Nelson, 1984; Rowley et al., 2002; Talbot et al., 2015; Umshler, 1975).

PS/M Geology

The PS/M primary obsidian source area lies between the Indian Peak and Caliente calderas (Figure 4.39), which formed in the middle Cenozoic Era (Best et al., 2013). Their formation about 36 Ma and subsequent activity between 25–18 Ma shaped the PS/M locale.

Between 13 and 11 Ma, rhyolitic lava-flows (75% SiO2) of the Steamboat Mountain Formation erupted, forming a dome and lava flows up to 250 m thick in areas around Prohibition Spring (Rowley et al., 2002; Williams et al., 1997). In some instances, the basal members of the flows cooled so rapidly upon contacting the ground that it formed discontinuous lenses of glass: the obsidian now present in the Prohibition Spring area (Rowley et al., 2002). Figure 4.40 illustrates the resultant phenomenon well: lenses of glassy obsidian forming at the bottoms of a series of overlapping rhyolitic flows emanating from a central dome area (Talbot et al., 2015). At the surface, these lenses of obsidian manifest as veins or ledges of solid obsidian, up to 1 m thick, with a low incidence of small phenocrysts (Rowley et al., 2002; Williams et al., 1997).

During the Pleistocene, PS/M obsidian nodules, some as large as boulders (> 25 cm per the Wentworth scale), eroded off the lenses and washed downhill to the east, consolidating with other material into massive sediment beds, up to 5 m thick (Rowley et al., 2002; Talbot et al., 2015; Wentworth, 1922; Williams et al., 1997). These sediments traveled tens of kilometers to the east, well past the town of Modena. As will be discussed below, the flow development is less clear on the western side of the hills, where nodules are much smaller, rarely exceeding 4 cm.

PS/M Archaeology

The PS/M geochemical signature was first identified by Umshler (1975), using samples from the secondary distribution near the town of Modena, Utah. Nelson (1984) similarly published an XRF sample taken near Modena. However, it was not until 1998 that avocational archaeologists Manetta and Farrel Lytle identified six primary sources, now referred to as the "Lytle sources," upslope in Nevada, more than 15 km west of the previously published sample locations and namesake (Rowley et al.,

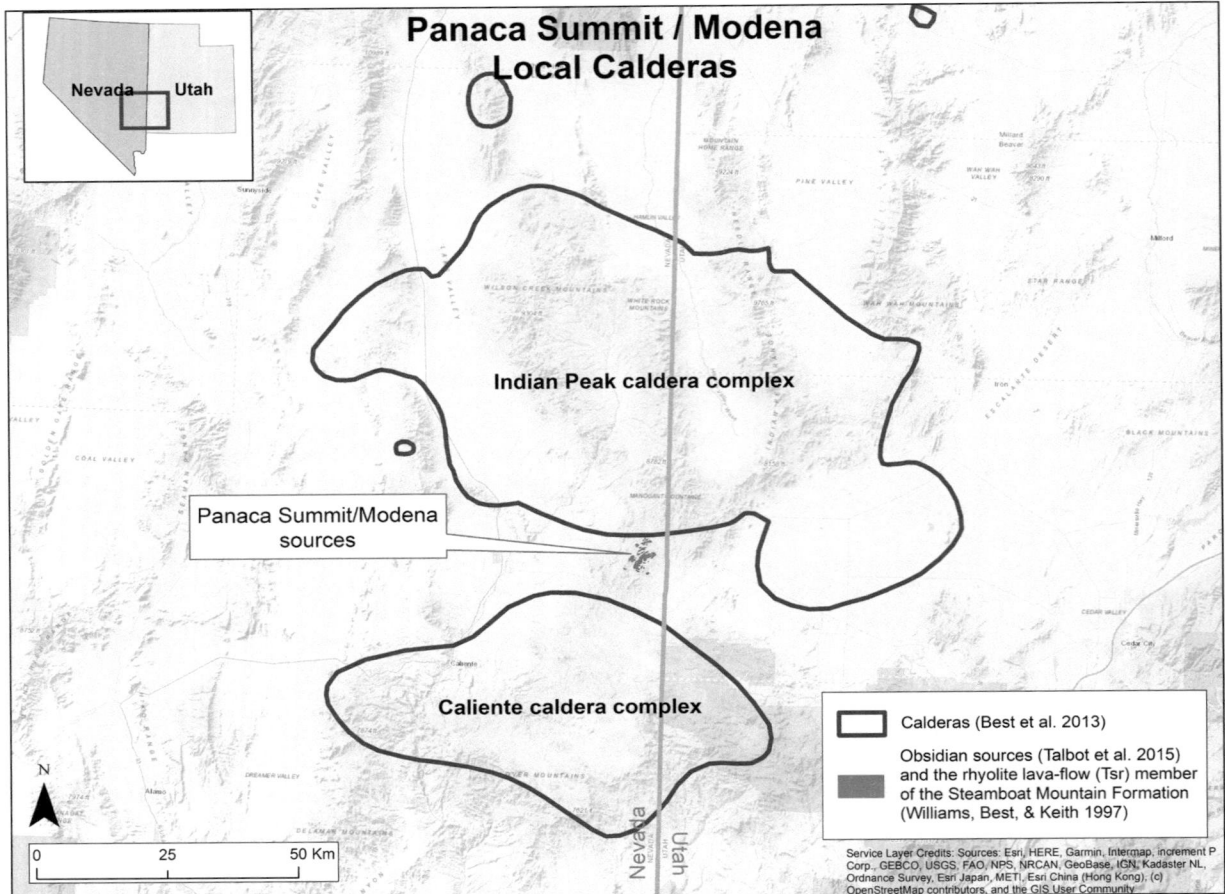

FIGURE 4.39. Panaca Summit/Modena location, relative to the Indian Peak and Caliente calderas.

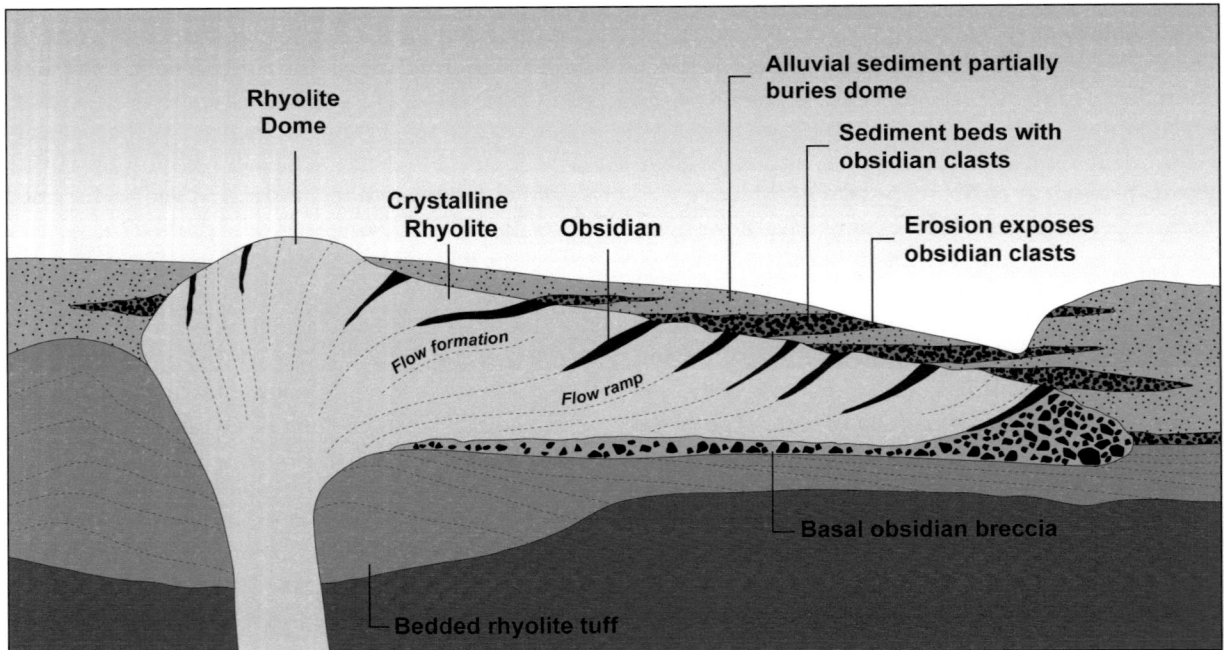

FIGURE 4.40. Illustration of discontinuous obsidian lens formations at Panaca Summit/Modena. Courtesy of the Museum of Peoples and Cultures, Brigham Young University.

FIGURE 4.41. The Lytle #1 primary source location, now just a massive field of natural and cultural flakes.

2002; Talbot et al., 2015). According to Rowley et al. (2002), all that remains of the original obsidian veins are the dense talus fields (Figure 4.41) of natural and cultural flakes recorded by the Lytles, the result of millennia of prehistoric mining activity, natural cracking, and erosion. While Rowley claims the obsidian ledges are "mined out" (2002, p. 2), Talbot et al. counter that while extensive mining did occur, it is "certainly not mined out" (Talbot et al., 2015, p. 39), as large nodules are abundant in the area, and no one has yet excavated the talus areas to confirm or deny the existence of remaining vein exposures. We also know that the PS/M sources were exploited from Paleoindian to at least Fremont times and that artifacts fashioned from PS/M obsidian have been identified at sites throughout Nevada, Utah, and as far west as Death Valley (Estes, 2009; Haarklau et al., 2005; Jones et al., 2003; Madsen, Schmitt, et al., 2015; Nelson, 1984; Talbot et al., 2015; Umshler, 1975).

Around the Lytle sources are dozens of small archaeological sites and perhaps hundreds of unrecorded lithic scatters. The natural corridor through the mountain pass at the southern end of the region, now occupied by Highway 319 and a railroad, has been the most thoroughly studied. Over 50 sites are recorded, and the corridor is considered a meeting point for the Virgin Anasazi and Fremont people (Talbot et al., 2015).

PS/M Past Work

The earliest XRF testing at this locality by Umshler (1975), Nelson & Holmes (1979), and Nelson (1984) provides insufficient locational data to be helpful here (only detailed to township-range sections or quarter sections). Hull (1994) provides an early dataset of XRF testing on 10 samples (Appendix D, Table D.1) from the region (converted from township and range descriptions to GPS centroids, which introduces several hundred meters of potential error). Jackson et al. (2009) provide some insight on the secondary flow but focused on Utah, not Nevada. Skinner (2021; Appendix D, Table D.2) provides eight XRF samples from PS/M. In 2019, I conducted a pilot survey and observed obsidian at various points around PS/M (Appendix B, Table B.6, $n = 14$). While these are not XRF test points, they provide a useful indicator of how obsidian is distributed on the hillside.

Talbot et al. (2015) provide the most comprehensive survey to date of the PS/M primary source region itself, the result of three seasons of field school surveys, and these are used extensively here for the flow analysis. Along with mapping the Lytle sources, they surveyed cobble density surrounding the talus fields, which is used in the flow prediction below. They also XRF tested 65 nodules (Appendix D, Table D.3), primarily

FIGURE 4.42. Anthropogenic dams at the Panaca Summit/Modena bottleneck; raised railroad bed and highway overpass.

from the eastern hillside region, which are mapped in Figure 4.46.

All this information was used in selecting the best flow prediction to use for the PS/M obsidian.

PS/M Flow Prediction

Using the process described in the beginning of this chapter, five flow distributions were created. During this process, however, natural and anthropomorphic challenges emerged.

First, as no known remaining obsidian ledges or veins remain, what is or is not "primary" is now subjective at this site. Talbot et al. (2015) describe the obsidian cobble field that surrounds the Lytle source areas and it is quite robust, producing nodules that fall into Wentworth's boulder classification. As such, this distribution field was used as the primary source (Figure 4.46). From the flow predictions that follow, this issue is simply an interpretative one of where primary flows end and secondary flows begin and likely has little impact on the final flow extent.

Second, the hillside where the PS/M primary resources originate drains eastward to a narrow channel, or bottleneck, at the bottom of Gold Springs Wash, between the foothills of Mount Elenore to the north and an unnamed ridge and hill to the south (see call-out at the natural bottleneck noted in Figure 4.45). This narrow passage is the conflux of the natural flow of Gold Springs Wash into the flats by the town of Modena and the routes of a Union Pacific railroad, on raised beds, and that of a state highway (Hwy 319), which includes an overpass over the railway (Figure 4.42). All three converge into a narrow natural passage that is only about 500 m wide and channels movement for more than 2 km as it travels east. The anthropogenic structures significantly stand above the natural topography and predate

modern DEM imagery. As such, their impact is incorporated into that imagery. When applying the flow prediction process described above, these obstacles form a dam that hinders accurate predictions for natural sediment flows.

Several methods were investigated to overcome this impediment. The first was to increase the smoothing aspect of the DEM to "average out" the dams. This had the negative impact of "blowing out", or over-smoothing, the naturally very flat terrain to the east of the channel, resulting in any flow that got past the dam to unrealistically and completely fill the basin to the east. Another method, provided by D'Avello et al. (2016), acts like a "cookie cutter," removing the offending portion of a DEM and replacing it with a patch that is the average of the surrounding edges. This approach did not work in this instance and seemed to only create a similar, more dense, linear dam.

As the intention is to model the flow of sediment from this natural channel eastward into the flats, a strategy was chosen to modify the weighted raster by including an artificial source, or "proxy," that originates at the dam itself. Since the original flow predictions make it clear that sediment moving off the Prohibition Flat hillside and travelling down Gold Springs Wash is channeled strictly through this passage, "leap-frogging" the dam should not have significantly impacted the eastward flow prediction. Figure 4.43 illustrates this solution with an artificial source 1000 m wide, spanning the bottleneck region. This approach is similar to the "donut" approach but bypasses the averaging step.

Another dilemma presented itself to the west. Skinner's sample SO-65-1738 appeared to be well out of range of the predicted flow (Figure 4.46). SO-65-1738 was more than 18 km to the northwest of the known primary sources and, more importantly, on the opposite

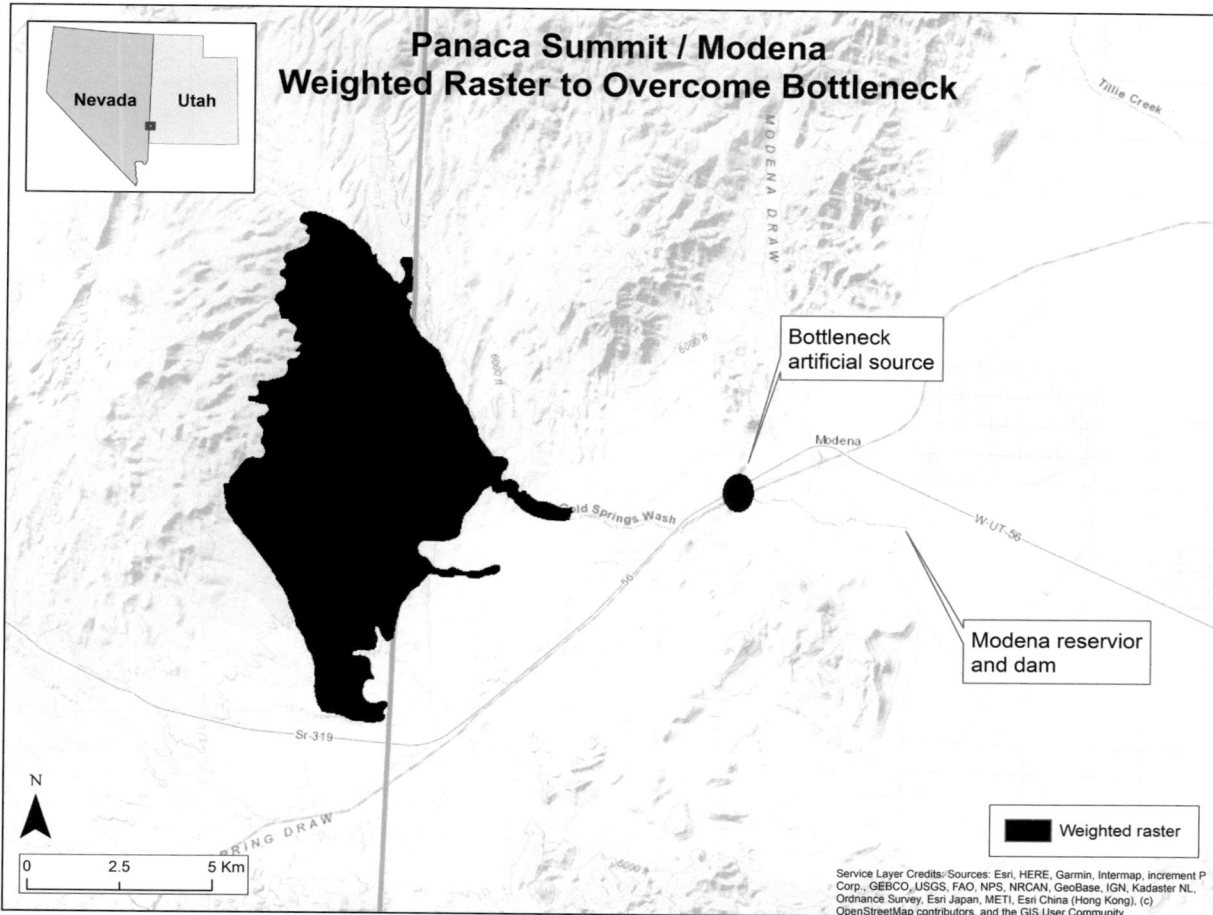

FIGURE 4.43. Weighted raster used to predict Panaca Summit/Modena flow showing artificial source used to overcome channel bottleneck.

side of the hydrographic basin ridgeline. This location suggested that a primary source exposure is, or was at one time, west of the ridgeline. During the 2020 field season, a survey near SO-65-1738 discovered a second sample of PS/M obsidian in a road cut in Flatnose Wash (sample #103 in Appendix B, Table B.4, confirmed by XRF test), clearly indicating that a western flow needed to be considered in the overall flow predictions.

To this end, a method like that in the bottleneck procedure above was used to create a proxy primary source. Three of Hull's samples are the westernmost samples on the ridge (M-04, M-06, and M-10). A polygon was created using these three samples, and this polygon then was used to create a weighted raster. Figure 4.44 illustrates the proxy primary source and the resultant 21 × 21 flow prediction generated using just this proxy source. The prediction flows westward along Gleason Canyon Wash, connecting with Flatnose Wash, and then captures sample SO-65-1738. Note that the eastern flow from the proxy source mimics the earlier predictions but is similarly restricted by the bottleneck region.

This proxy primary source was incorporated into the weighted DEM and used to generate 3 × 3, 5 × 5, 7 × 7, 11 × 11, and 21 × 21 flow predictions using the method described above. These are presented in "stacked" form in Figure 4.47, with the 3 × 3 nearest neighborhood flow represented by the darkest shade and the 21 × 21 flow represented by the lightest shade.

In the east, the 21 × 21 flow abruptly terminates just as it escapes from the bottleneck and passes south of the town of Modena. Here the eastern 21 × 21 flow hits a real dam, the Modena reservoir. While the eastern 11 × 11 smoothing appears to allow the flow to move around the dam, the 21 × 21 smoothing is too much, creating a wide raised area that stops this flow from continuing. A comparison to the known sample points by Hull (1994; Appendix D, Table D.1), Talbot et al. (2015; Appendix D, Table D.3), Skinner (2021; Appendix D, Table D.2), and my own pilot project (Appendix B, Table B.6) shows good concordance with this 11 × 11 flow to the east of the PS/M ridge (Figure 4.48). For this reason, fieldwork in the east was based on this flow prediction, and the final

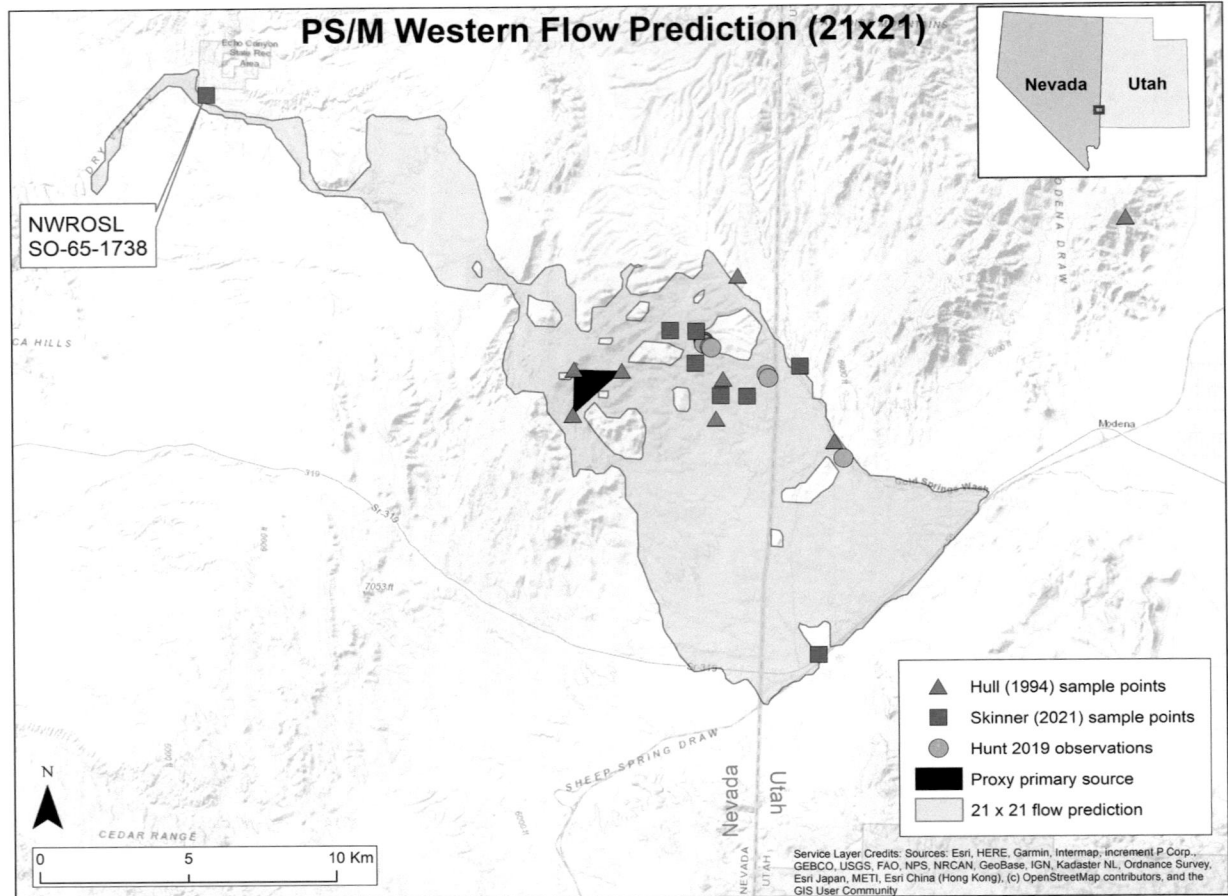

FIGURE 4.44. Panaca Summit/Modena western flow prediction (21×21) derived from proxy primary source.

flow outlines and transects for the 11 × 11 flow are shown in Figure G-14.

To the west, the 21 × 21 flow appeared to provide the best prediction, based primarily on the placement of sample SO-65-1738 (Figure 4.49). The final flow outlines and transects for the 21 × 21 flow are shown in Figure G.15.

Survey Results

The Panaca Summit/Modena secondary distribution was surveyed during the summers of 2020 and 2021. The observed extent is illustrated in Figure 4.50. The PS/M extent covers an area of ~330 km² with a perimeter of ~165 km. During the survey, 126 observation points were recorded, and 104 natural obsidian samples were collected (Appendix B, Table B.4). Of these collected samples, 28 were submitted to NWROSL for XRF testing (Appendix C, Table C.4) and were confirmed as "Modena" obsidian (triangles in Figure 4.50).

The surveyed flow encompasses almost all previous sample points recorded by Hull (1994), Talbot et al. (2015), Skinner (2021; Appendix D, Table D.2), and myself (Appendix B, Table B.6), with mostly

minor exceptions. On the eastern slope, a single previously recorded point is ~570 m outside the surveyed extent, and two are less than 300 m outside the extent. The placement of these points would not materially affect the predicted secondary distributions. The only significant anomaly is to the northeast, where Hull's (1994) M-01 appears to be more than 240 m above the Escalante Valley (Figure 4.48). While this point is interpolated from a township and range location, the range of error still places it considerably above the valley bottom. During the 2020 survey season, the drainage below the elevation point was surveyed and no evidence of obsidian flowing downhill was observed. This finding appears to be a recording error.

Following the modified confusion matrix methodology described in the "Analyzing Survey Results" section of this chapter, the optimal smoothing level for PS/M occurs at the 13 × 13 nearest neighbor average (Table 4.6). At this level, 54 percent of the actual survey region was predicted by the model.

The model performed adequately for initiating surveys but suffered in two key areas. In the east, we see that the observed flow extends much further south and east

TABLE 4.6. Confusion Matrix Results for Panaca Summit/Modena.

Smoothing	Predicted Flow Area (km²)	TP	FP	% Survey Predicted	% Prediction Inside Observed	% Prediction Outside Observed	TP/ Observed	FP/ Observed	(TP-FP)/ Observed
3×3	93.3	90.5	2.9	27%	97%	3%	27%	1%	26.6%
5×5	106.1	102.2	4.0	31%	96%	4%	31%	1%	29.8%
7×7	112.4	107.7	4.7	33%	96%	4%	33%	1%	31.2%
9×9	143.6	132.7	10.9	40%	92%	8%	40%	3%	36.9%
11×11	177.3	152.9	24.4	46%	86%	14%	46%	7%	39.0%
13×13	**222.9**	**176.8**	**46.1**	**54%**	**79%**	**21%**	**54%**	**14%**	**39.6%**
15×15	233.7	173.7	60.1	53%	74%	26%	53%	18%	34.5%
17×17	221.9	169.0	52.9	51%	76%	24%	51%	16%	35.2%
19×19	154.1	136.5	17.6	41%	89%	11%	41%	5%	36.0%
21×21	156.9	136.9	20.0	42%	87%	13%	42%	6%	35.5%
23×23	162.5	138.7	23.7	42%	85%	15%	42%	7%	34.9%
25×25	165.6	139.5	26.0	42%	84%	16%	42%	8%	34.4%

past the bottleneck area (annotated as "A" in Figure 4.50) than the prediction allows. At the same time, the eastern side likely would benefit from a higher smoothing than 11×11, but anthropogenic modifications impacted these predictions. This area is an enormous basin bottom, and the unpredicted flow in this area demonstrates the difficulty the model has with these extremely low slope/low energy environments, in this case, not filling the basin accurately. This area is also comprised of large areas of private property and agricultural land, complicating accurate survey.

To the west, the area annotated as "B" has a high occurrence of small obsidian pebbles, typically less than 2 cm in diameter. These occupy the hills to the south of the Gleason Canyon Wash and suggest additional, unknown primary obsidian sources in that region, perhaps a pyroclastic tuff or ancient obsidian source that has degraded to marekanites (Apache tears). As discussed earlier, model accuracy is incumbent on known primary sources, some of which may still be unknown at PS/M.

Topaz Mountain

Location: Juab County, Utah
Alternative Names: None
Hull (1994) Sample Points: n = 10 (Appendix D, Table D.1)
Skinner Sample Points: n = 11 (Appendix D, Table D.2)
Hunt 2019 Observation Points: n = 10 (Appendix B, Table B.6)
ORB Paleoindian Artifacts: n = 130 (Appendix A, Table A.37)

The Topaz Mountain (TM) obsidian originates in the Thomas Range in Juab County, Utah (Figure 4.53). Four separate TM primary sources are situated along

ridges of the Thomas Range to the north of Topaz Mountain and one newly recorded source resides close to the basin bottom in the north end of the range. These sources erode in multiple directions: eastward into Pismire Wash and the basin bottom between the Thomas Range and Keg Mountain (Figure 4.51), westward into the valley named The Dell between the Thomas Range and Spor Mountain, southwest into Fish Springs Flat, and north along the east side of the Black Rock Hills.

TM Geology

The Thomas Range is a remnant structure of the western edge of the Thomas caldera, which formed about 42 Ma and then collapsed around 38 Ma (Lindsey, 1982). The mountain range was further modified during the basin-and-range faulting period, circa 21 Ma, also signaling the beginning of an extensive period of alkali-rhyolitic eruptions in the region. Spor Mountain, just 2–3 km to the west of Topaz Mountain, experienced rhyolitic eruptions around 21 Ma, while the Thomas Range rhyolitic eruptions occurred much later, between 6.3 ± 0.4 and 6.8 ± 0.3 Ma (Lindsey, 1979, 1982). These most recent rhyolitic eruptions—from at least 12 separate vents across the range, with thicknesses up to 700 m and a total volume of up to 50 km³—have been named the Thomas Range Rhyolite (Figure 4.53).

The Thomas Mountain Rhyolite is a high-silica, fluorine-rich (up to 1.5% wt.) rhyolite known for producing topaz, a widely collected gemstone (Christiansen et al., 1984, 1986). The obsidian members of the Thomas Mountain Rhyolite were created as the result of rapid cooling of the magma, appear as discontinuous, "steeply dipping" lenses (Lindsey, 1982, p. 27; Staatz & Carr, 1964) and were identified at four locations (Figure 4.53) within the Thomas Range (Jackson et al., 2009). The obsidian contains low percentages of phenocrysts

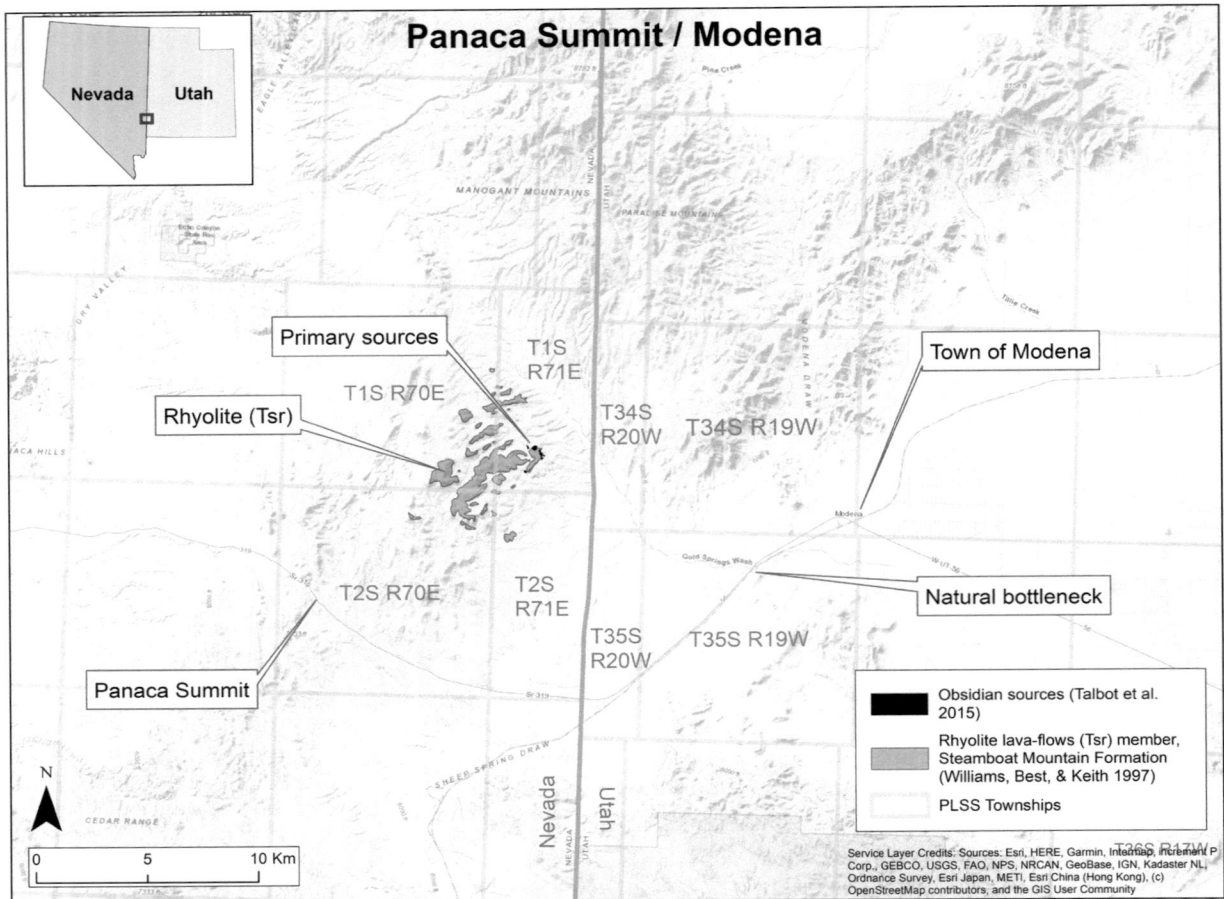

FIGURE 4.45. Panaca Summit/Modena regional view.

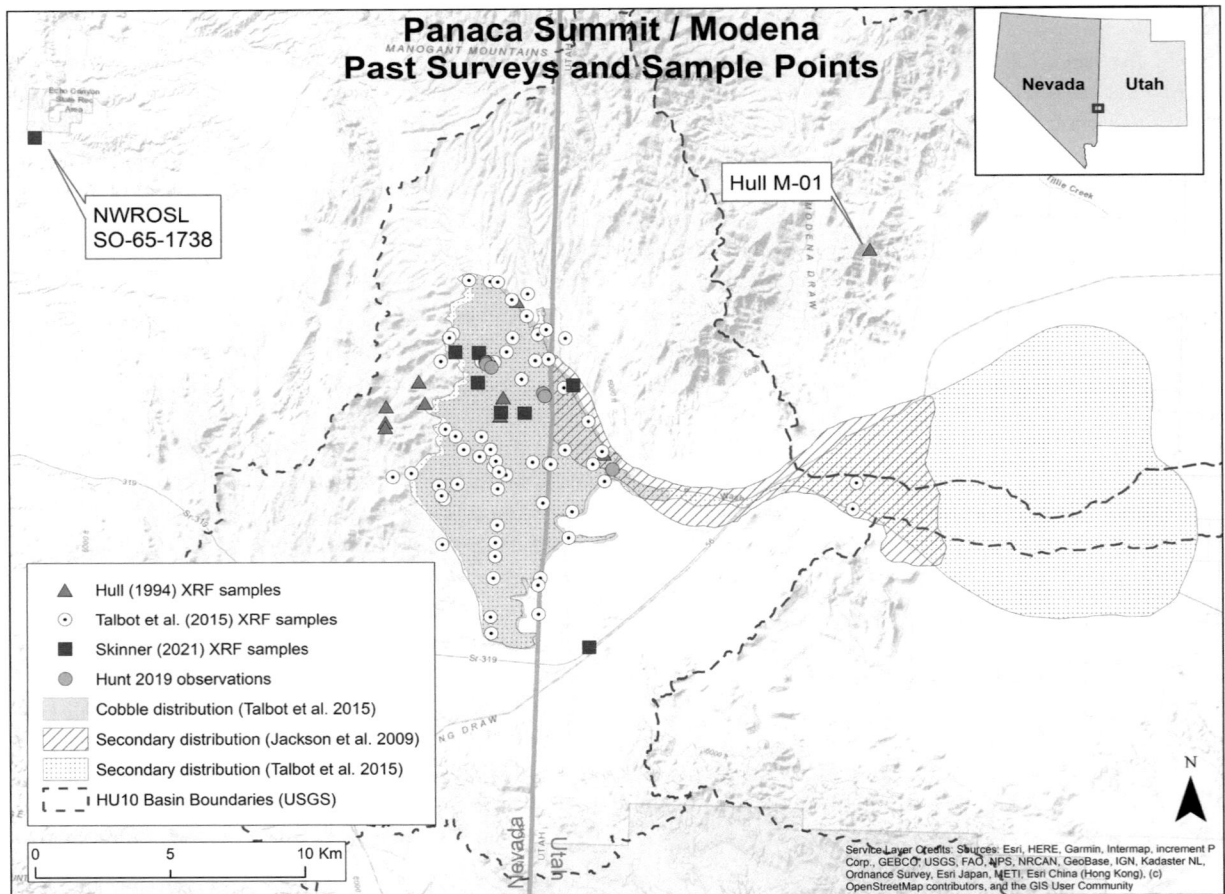

FIGURE 4.46. Panaca Summit/Modena past surveys and sample points.

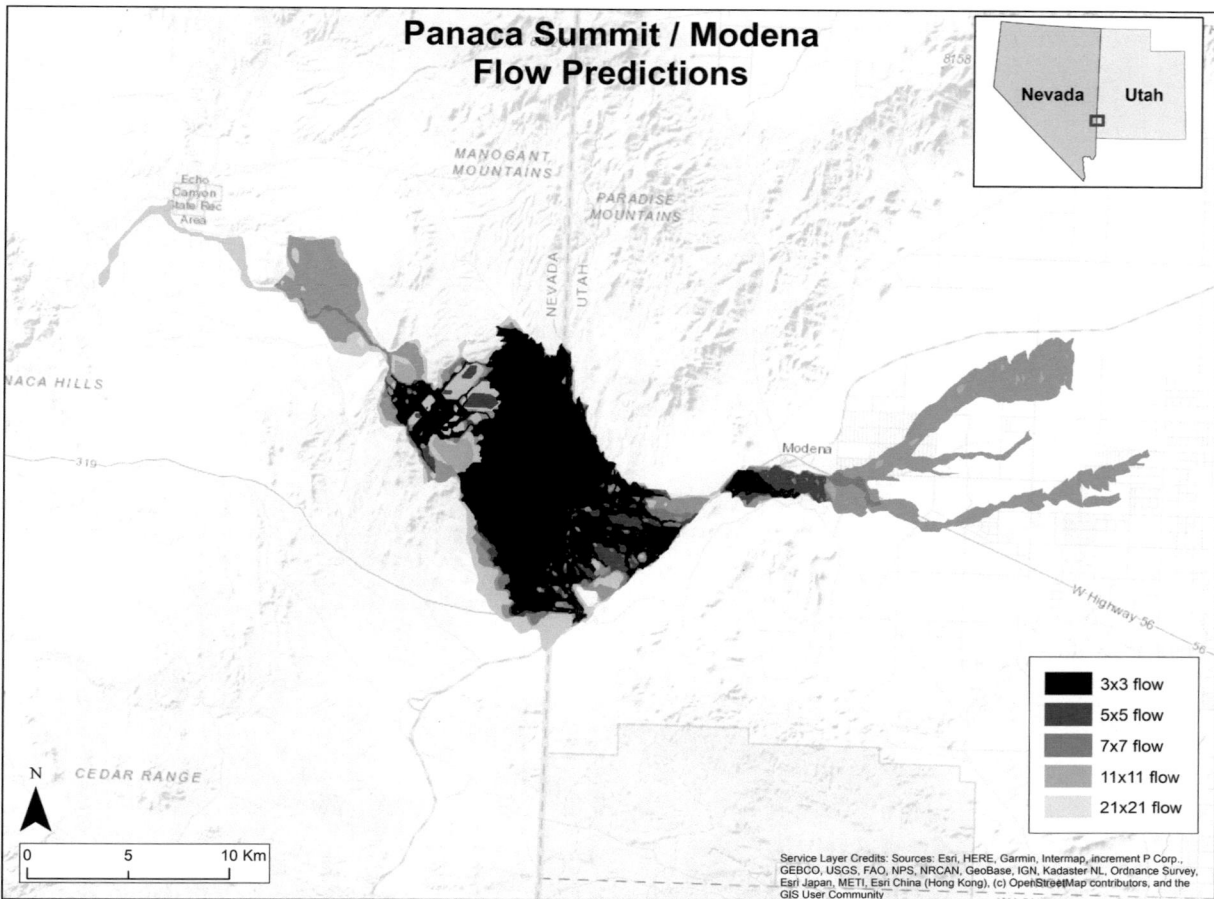

FIGURE 4.47. Panaca Summit/Modena flow predictions.

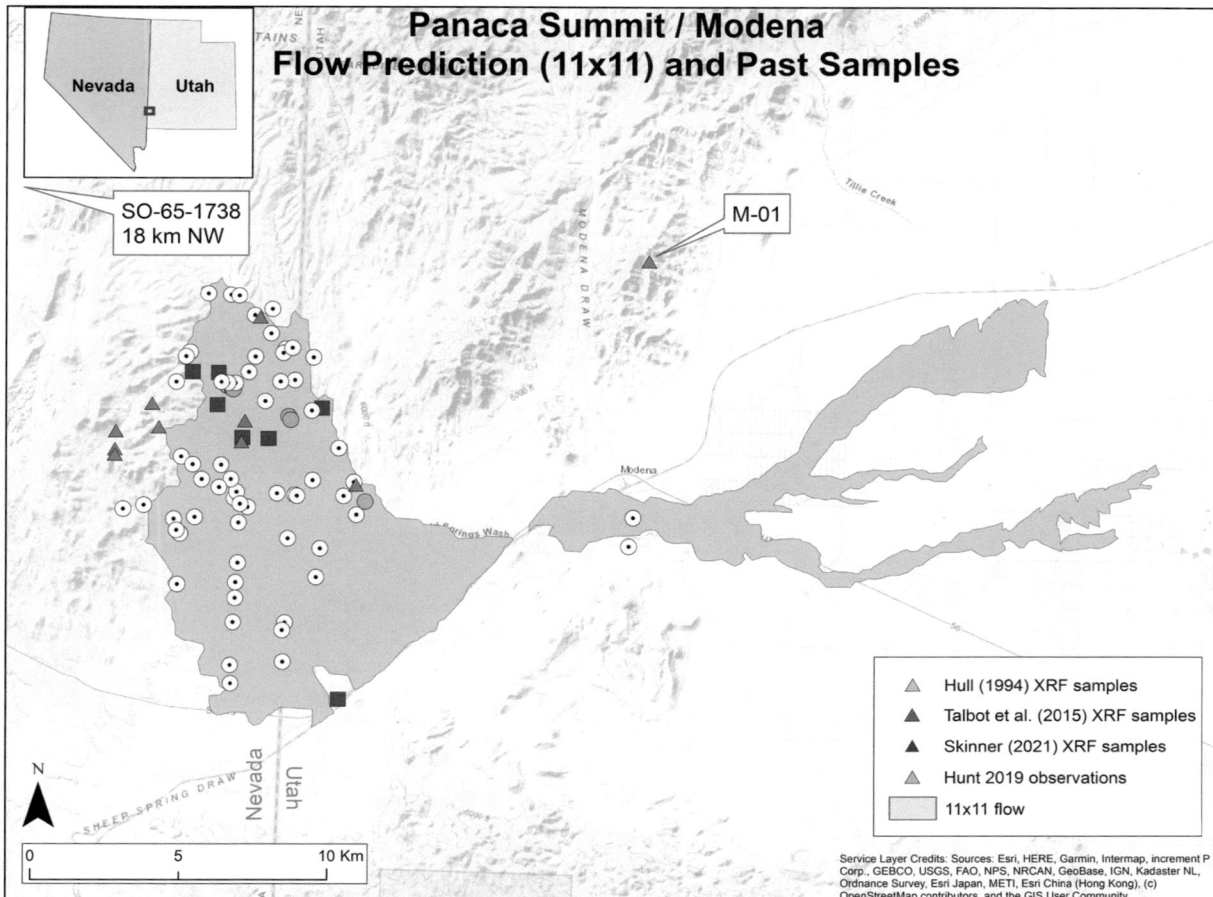

FIGURE 4.48. Panaca Summit/Modena 11×11 flow prediction in comparison with past sampling.

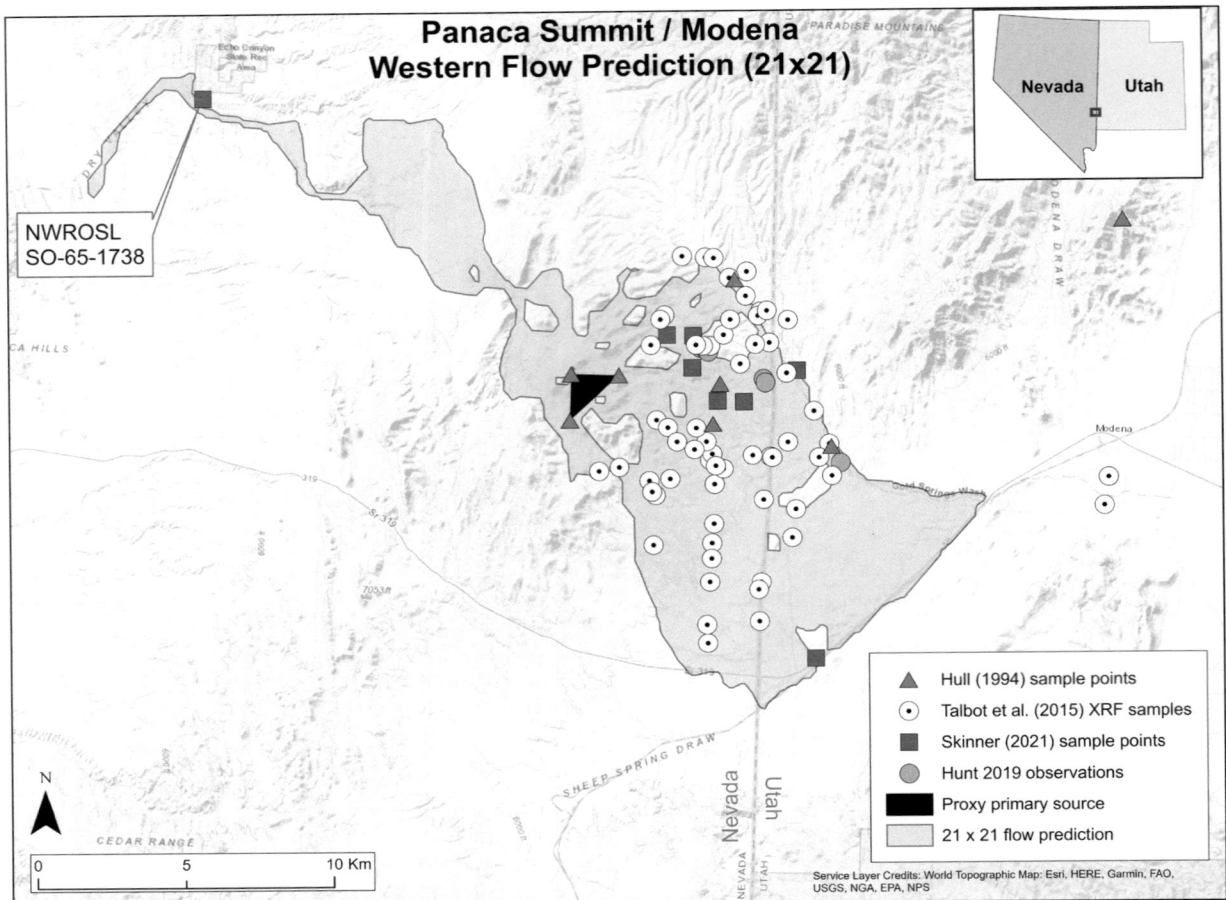

FIGURE 4.49. Panaca Summit/Modena western flow prediction using a proxy primary source.

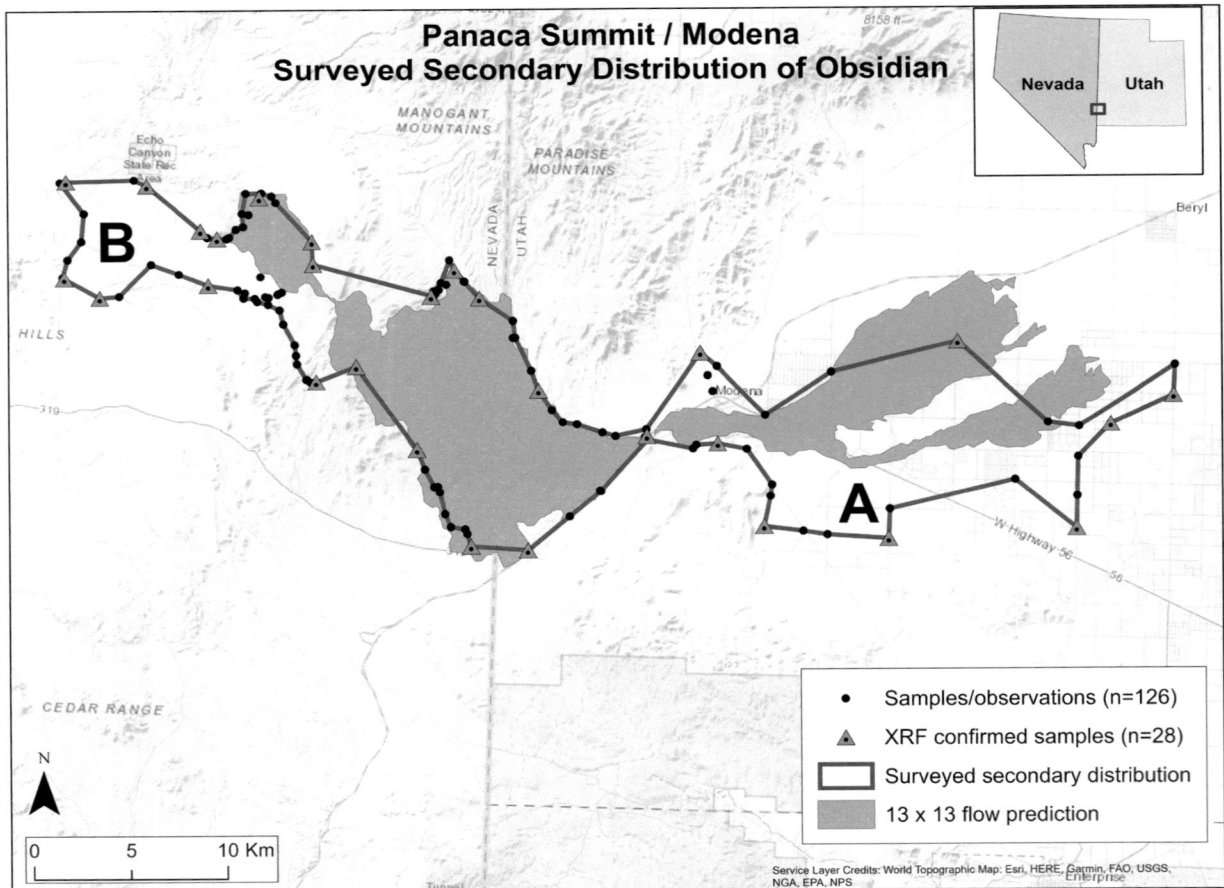

FIGURE 4.50. Panaca Summit/Modena surveyed secondary distribution of obsidian.

FIGURE 4.51. Looking to the east from the Thomas Range, into the expansive Pismire Wash area [near 12T 319783 4401463].

(typically less than 4–5 percent) and some is porphyritic (Staatz & Carr, 1964, p. 95).

More recently, around 18,000 cal BP, the Thomas Range was surrounded by Pleistocene Lake Bonneville at its height (Chen & Maloof, 2017b; Oviatt & Jewell, 2016; Utah Geospatial Reference Center, 2017), as illustrated in Figure 4.54. After Lake Bonneville receded, the valley bottoms, which include the flats below Pismire Wash, Fish Springs Flat, and the flats around the Black Rock Hills, were covered in lacustrine fine silt, sandy loam, and pebble fields, which remain today.

The Spor Mountain/Thomas Range region is rich in commercially-useful elements and minerals, such as uranium and beryllium, and mines are abundant in the area, including the large Brush Wellman beryllium mine at the south end of Spor Mountain (Lindsey, 1998). There is also an active commercial rockhounding and topaz-collecting business operating at the base of Topaz Mountain.

TM Archaeology

Three Topaz Mountain primary obsidian sources were recorded in 1981 (42Jb275, 42Jb276, and 42Jb277) and are notable in their high altitude (~2130 m) exposures and difficulty to access on the steep ridges along the imposing western crests of the Thomas Range (Cartwright, 1981; Raymond, 1981a, 1981b). The authors of the original site reports note that quarrying activity is evident

and that the exposures saddle multiple drainages, allowing for extensive colluvial and alluvial action to both the east and west. To the west, sites 42Jb296, 42Jb440, and 42Jb450 are noted lithic scatters with potential surface quarrying activity of the colluvial cobbles (Montgomery, 1981; A. Nielsen, 1990; G. Nielson, 1990). To the east, 42Jb278 is a primary obsidian exposure but composed only of small nodules (Jackson et al., 2009). The regional survey by Jackson and colleagues (2009) provides the most comprehensive examination of an area with surprisingly little previous archaeological focus.

TM Past Work

The earliest XRF testing at this locality by Nelson & Holmes (1979) and Nelson (1984) provides insufficient locational data to be helpful here (only detailed to township-range sections or quarter sections). Hull (1994) provides an early dataset of XRF testing on 10 samples (Appendix D, Table D.1) from the region (converted from township and range descriptions to GPS centroids which introduces several hundred meters of potential error). Skinner (2021; Appendix D, Table D.2) provides 11 XRF samples from TM. In 2019, I conducted a pilot survey and observed obsidian at various points around TM (Appendix B, Table B.6, $n = 10$). While these are not XRF test points, they provide a useful indicator of how obsidian is distributed in the washes to the east and southwest. Jackson et al. (2009) provide some insight on the secondary flow, but this data seems limited when compared to the other point observations above (Figure 4.55).

Clearly, from the point scatter, several surveyors have observed obsidian flowing to the west, into the valley between the Thomas Range and Spor Mountain, known as The Dell. Similarly, my own observations far to the east and southeast in Pismire Wash indicate that the secondary distribution extends much further into the valley than suggested by Jackson et al. (2009). Finally, Skinner (2021; Appendix D, Table D.2) records a sample (SO-65-1434) far to the northwest of all the other samples—this area was investigated during my survey fieldwork and resulted in recording a new primary source area (discussed below).

All this information was used in selecting the best flow prediction to use for the TM obsidian.

TM Flow Prediction

Using the process described in the beginning of this chapter, five flow distributions were created.

The starting requirement for all flow prediction is the location of the primary sources. Prior to the 2020 field season, the primary source outlines were derived solely from Jackson et al. (2009), as seen in Figure 4.53. Using these primary sources as the starting points, the downslope flows were predicted for 3×3, 5×5, 7×7, 11×11, and 21×21 nearest neighbor smoothed DEMs. These are presented in "stacked" form in Figure 4.56, with the 3×3 nearest neighborhood flow represented by the darkest shade and the 21×21 flow represented by the lightest shade.

A comparison to the known sample points by Hull (1994) (Appendix D, Table D.1), Skinner (2021; Appendix D, Table D.2), and my own pilot project (Appendix B, Table B.6) showed good concordance with the predicted flows (Figure 4.57), especially the 21×21 flow, though the predicted flows extended significantly beyond past sampling. The flow into Fish Springs Flat and north into the Dugway Valley suggested an expansive secondary distribution of several hundred square kilometers. The transect map used during the 2020 field season is illustrated in Figure G.16.

However, like the situation in western PS/M, Skinner's SO-65-1434 at the north end of the Thomas Range, appeared well out of range of the flow prediction based on the four previously recorded primary sources. This divergence suggested the presence of an unrecorded primary source in that area. This vicinity was investigated at the end of the 2020 field season, resulting in the discovery of an additional primary source (described below) eroding from an exposed tuff. Using this information, the flow prediction was expanded (Figure 4.58)

and used to create a localized transect map (Figure G.17) for the 2021 field season.

Survey Results

The Topaz Mountain secondary distribution was surveyed during the summers of 2020 and 2021. The observed extent is illustrated in Figure 4.59. The full TM extent covers an area of ~309 km² with a perimeter of ~157 km. During the survey, 150 observation points were recorded, and 107 natural obsidian samples were collected (Appendix B, Table B.5). Of these collected samples, 22 were submitted to NWROSL for XRF testing (Appendix C, Table C.5) and were confirmed as "Topaz Mountain" obsidian (triangles in Figure 4.59).

The surveyed flow encompasses almost all previous sample points recorded by Hull (1994; Appendix D, Table D.1), Skinner (2021; Appendix D, Table D.2), and myself (Appendix B, Table B.6), with mostly minor exceptions (two points are less than 210 m outside the survey outline). However, Hull's sample, T-4, which appeared appropriately positioned in the 21×21 flow prediction (Figure 4.57), is outside the observed survey outline by ~2 km (Figure 4.59). The most likely explanation, even allowing for error inherent in the conversion of the original township and range coordinates to centroid UTM coordinates, is that the flow does, or did, extend into that area but was not observed during my survey. This area is difficult to access, but further survey in that area is warranted in the future.

Skinner's sample (SO-65-1434) triggered further investigation and survey to the north of the Thomas Range, leading to the addition of a new Topaz Mountain obsidian source location. This source manifests as an ash-flow tuff (Figure 4.52) with embedded obsidian nodules. These rarely exceed 4 cm in diameter and are predominantly < 1 cm in size. While this source may have produced little in the way of raw materials for tools, it cast a significant signal north for hunter-gatherers to encounter.

Following the modified confusion matrix methodology described in the "Analyzing Survey Results" section of this chapter, the optimal smoothing level for TM occurs at the 11×11 nearest neighbor average (Table 4.7). At this level, 63 percent of the actual survey region was predicted by the model.

As has been seen in other source regions, the model's predictions suffer in the large flat basin bottoms. At Topaz Mountain, to the west in the Fish Springs Flat, the prediction is both too extensive (traveling north to the Fish Spring Wildlife Refuge) and not expansive enough (failing to capture flow to the extreme southwest as the basin abuts the eastern edge of the Fish Springs Range). Similarly, in the flow predicted from the new northern

FIGURE 4.52. Northern primary source in tuff. Left, the pink tuff topped by gray conglomerate. Right, close-up of pink tuff and embedded obsidian pebbles [near 12S 311935 4409623].

TABLE 4.7. Confusion Matrix Results for Topaz Mountain.

Smoothing	Predicted Flow Area (km²)	TP	FP	% Survey Predicted	% Prediction Inside Observed	% Prediction Outside Observed	TP/ Observed	FP/ Observed	(TP-FP)/ Observed
3×3	183.9	83.4	100.5	27%	45%	55%	27%	33%	−5.6%
5×5	129.0	73.3	56.2	24%	57%	44%	24%	18%	5.5%
7×7	243.6	118.3	125.6	38%	49%	52%	38%	41%	−2.4%
9×9	256.3	168.2	88.1	54%	66%	34%	54%	29%	25.9%
11×11	**268.6**	**194.7**	**73.9**	**63%**	**72%**	**28%**	**63%**	**24%**	**39.1%**
13×13	280.8	198.3	82.4	64%	71%	29%	64%	27%	37.5%
15×15	363.6	230.6	133.1	75%	63%	37%	75%	43%	31.5%
17×17	380.9	233.7	147.2	76%	61%	39%	76%	48%	28.0%
19×19	422.5	258.7	163.8	84%	61%	39%	84%	53%	30.7%
21×21	457.6	268.9	188.7	87%	59%	41%	87%	61%	26.0%
23×23	472.9	267.3	205.6	87%	57%	43%	87%	67%	20.0%
25×25	476.5	267.1	209.5	86%	56%	44%	86%	68%	18.7%

source, even the 11×11 prediction expands well into the Dugway Proving Grounds, but the observed flow vanishes much earlier, reminiscent of the Ferguson Wash flow. As in that case, these areas were impacted by the Lake Bonneville highstand (Figure 4.60) and that may be confounding model accuracy.

Conclusion

The goal of this chapter is to determine if a universal methodology, using known primary obsidian source data, can be applied to determine the extent and scale of a source's secondary distribution. This distribution represents the exposure component of the discoverability signal (Equation 3.2) that this source would have presented on the landscape to hunter-gatherers seeking toolstone. While the accuracy and precision of matching the exact flow would be optimal, in terms of discoverability the ultimate goal is one of exposure scale (E)

and the scale factor of that signal in comparison to other sources.

$$D = E * \frac{1}{d^2} \qquad \text{(Eq. 3.2)}$$

Using the best fit equation (Equation 4.4 above), the optimal DEM smoothing was determined for each of the five test sources. These are summarized in Table 4.8. As noted in the Ferguson Wash section, this source produced results far out of the norm, and this was attributed to the full immersion of the site by Lake Bonneville. For this reason, those results are excluded here.

From these results, limited as they are, we see that the average correctly predicted flow (TP/observed) is 66 percent. However, just in terms of scale factor of the flow, when comparing the size of the predicted flow (regardless of precision) to the size of the observed extent, this value improves dramatically to 81 percent. This alone

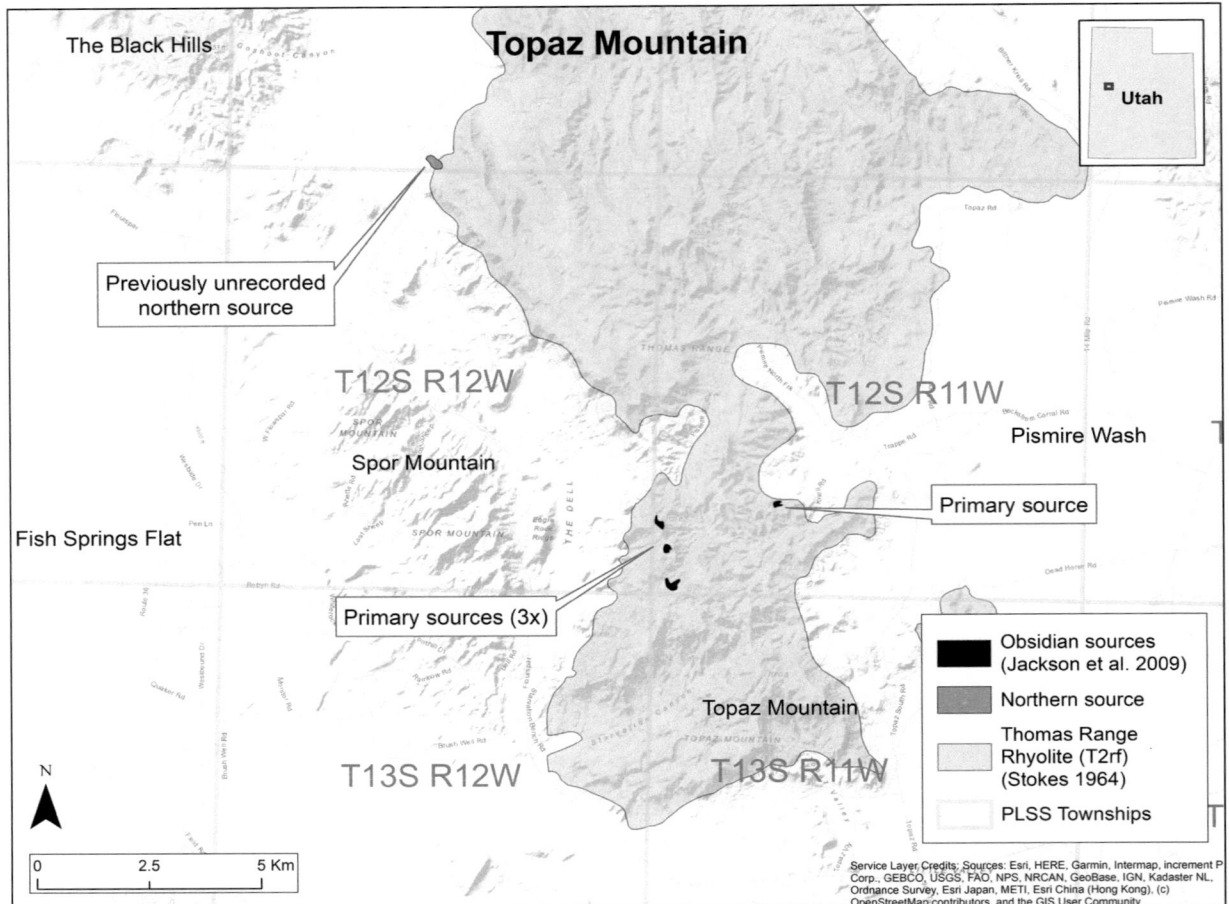

FIGURE 4.53. Topaz Mountain regional view.

TABLE 4.8. Best Fit Smoothing Summary.

Source	Observed Extent (km²)	Predicted Extent (km²)	Best Fit Smoothing	Best Fit Extent (km²)	% Survey Predicted	Scale Factor (Prediction/Observed)
BRA	353	288	13 × 13	227	64%	82%
MM	160	142	23 × 23	142	82%	89%
PS/M	330	223	13 × 13	223	54%	68%
TM	309	269	11 × 11	269	63%	87%
Average	**288**	**230**	**15 × 15**	**215**	**66%**	**81% ± 10**

suggests that the scale factor is consistent when comparing prediction results.

If the average best fit smoothing (15 × 15) is applied to all four sources, we see further improvement in these results (Table 4.9).

This level of smoothing (15 × 15), which I am naming the smoothing index, will now be applied in Chapter 5, as E is calculated for each of the obsidian and fine-grained volcanic sources that were utilized in the final cleaned Paleoindian dataset from the ORB delta (Appendix A).

TABLE 4.9. Scale Factor Results with 15 × 15 Smoothing.

Source	Observed Extent (km²)	15 × 15 Extent (km²)	% Survey Predicted	Scale Factor
BRA	353	303	66%	86%
MM	160	128	75%	80%
PS/M	330	234	49%	71%
TM	309	364	75%	118%
Average	**288**	**257**	**66%**	**89% ± 20**

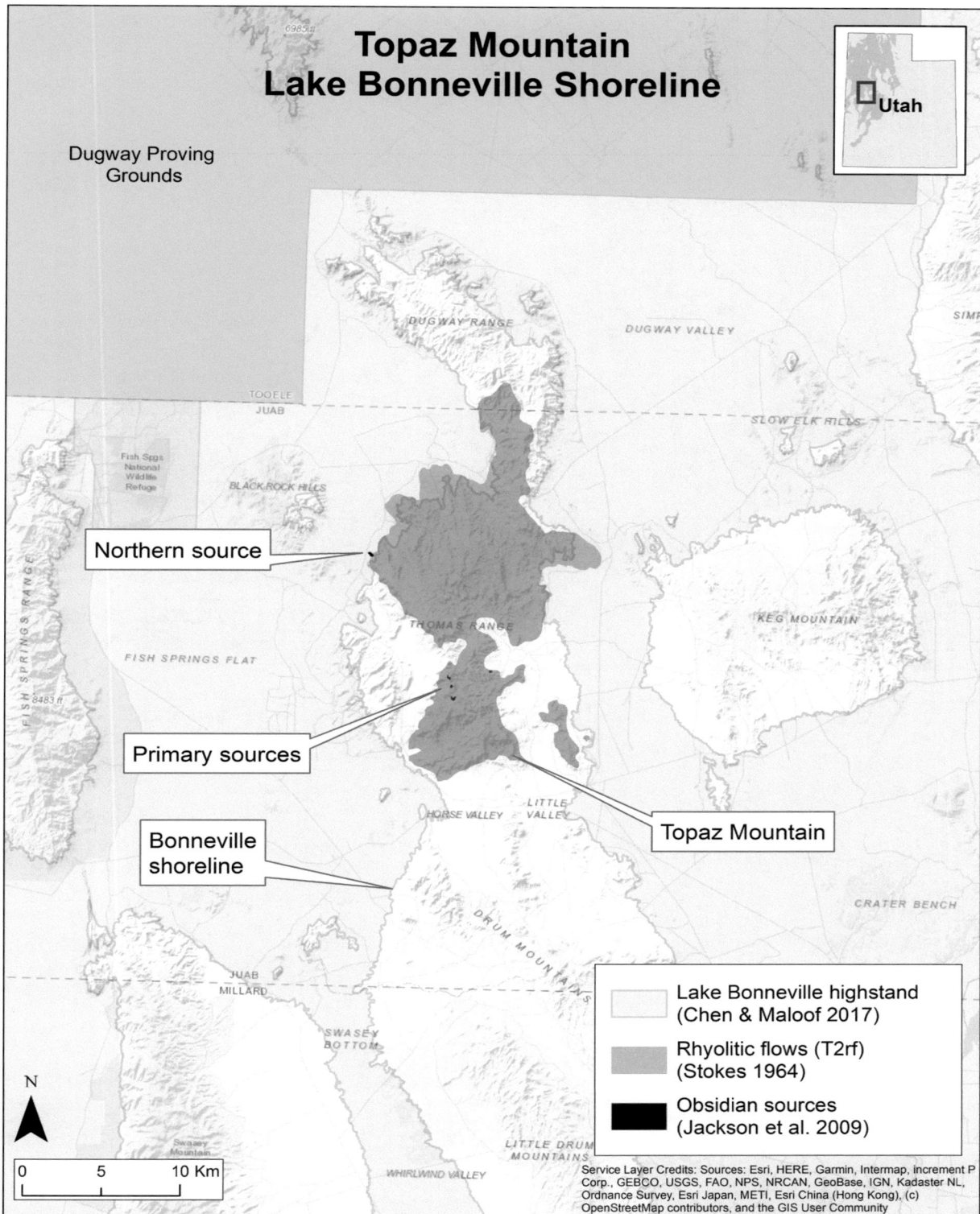

FIGURE 4.54. Topaz Mountain/Thomas Range primary sources in relation to the Lake Bonneville highstand.

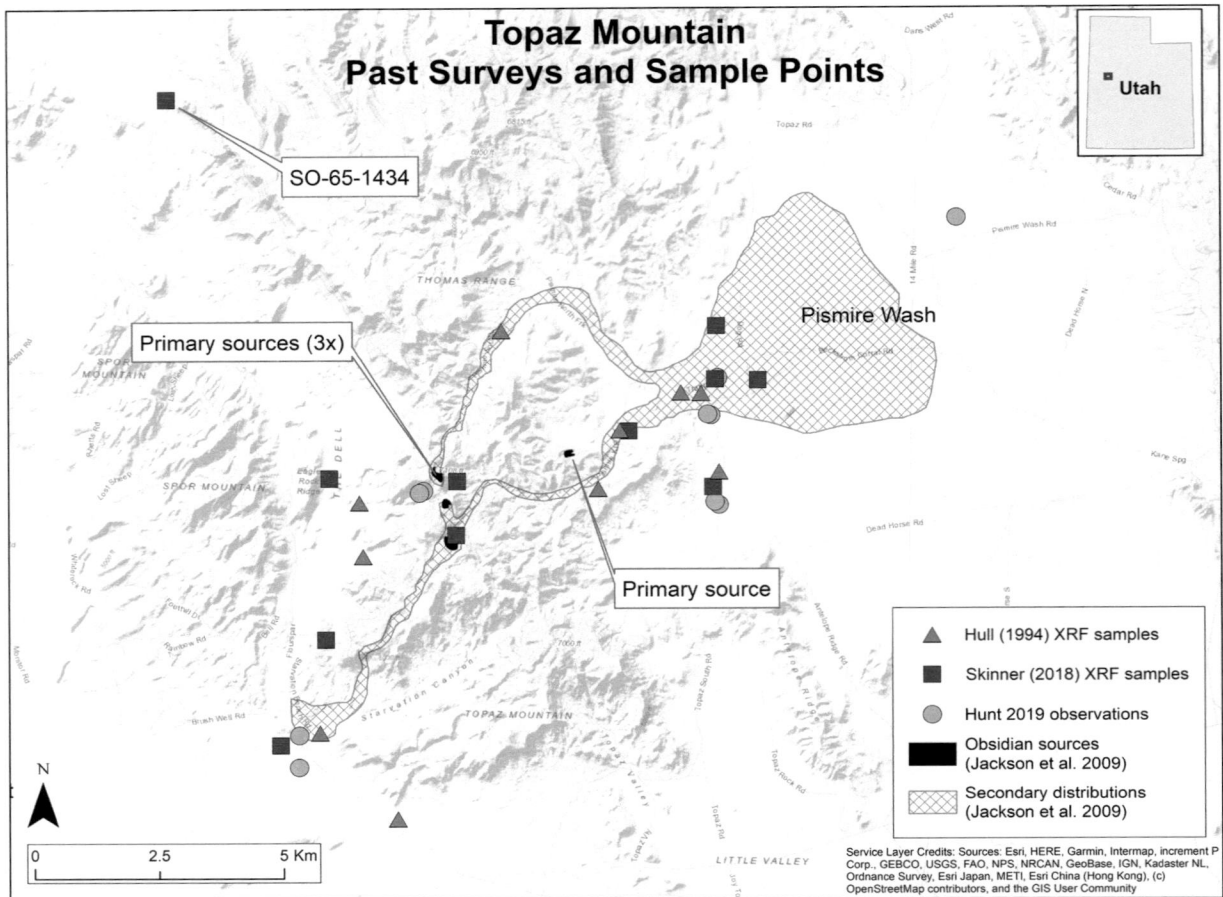

Figure 4.55. Topaz Mountain past surveys and sample points.

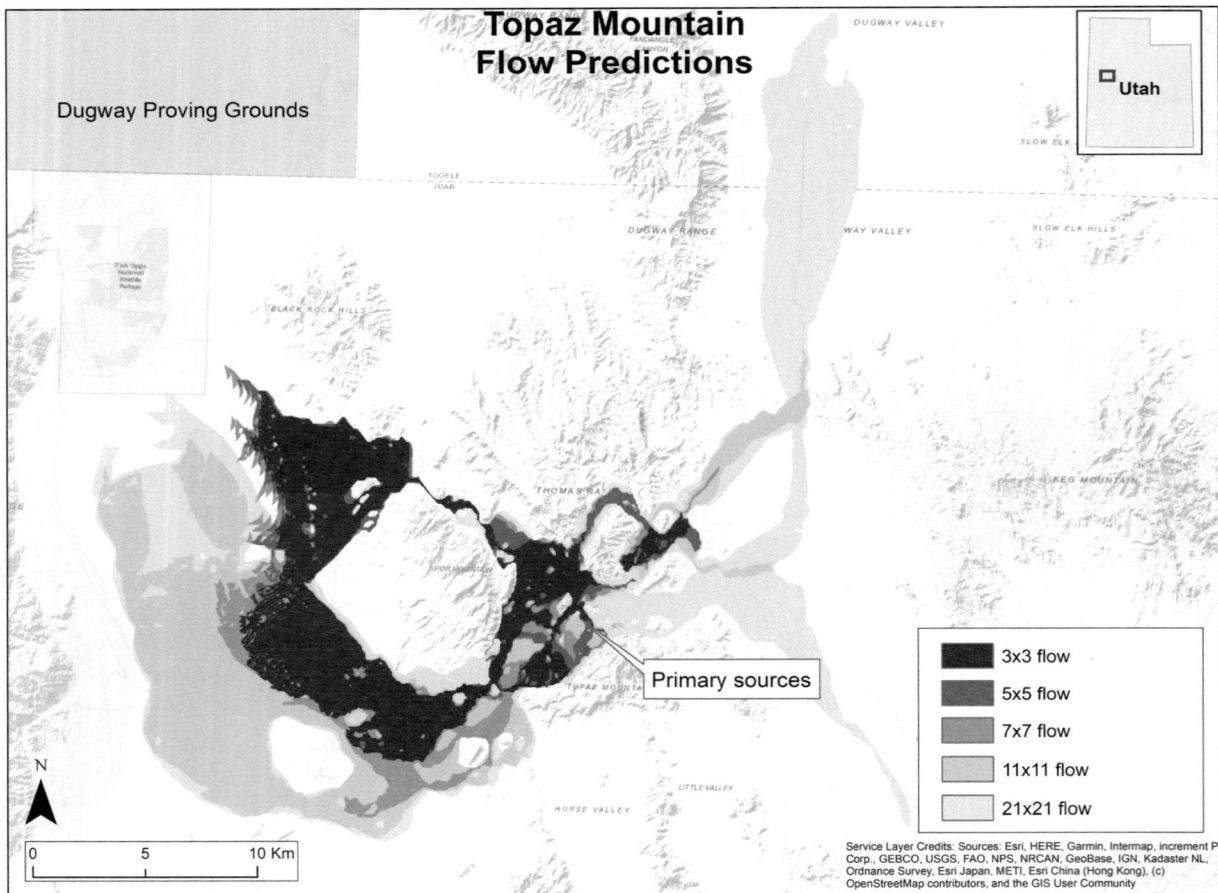

Figure 4.56. Topaz Mountain flow predictions.

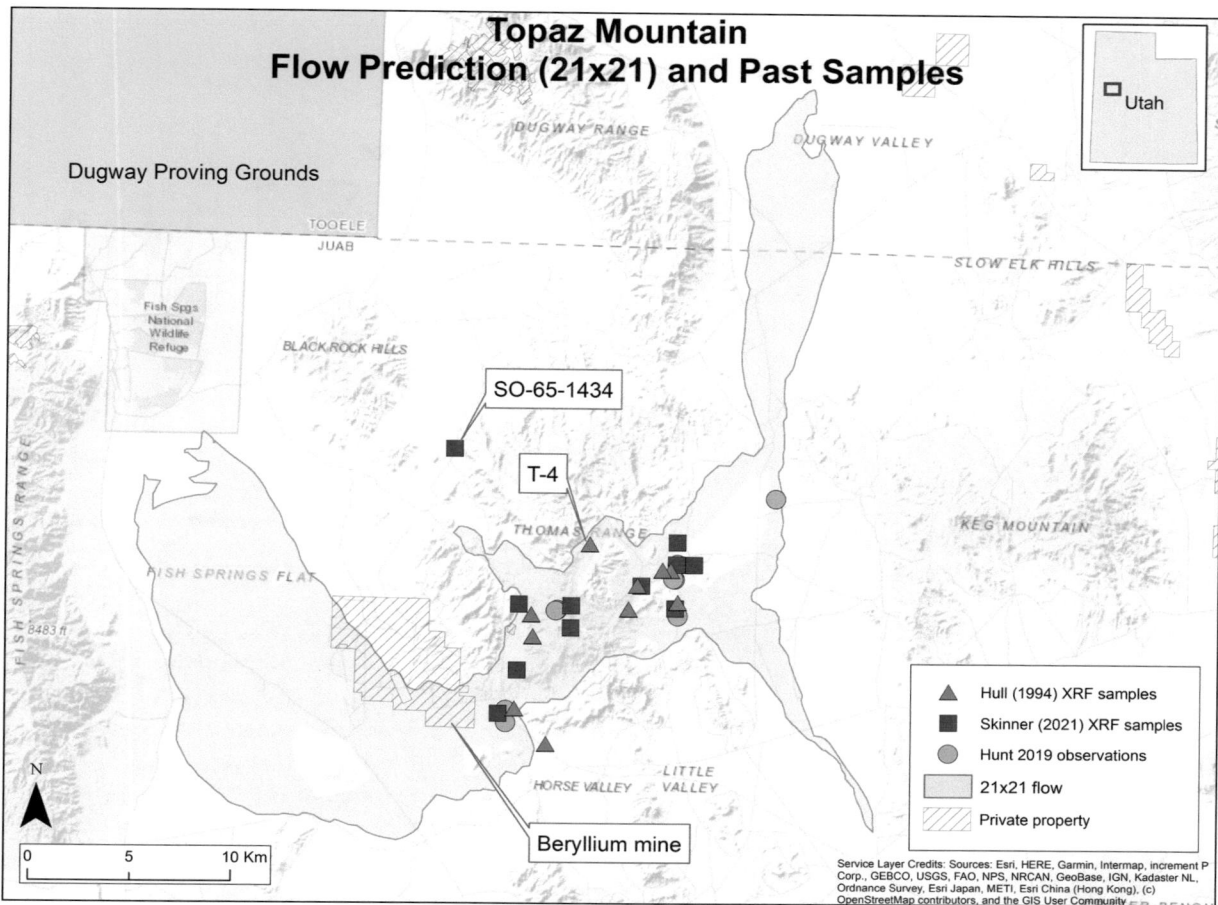

FIGURE 4.57. Topaz Mountain 21×21 flow prediction in comparison with past sampling.

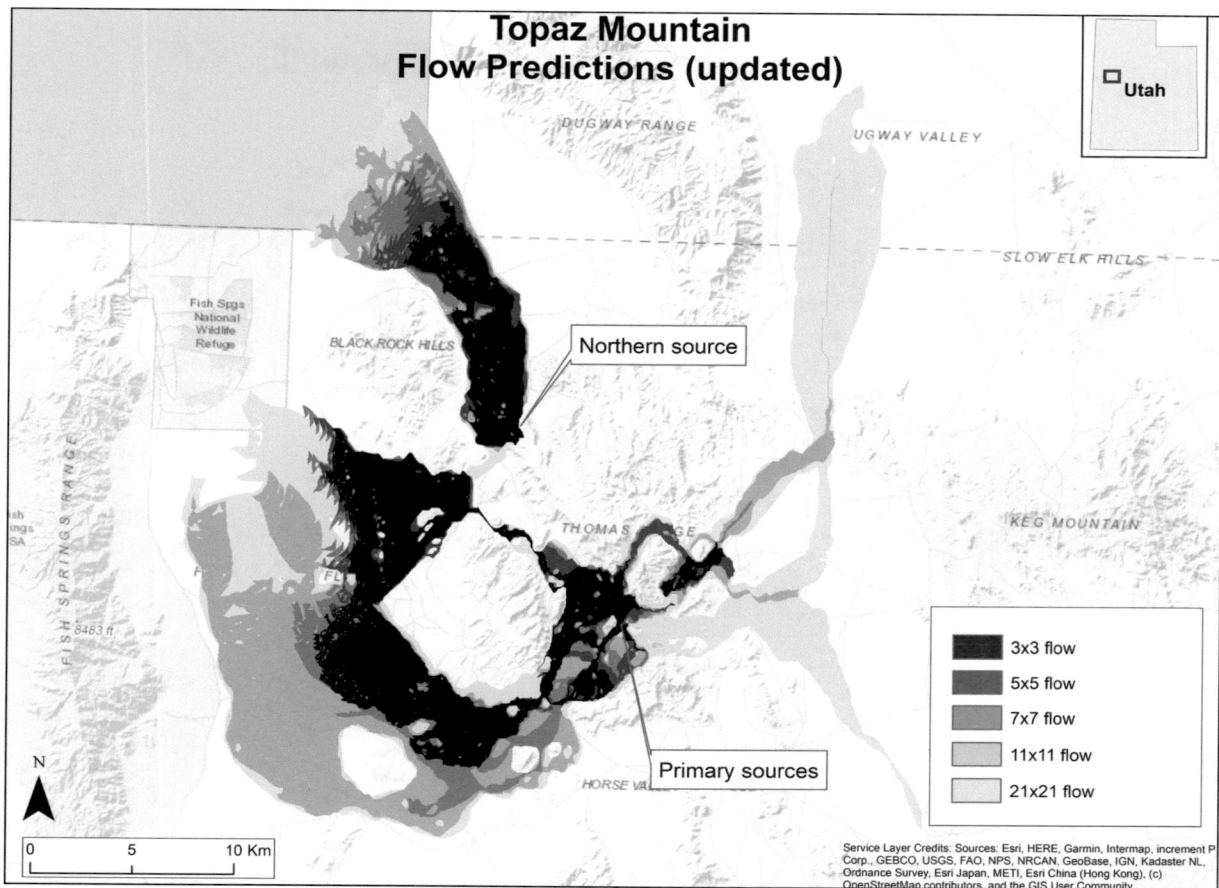

FIGURE 4.58. Topaz Mountain expanded flow predictions.

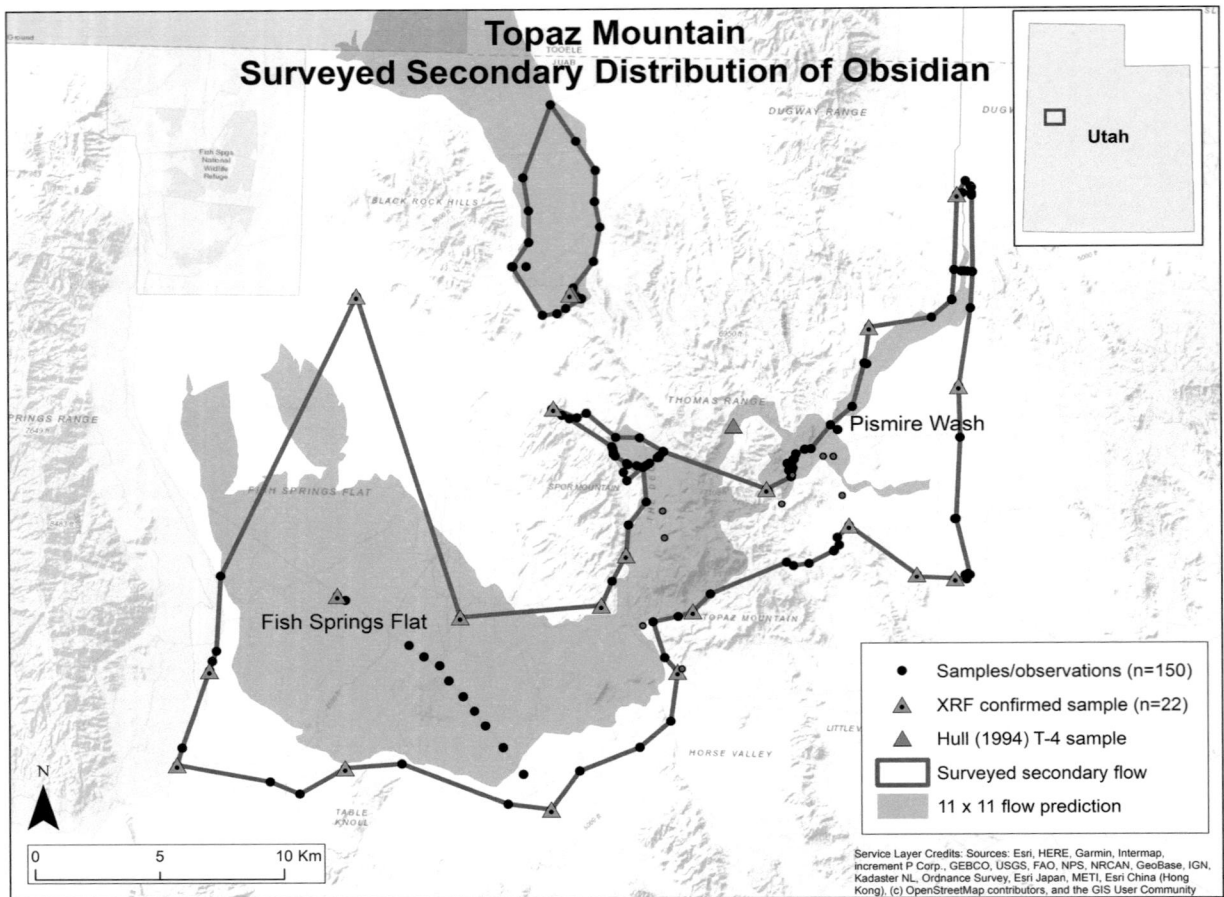

FIGURE 4.59. Topaz Mountain survey results.

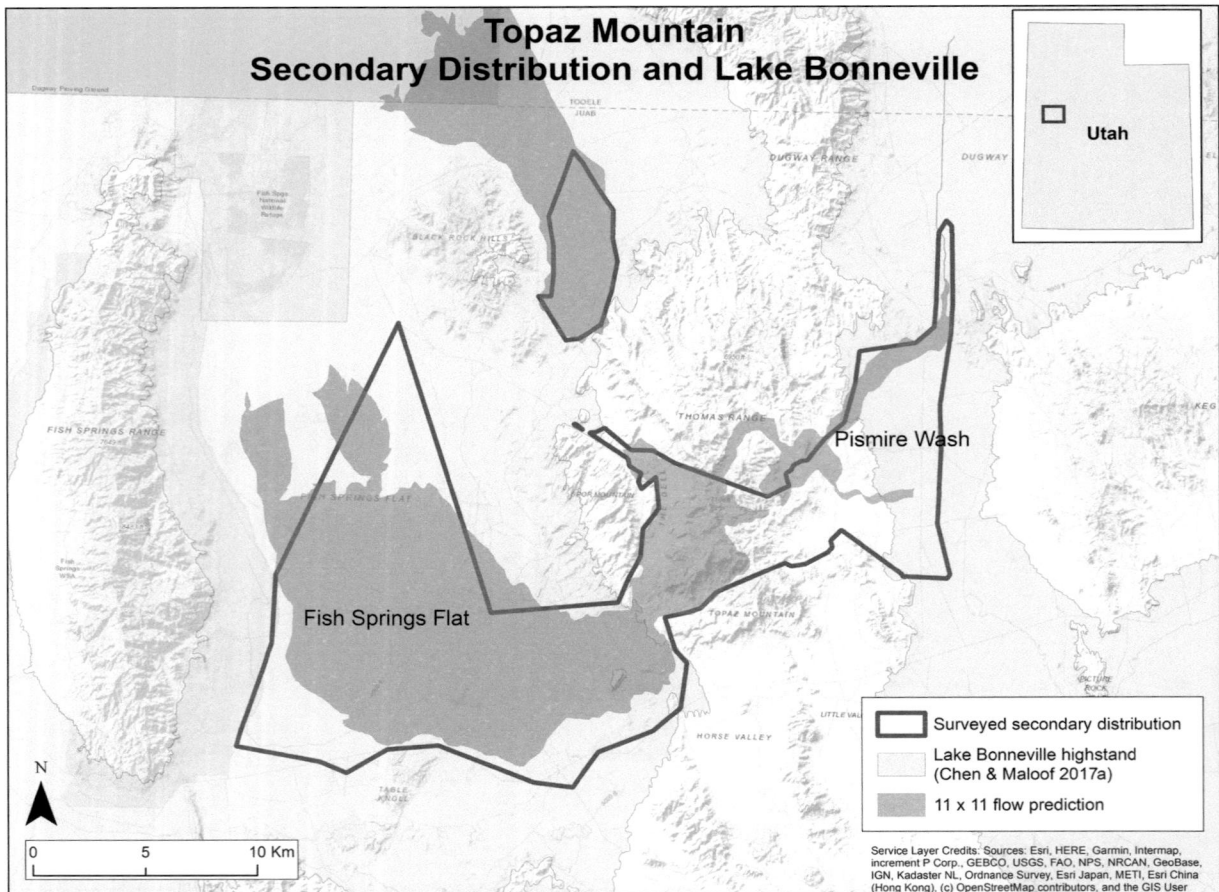

FIGURE 4.60. Topaz Mountain secondary distribution in relation to Lake Bonneville.

5

Flow Predictions for Toolstone Sources Used by the Paleoindian Occupants of the Old River Bed Delta

The purpose of this chapter is to quantify the discoverability of the obsidian and fine-grained volcanic (FGV) toolstone sources used within the Old River Bed (ORB) assemblage (Madsen, Schmitt, et al., 2015). The previous chapter provides a guide for the level of digital elevation model (DEM) smoothing needed to predict the secondary distributions of these sources and then extract a discoverability value from the extent of the sources.

Accomplishing this goal requires a dataset of geolocated Paleoindian artifacts associated with dated channels within the ORB delta/wetlands. The steps taken to generate this dataset, and the dataset itself, are detailed in Appendix A (https://collections.lib.utah.edu /ark:/87278/s6mntfnx). The process described in that appendix provides a total of 442 Paleoindian artifacts in association with a dated ORB channel and with an assigned geochemical (source) type (Table 5.1). Each of these sources will be described briefly in the following sections, and an exposure (E) value, as described in Chapter 4, will be calculated for each. Those samples returning an "unknown" geochemical signature ($n = 12$) will be dropped from further analysis.

METHODOLOGY

A distinction needs to be made between the sources surveyed in Chapter 4 and those representing the full complement of toolstone sources used in the ORB (Table 5.1). The sources surveyed in Chapter 4 served as test examples for the flow prediction methodology. Part of the selection process for those test areas included the requirement of an adequate existing description of the primary source. This qualification allowed initial pre-

dictions that were tested by fieldwork and, in some cases, led to the discovery of additional primary sources. The data available for characterizing the primary source areas for each of the remaining sources in Table 5.1 varies significantly. Some sources (e.g., Brown's Bench) are widely studied with many sample points by multiple authors, while other sources (e.g., Paradise Valley) are represented by only a few sample points or by sample points that are generalized to township-range sections with much lower spatial precision. I also have relied primarily on samples recorded using a GPS device, though even some of those are limited in precision. In cases where overlap in sample sets occurs between two authors, the data points with the greatest available precision were chosen.

In cases where only sporadic samples on the landscape are available (e.g., Currie Hills) and these samples isolated to a single topographical flow path (e.g., Cedar Mountain), GIS tools were used to apply a 20 m buffer around these points. These buffers were then used to create the weighted rasters (see "Establish a Catchment Region" in Chapter 4) by capturing several raster cells to act as seeds, or proxy sources, for calculating flow accumulations. Where extended cobble fields are known from the literature (e.g., Panaca Summit/Modena and Bear Gulch) or can be inferred by high sample density (e.g., Brown's Bench and Owyhee), points were aggregated to form a polygon or polygons that effectively represent a cobble field and then used to create the weighted raster.

However, for many samples reported in the literature, whether the sample was originally collected from a primary or secondary context is unknown. This lack of information exposes one weakness of the prediction model in that it assumes the most elevated, or upslope, seed is a primary source and that there is no distribution above it in elevation. This problem is one that only more fieldwork at each source location can eliminate. For now, the scale of a source's discoverability is represented by the flow prediction from known sample points. Much more work needs to be done here.

Fine-Grained Volcanics

Chapter 4 discusses the physical characteristics and formation processes of obsidian; however, within the Great Basin, non-glassy volcanic rock has long been recognized as a key raw material in lithic assemblages (Arkush & Pitblado, 2000; Beck & Jones, 1990; Jones & Beck, 1990). Over the years, a number of appellations have been applied to this material, from the most commonly used, "basalt" (Graf, 1995; Jones & Beck, 1990; Rice, 1972; Sargeant, 1973; Tuohy, 1968), to "glassy basalt" (Arkush & Pitblado, 2000, p. 12), "fine-grained eruptives" (Rogers, 1939, p. 16), and perhaps even "dull obsidian" (Amsden, 1937, p. 78). Over time, researchers recognized that these artifacts were usually not fashioned from actual "basalt" but rather from fine-grained volcanic rock within a range of silica-alkali compositions (Figure 5.1), primarily composed of andesite, dacite, trachyandesite, or trachydacite (Duke, 2011, 2013; Jones et al., 1997; Le Bas, 1986; Page, 2008). Within archaeological literature, the attribution "fine-grained volcanic(s)," or FGV(s), is now the standard term for this family of toolstone raw material.

While obsidian provenance analysis via X-ray fluorescence (XRF) has been in practice for more than half a century (Cann & Renfrew, 1964; Jack & Heizer, 1968), XRF testing on non-glassy volcanic material is a relatively recent endeavor (Shackley, 2010). In the 1990s, pioneering efforts by workers like Latham et al. (1992), Weisler and Woodhead (1995) and Jones et al. (1997) demonstrated that XRF could, in fact, be used to geochemically identify FGVs. Unlike obsidian, which is formed from "supercooled liquid silica melt" (Hughes, 1986, p. 21) and is therefore compositionally homogenous, FGVs represent the same melt differentially cooled and crystalized, raising concerns of geochemical heterogeneity, which could lead to inaccurate and irreproducible XRF readings. These concerns have been alleviated, and with appropriate sample selection, XRF is now considered a standard means of identifying FGV geochemical types (Jones et al., 1997; Craig Skinner, personal communication, May 31, 2021).

The geographical sourcing of FGV types within the Great Basin has been led by workers such as Jones et al.

Table 5.1. Old River Bed Delta Paleoindian Toolstone Sources.

Sources	Totals
Badlands	18
Bear Gulch	1
Black Rock Area	10
Brown's Bench	41
Brown's Bench Area	5
Cedar Mountain	8
Currie Hills	3
Deep Creek	10
Ferguson Wash	1
Flat Hills	182
Kane Springs Wash Caldera	1
Malad	4
Mineral Mountains	9
Owyhee	2
Panaca Summit/Modena	1
Paradise Valley	3
Pumice Hole Mine	1
Topaz Mountain	130
Unknown 1	1
Unknown FGV	6
Unknown obsidian	5
Total	**442**

Note: Bolded sources are documented in Chapter 4.

(1997), Page (2008), Skinner (Page & Skinner, 2008; see also Appendix D, Table D.2, https://collections.lib.utah.edu/ark:/87278/s6mntfnx), and Duke (2011, 2013). The work by Page (2008) is of particular importance to this project as he identifies the sources of five FGV types/subtypes (Badlands A, Cedar Mountain B, Currie Hills, Deep Creek A, and Flat Hills A, C, D, and E) that appear in the ORB dataset. The total alkali-silica range of these samples is illustrated by the hatched area in Figure 5.1 Understanding the geographical location of these FGV sources allows their inclusion in my final discoverability analysis and increases the overall size of the artifact dataset (*n* = 442).

ORB Sources

Badlands

Source Type: Fine-grained volcanic; trachyandesite (Page, 2008)

Location: Western Tooele County, Utah and eastern Elko and White Pine Counties, Nevada. The Badlands A subtype is present ~60 km east at Wildcat Mountain, Tooele County, Utah.

Alternative Names: None, but two subtypes (A and B) and its distribution geographically overlaps with the Deep Creek FGV distribution.

Page (2008) Sample Points: n = 14 (see Table D.5)

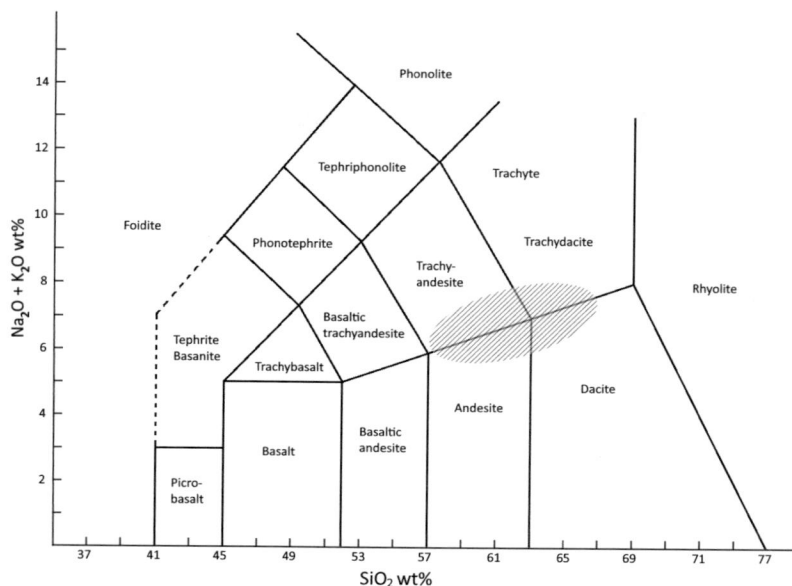

FIGURE 5.1. Total Alkali Silica (TAS) diagram showing the general range (hatched region) of alkali-silica profiles from several known fine-grained volcanic (FGV) sources identified in Old River Bed delta artifacts (after Le Bas, 1986; Le Bas & Streckeisen, 1991; Page, 2008).

Skinner Sample Points: *n* = 27 (see Table D.2)
ORB Paleoindian Artifacts: *n* = 18 (Table 5.1)

The distributions of Badlands and Deep Creek FGV types are found largely overlapping to the northwest of the Deep Creek Range in western Tooele County, Utah and southeast of White Horse Mountain in Elko County, Nevada. For the purposes here, it would make sense methodologically to combine the Badlands and Deep Creek types into a single discoverability signal, save for an exposure of Badlands A FGV present at Wildcat Mountain (see inset in Figure 5.2). This exposure, roughly 70 km northeast of the Old River Bed sites, and deep within the Utah Test and Training Range-South military zone, is significantly closer to the ORB than the western exposure. For this reason, the Badlands and Deep Creek FGV types are presented separately, though they share many of the same landscape attributes.

Compared to our understanding of many of the other areas discussed here, the geology of this region has not been examined in detail. Crafford (2007) defines the region's low-lying, unnamed ridges as andesite or dacite flows from 30 to 45 Ma (*Ta1* in Figure 5.2). Aside from these volcanic flows, the area is largely comprised of more recent sedimentary deposits and alluvium. To the east, at Wildcat Mountain, Moore and Sorensen (1979) suggest a late Permian or early Pennsylvanian origin (roughly 300 Ma) for the mountain, with a Tertiary (2.6–66 Ma) basalt on the west side, but go no further. Clark et al. (2016) document the latitic/trachyandesite

intrusions on the west side of Wildcat Mountain (*Tlw* in the Figure 5.2 inset) and suggest a possible Eocene age (roughly 34–56 Ma; they specifically note that the geology was not dated), in line with the timing of regional volcanism (see the "Regional Geology" section of Chapter 4).

Archaeologically, most of our understanding of this area and of the Badlands FGV geochemical type comes from work by Page (2008), who classifies the source as a trachyandesite and other unknown FGV types. Duke (2013) makes the point that the Badlands type has no distinct primary source location, so all samples are in a context of secondary distribution.

Two sets of sample points were used for the flow prediction. Page (2008) provides 14 FGV samples in secondary context for the western distribution region. Skinner (Table D.2), who provided the XRF analysis for Page, provided 28 sample points, of which 14 were unique from Page (2008). Three of these samples are located at Wildcat Mountain and characterize the Badlands A signature for that exposure. One of the Skinner samples is located more than 100 km to the west in Mahoney Canyon on the east side of Big Bald Mountain, Nevada. This single, distant sample was excluded from the flow calculations as it will have no impact on the overall ORB discoverability calculations for the majority exposure extent for the Badlands FGV, which is quite close to the ORB delta.

The points were combined (*n* = 28), buffered to 20 m, and the 15 × 15 flow is predicted in Figure 5.2.

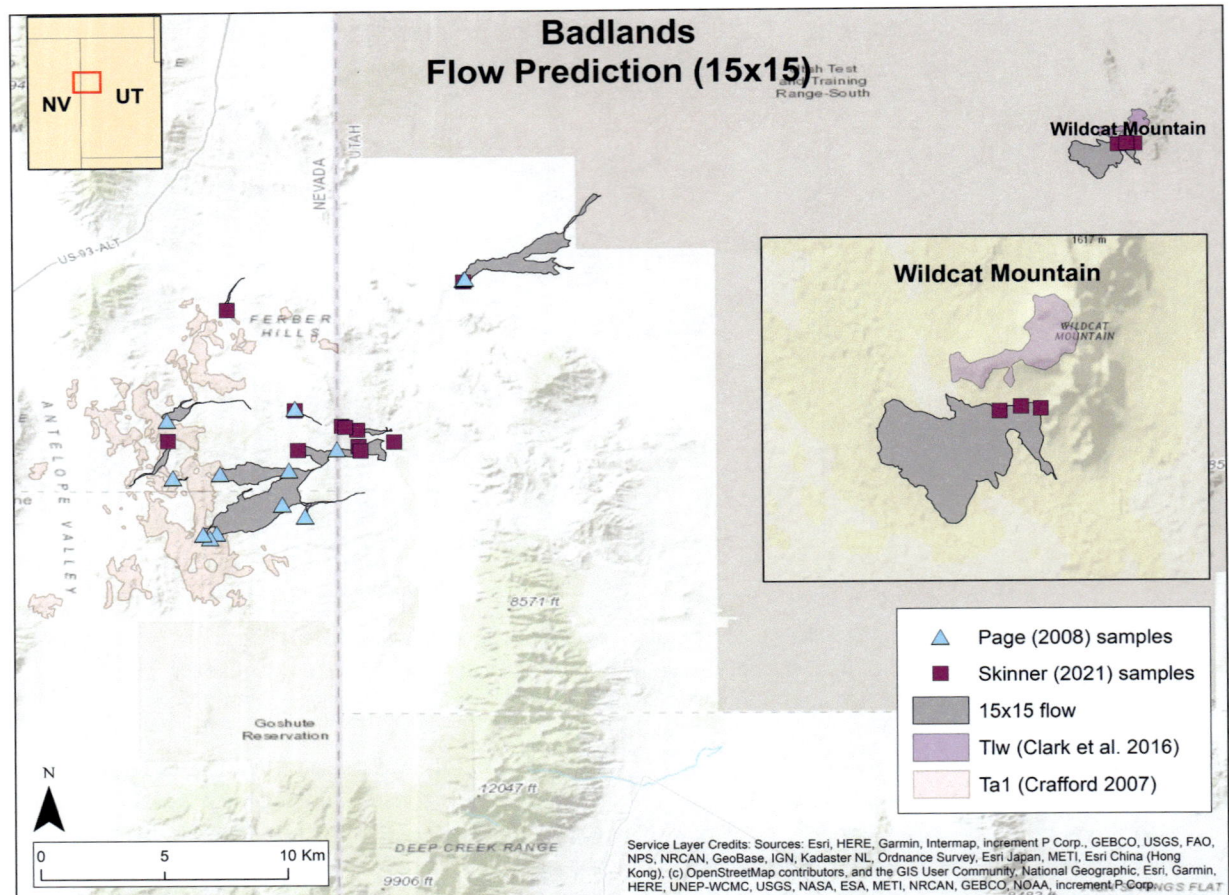

FIGURE 5.2. Badlands fine-grained volcanics (FGV) 15×15 flow prediction.

The Badlands FGV source has an exposure (E) value of 72 km².

Bear Gulch

Source Type: Obsidian

Location: Clark County, Idaho

Alternative Names: Big Table Mountain (Willingham, 1995), Camas/Dry Creek (Michels 1983, cited in Bailey, 1992; Wright et al., 1990), Centennial (Sappington, 1981), F.M.Y. 90 Group (Griffin et al., 1969), Spring Creek (Gallagher, 1979), Reas Creek (Fowler, 2014), Warm Creek Spring (Kimball 1976, cited in Holmer, 1997), West Camas Creek (Gallagher, 1979)

Skinner Sample Points: $n = 7$ (Table D.2, two samples share identical locations with two others) Richard Holmer (personal communication, July 24, 2019): $n = 4$ (Table D.4)

ORB Paleoindian Artifacts: $n = 1$ (Table 5.1)

The Snake River Plain experienced a series of explosive eruptions of high-silica rhyolites over the last 16 Ma.

These occurred as the North American continental plate moved in a southwest direction over a mantle hot spot (Figure 5.3) which now, after effectively cutting across the northern Basin and Range Province, resides beneath the Yellowstone caldera (Morgan & McIntosh, 2005). These pyroclastic eruptions produced massive ash-flow sheets, the basal units of which, in some instances, cooled quickly enough to form artifact-grade obsidian (Hughes & Smith, 1993; Morgan & McIntosh, 2005).

The origins of the obsidian found in the Bear Gulch area, south of Big Table Mountain and within the Centennial Mountains of Idaho, are geologically poorly understood. First identified as geochemically distinct by Griffin et al. (1969), Sappington (1981) reported that its origins were variously attributed to either an obsidian welded tuff or an ignimbrite, but suggested it is best characterized as a vitrophyre. Willingham (1995) argues that the obsidian boulders and cobbles are the product of obsidian outcrops exposed during Pliocene (5.33–2.58 Ma) uplift of the mountains around Big Table Mountain and the subsequent erosion of the same. Homing in on the primary source location was equally

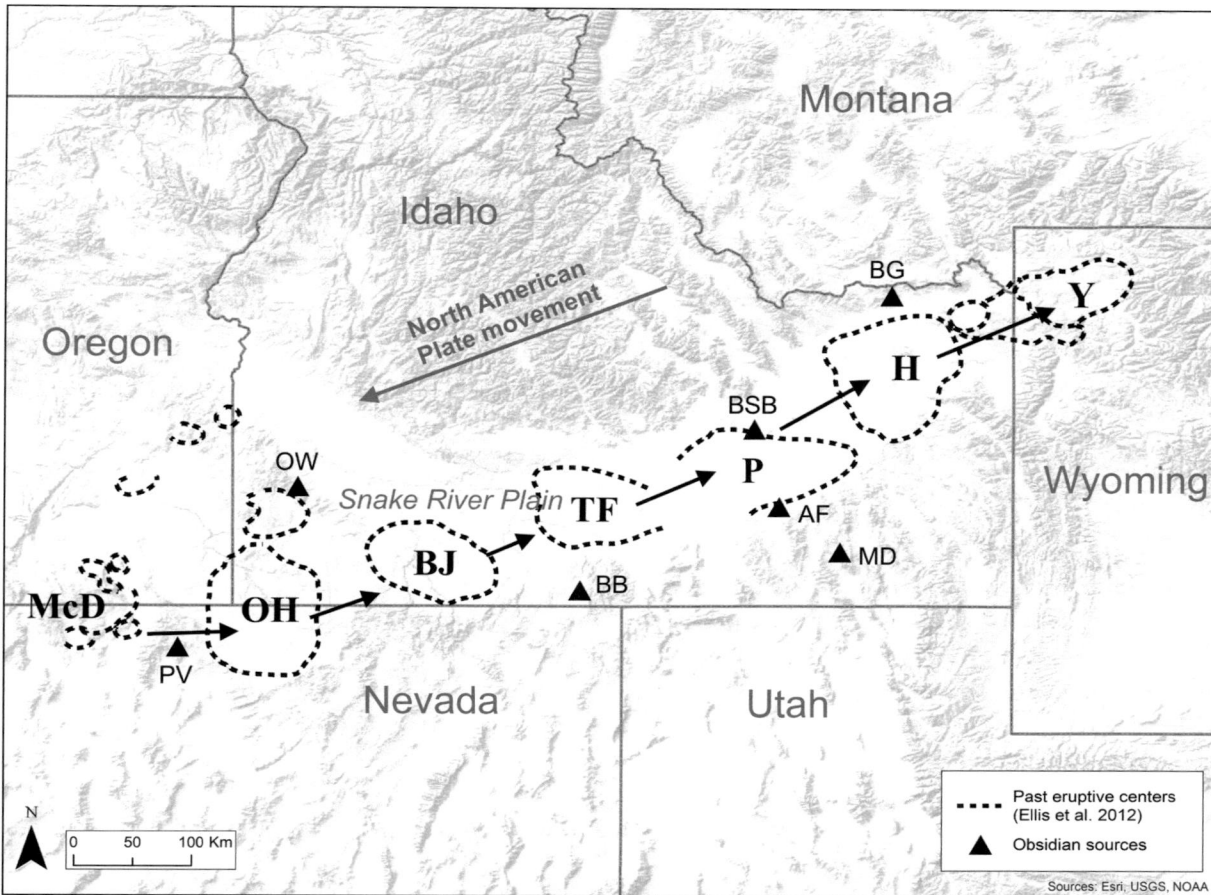

FIGURE 5.3. Progression of the Yellowstone hot spot and resultant eruptive centers across the Snake River Plain; large abbreviations: McD, McDermitt (~16.1 Ma); OH, Owyhee Humboldt (~14 Ma); BJ, Bruneau-Jarbridge (~12.7 Ma); TF, Twin Falls (~10.8 Ma); P, Picabo (~10.2 Ma); H, Heise (~6.6 Ma); and Y, Yellowstone (~2.05 Ma). Black triangles are common obsidian source locations: AF, American Falls; BB, Brown's Bench; BG, Bear Gulch; BSB, Big Southern Butte; MD, Malad; OW, Owyhee; PV, Paradise Valley. Eruptive center data from Ellis et al. (2012).

difficult, made more challenging by the host of names attached to the obsidian (see list above), including that of a nearby obsidian with a similar name (Centennial Valley) but a distinctly different geochemical signature. Hughes and Nelson (1987) established the central source area around Bear Gulch and attached the current appellation.

The detection of Bear Gulch obsidian in numerous archaeological sites over a widespread geographical area, was a key motivator in the search for its source location. First recognized in samples found in Yellowstone National Park (described then as "Field Museum Yellowstone 90", or "FMY 90"), Bear Gulch obsidian is found in archaeological sites throughout states to the east (Minnesota, Ohio, Illinois, Indiana), to the south in Iowa and along the Mississippi Valley, and north into Montana and Alberta (Hughes, 2007b; Hughes & Nelson, 1987; Scheiber & Finley, 2011; Willingham,

1995). The resource has been used by Native Americans for millennia, appearing in assemblages ranging from Paleoindian to Hopewell (Hughes, 2007b; Willingham, 1995). Willingham reports multiple large quarries at Big Table Mountain, many with "debitage backfill over one meter thick" (1995, p. 3).

Willingham (1995) provides the best and most current regional outline of the source (Figure 5.4), encompassing almost 63 km², but includes no specific details of primary source outcrops. The known boundaries of this source include the southern side of Big Table Mountain, Castle Peak, and Bear Gulch, and extend southeast along a ridge, almost to Button Butte. In this case, this extent was methodologically treated in the same manner as the cobble field on the east slope of Panaca Summit/ Modena and its outline converted to a polygon that was used to calculate the flow prediction. Notably the prediction captures all of the sample points provided by

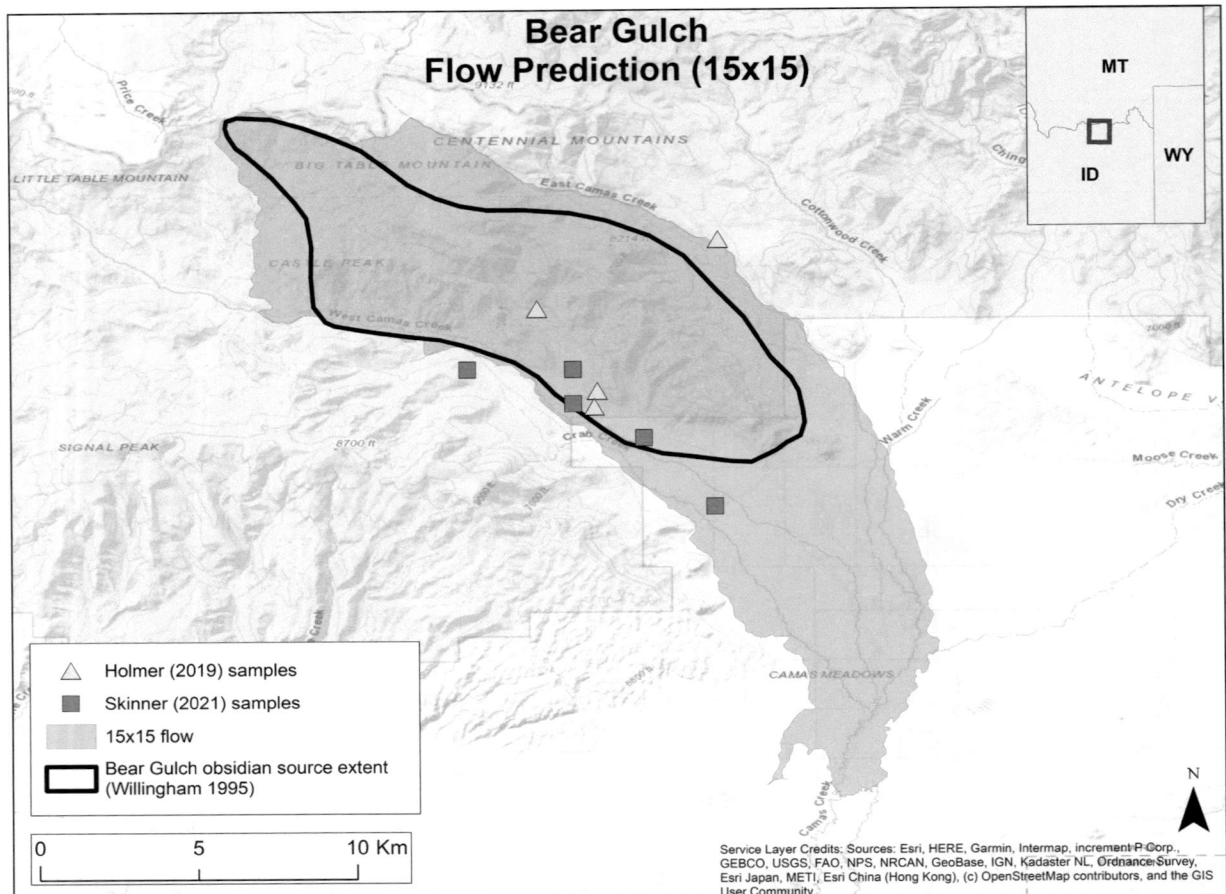

FIGURE 5.4. Bear Gulch obsidian 15×15 flow prediction.

Holmer (1997; Table D.4) and five of the seven samples provided by Skinner (2021; Table D.2), with the only two exceptions (two samples that share the same location) occurring about 500 m from the predicted flow edge. The Bear Gulch obsidian source has an exposure (*E*) value of 129 km².

Brown's Bench, Brown's Bench Area, and Butte Valley Group A

Source Type: Obsidian
Location: Twin Falls and Cassia Counties, Idaho
Alternative Names or Localities: Browns Bench (Bowers & Savage, 1962), Brown's Bench Ranch (Hughes, 1990), Cedar Creek (Bailey, 1992), Coal Bank Creek (Jones et al., 2003), Coal Bank Spring (Page & Bacon, 2016), Cottonwood Ranch (Hughes, 1990), Goose Creek, Hudson Ridge, Jackpot (Skinner, 2021), Little House Creek (Bailey, 1992), Murphy Springs (Page & Bacon, 2016), Rock Creek (Gallagher, 1979), Mahogany Butte (Fowler, 2014), Three Creeks (Gallagher, 1979), Three Creek Landfill, Three Creek 2 (Bailey, 1992), and Twin Meadows (Hughes, 1990)

Page and Bacon (2016) Sample Points: Brown's Bench type (*n* = 58), Brown's Bench Area type (*n* = 12), Butte Valley Group A type (*n* = 28; Table D.6).
Richard Holmer (personal communication, July 24, 2019): *n* = 18 (Table D.4)
Skinner Sample Points: Brown's Bench type (*n* = 45), Brown's Bench Area type (*n* = 4), Butte Valley Group A type (*n* = 7; Table D.2)
ORB artifacts: Brown's Bench type (*n* = 41), Brown's Bench Areas type (*n* = 5), Butte Valley Group A (*n* = 0; Table 5.1)

In the central Snake River Plain, the Bruneau-Jarbridge (BJ) and Twin Falls (TF) eruptive centers (Figure 5.3) produced a succession of massive rhyolitic ignimbrites, beginning around 13 Ma (Ellis et al., 2012). The Bruneau-Jarbridge center produced at least nine of these intensely-welded ignimbrites between 12.8 and 10.5 Ma, creating accumulations over 500 m thick which are characterized as the Cougar Point Tuff (Bonnichsen et al., 1988, 2008; Cathey & Nash, 2004; Ellis et al., 2012). These ignimbrite eruptions were expansive and considered to have been regionally devasting, with one such eruption, Cougar Point Tuff XIII, ejecting more than 1,000 km³ of material across the plain (Ellis et al., 2012). The region was also subjected to numerous large-volume rhyolitic lava flows following individual ignimbrites (Bonnichsen et al., 2008). The end result was a cumulative volume of tens of thousands of cubic-kilometers of rhyolitic magma spread across southern Idaho, northern Nevada, and northwestern Utah (Bailey, 1992; Bonnichsen et al., 2008; Reid et al., 2015).

The Brown's Bench fault in southern Idaho (BB in Figure 5.3) exposes at least 13 such ignimbrites, most of which likely correlate with the Cougar Point Tuff succession, but about which little more is known (Ellis et al., 2012). The ignimbrites produced vitrophyre sources as they cooled, creating a widespread obsidian source in the Brown's Bench region with cobbles up to 30 cm in diameter (Bailey, 1992; Reid, 2014; Sappington, 1981).

That Brown's Bench obsidians have been exploited as toolstone sources since the Pleistocene/Holocene transition is widely accepted. Brown's Bench obsidian is present in numerous archaeological contexts within the Snake River Plain region and appears in many other sites outside of Idaho, some up to 250 km away (Arkush & Pitblado, 2000; Bailey, 1992; Beck & Jones, 1990, 1994; Bowers & Savage, 1962; Fowler, 2014; Hildebrandt et al., 2016; Hockett, 1995; Hughes, 1990, 2013; Hughes & Smith, 1993; Jones et al., 2003; King, 2016; Madsen, Schmitt, et al., 2015; Page & Skinner, 2008; Reid, 2014; Scheiber & Finley, 2011). However, understanding the primary sources and regional extents of the Brown's Bench obsidians is complicated by several factors, including the multiple volcanic eruptions and modes (ignimbrite vs. lava) noted above, the massive scale of these eruptions both in volumetric and areal extents, the patchwork of past geological and archaeological studies using variable naming conventions (see alternative names list above), and even the persistence of placeholder names for initially unknown sources (e.g., the Butte Valley Group A). Butte Valley is more than 200 km away from the region, but this major Brown's Bench geochemical subtype carries this name as a result of its first characterization as an unknown "Group A" in the analysis of artifacts at the Butte Valley site in Nevada by Jones and Beck (1990). These authors were also the first to recognize the unknown Group A obsidian as a member of the Brown's Bench family (Jones et al., 2003), yet the name persists in the literature. This work demonstrates that at least three geochemical types are present within the greater Brown's Bench region. These are now largely standardized on the names Brown's Bench, Brown's Bench Area, and Butte Valley Group A (but see Page & Bacon, 2016 for suggested name updates: Browns Bench Variety 1–3).

Page and Bacon (2016) documented an extensive survey and sampling of the Brown's Bench region with the dual goals of refining the spatial extents and the geochemical characterizations of the Brown's Bench obsidians. The authors explored whether the three geochemical signatures represent three geographically distinct source areas. Their survey's areal extent results are illustrated in Figure 5.5. What becomes clear from their survey is that the three Brown's Bench geochemical types are spatially overlapping, leaving no distinct source areas. In terms of determining how "discoverable" or how large a signal the Brown's Bench obsidians presented on the landscape, these three types are combined into a single type, simply referred to as "Brown's Bench" going forward. When analyzing the Old River Bed delta data (see Chapter 6), artifacts from these geochemical types will be similarly grouped.

As surveyed by Page and Bacon (2016), the BB areal extent is approximately 3580 km², BBA is ~800 km², and BVGA is ~1445 km². Both BBA and BVGA are almost completely subsumed within the larger BB extent.

The Brown's Bench region presents the most complicated distribution of a geochemical type (or group of types) that was used as toolstone in the ORB. Figure 5.6 illustrates the combined distribution of sample points from Page & Bacon (2016) and Skinner (2021; Table D.2). The contexts of Skinner's northern sample points, whether in primary source locations (some do appear at elevation) or secondary (particularly those along the rivers), are unknown. The northern points are, in general, also at considerable distance from the southern point cluster.

With this consideration in mind, the BB, BBA, and BVGA datasets from Page and Bacon (2016), Holmer (personal communication, July 24, 2019; Appendix D, Table D.4), and Skinner (2021; Table D.2) were combined and flow predictions generated using two methods. The region surveyed by Page and Bacon was treated as a single cobble field (as on the eastern slope of the Panaca Summit/Modena source) and generated 20 m buffers around the remaining points. Together, these areas were used as the proxy sources for a 15 × 15 flow prediction.

The combined Brown's Bench obsidian source has an exposure (E) value of 5173 km².

Cedar Mountain

Source Type: Fine-grained volcanic; andesite and other unknown igneous types (Page, 2008)
Location: Tooele County, Utah
Alternative Names: None, but nine subtypes (A–I)
Page (2008) Sample Points: n = 28 (samples comprised of a mix of subtypes A–I; Appendix D, Table D.5)

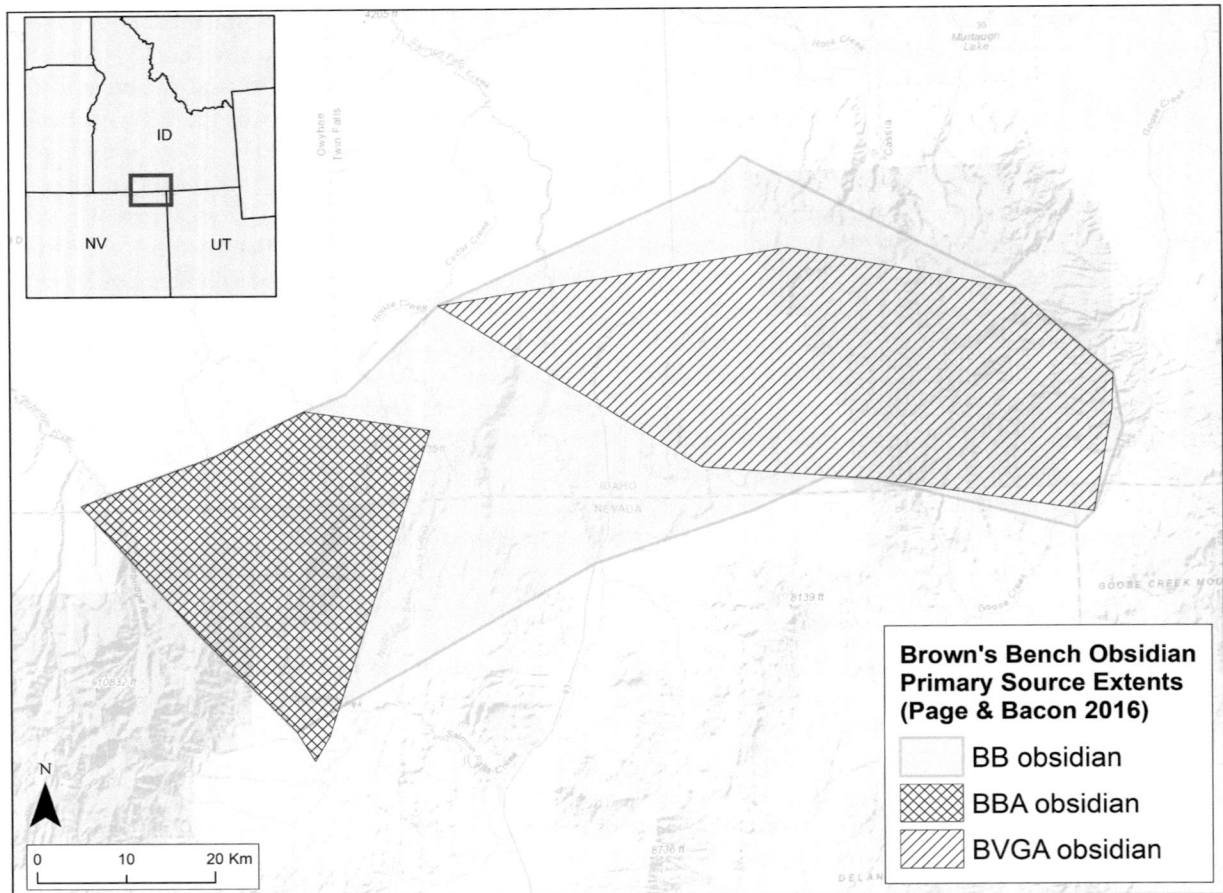

FIGURE 5.5. The primary source extents of the three main obsidian geochemical types associated with Brown's Bench: Brown's Bench (BB), Brown's Bench Area (BBA), and Butte Valley Group A (BVGA), after data and description in Page and Bacon 2016.

Skinner (2021) Sample Points: *n* = 1 (Appendix D, Table D.2, subtype B)
ORB Artifacts: *n* = 8 (Table 5.1)

The Cedar Mountain Range lies about 100 km southwest of Salt Lake City, Utah, and its ridge forms a portion of the eastern border of the Dugway Proving Grounds military installation. The range is Paleozoic in origin (composed of various sedimentary formations) and capped with basaltic andesite and rhyolite from early Tertiary volcanic activity, approximately 40 Ma (Clark et al., 2016; Hintze, 1988; Maurer, 1970; Page, 2008). At its height, Lake Bonneville surrounded the range (Chen & Maloof, 2017a) and Maurer (1970) notes that large areas of the Tertiary volcanic rock are now overlain by recent sand dunes.

The Cedar Mountain FGV source was extensively documented by Page (2008), who provides the most complete dataset of andesite samples. Page classifies the Cedar Mountain FGV into nine subtypes (A–I), but geographically these are widely distributed within

the local area. For the purposes of determining a discoverability signal, 20 m buffers of the complete set of Cedar Mountain subtypes were used to generate the flow predictions (Figure 5.7). Page (2008) notes that large cobbles are readily available and that these have been distributed by alluvial transport within an area of about 5 km in diameter and up to 10 km southeast of the source, well in line with the scale of the flow prediction here. Archaeologically, Duke (2011, p. 110) notes that the abundance of phenocrysts in the Cedar Mountain FGV is approaching a level that may limit its knapping utility.

The Cedar Mountain prediction (Figure 5.7) presents a discoverability exposure (*E*) signal of 37 km².

Currie Hills

Source Type: Fine-grained volcanic; dacite, trachydacite, trachyandesite, and other igneous types (Page, 2008)
Location: Elko County, Nevada
Alternative Names: None

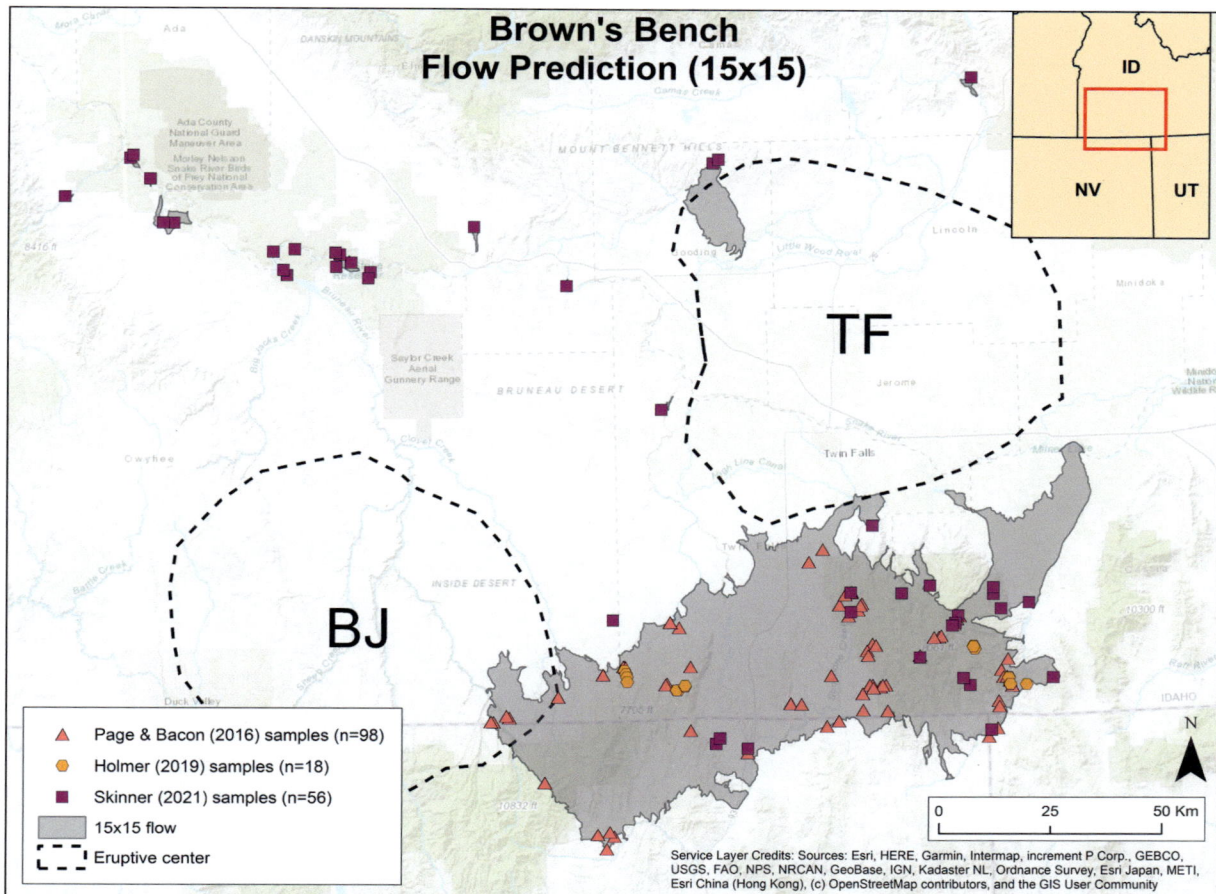

FIGURE 5.6. Brown's Bench obsidian 15×15 flow prediction and Brown's Bench, Brown's Bench Area, and Butte Valley Group A sample point distributions (Page & Bacon, 2016; Holmer, personal communication, July 24, 2019; Skinner, 2021) in relationship to the putative Bruneau-Jarbridge and Twin Falls eruptive centers (Ellis et al., 2012).

Jones (Personal Communication, July 10, 2021) Sample Points: $n = 1$

Skinner Sample Points: $n = 1$ (Appendix D, Table D.2)

Observation Points by Hunt, 2021: $n = 3$ (Appendix B, Table B.7, https://collections.lib.utah.edu/ark:/872 78/s6mntfnx)

ORB Artifacts: $n = 3$ (Table 5.1)

The Currie Hills FGV is found in Elko Country, Nevada, 30 km directly west of the Badlands and Deep Creek FGV locations. As discussed above, the geology of this area is poorly documented, but Crafford (2007) defines the region's low-lying, unnamed ridges as andesite or dacite flows from 30 to 45 Ma (*Ta1* in Figure 5.2). Aside from these volcanic flows, this area is also largely comprised of more recent sedimentary deposits and alluvium.

The first recording of the Currie Hills FGV extent appears in DeChambre (1979, p. 1) which reports a lithic scatter of "fine grained, black basalt" with "nodules of source material" in the southern Currie Hills

(26Ek1976). This finding was followed by Murphy (1981, p. 1) who records "a large basalt quarry which covers at least ¼ mile by 1 mile" (26Ek3870), approximately 2 km west of 26Ek1976. In Murphy (1981, p. 1), part of the site "is a series of hills where the nodules of basalt are weathering out." An additional lithic scatter (26Ek7320) was recorded by Zerga (1988) just over 19 km to the north with natural cobbles to 8 in (~20 cm).

To predict the flow extent, shapefiles provided by Daron Duke (personal communication, July 11, 2021) for sites 26Ek1976 and 26Ek7320 were used. The site report for 26Ek3870 provided a detailed map that was georeferenced, and a shapefile was generated from that image, which corresponds with a similar, but smaller, polygon from Duke. Tom Jones (personal communication, July 10, 2021) provided two sample locations, one within 100 m of 26Ek7320 and the other along state highway 93A. The latter was excluded here because it was unclear if its context was affected by road construction. Skinner also reported one XRF sample (Appendix D, Table D.2). Finally, during a site visit in 2021, I recorded

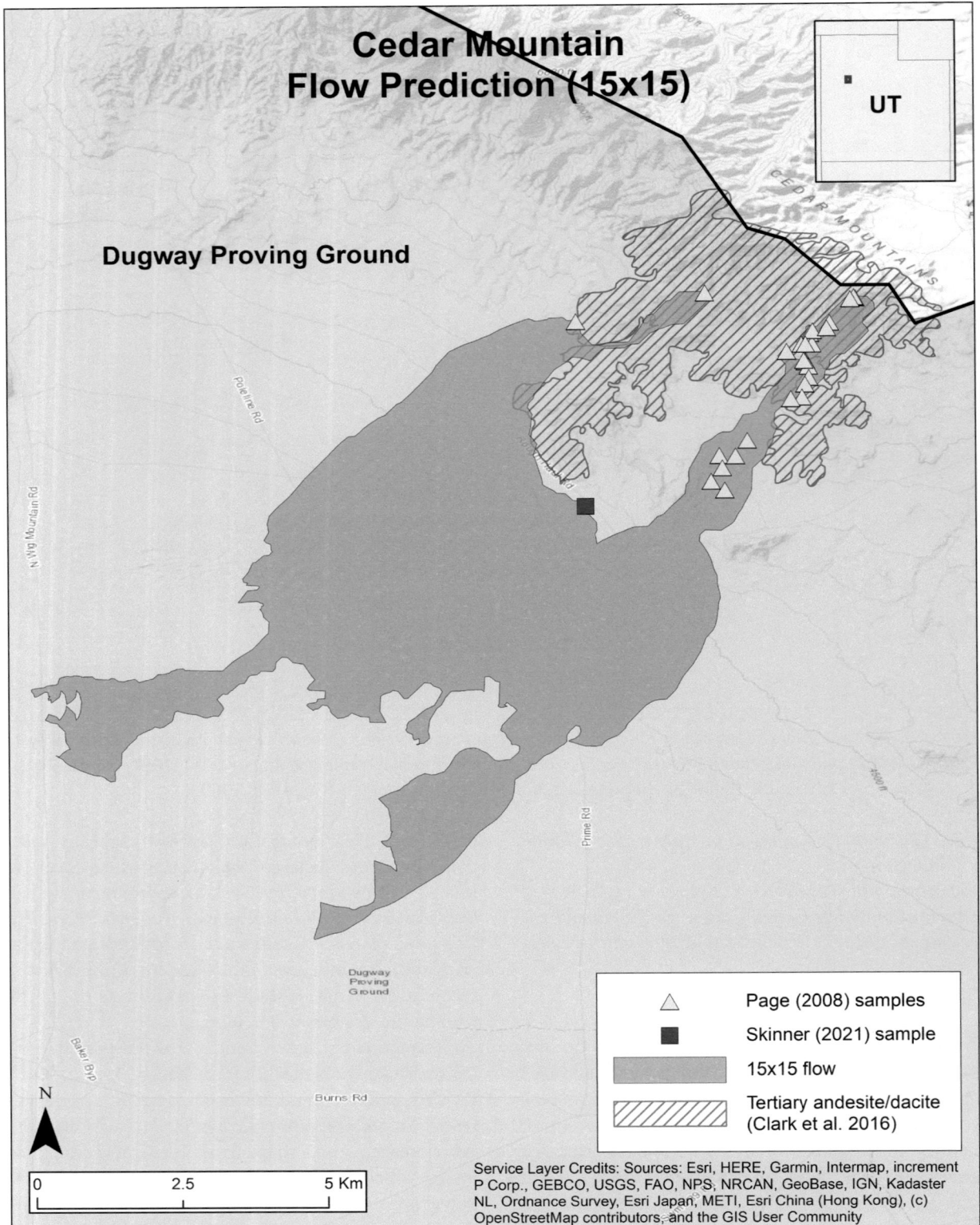

FIGURE 5.7. Cedar Mountain fine-grained volcanics (FGV) 15×15 flow prediction.

three FGV observations (Appendix B, Table B.7). From the broad sampling distribution, this source is still largely unknown and suggests a large expanse that will be exposed by further fieldwork. A weighted raster was generated using the known quarry site polygons and 20 m buffers around individual sample points.

With the information we have now, the Currie Hills prediction (Figure 5.8) presents a discoverability exposure (E) signal of 26 km^2.

Deep Creek

Source Type: Fine-grained volcanic; andesite and trachyandesite (Page, 2008)

Location: Western Tooele County, Utah and eastern Elko and White Pine Counties, Nevada.

Alternative Names: None, but four subtypes (A–D) and geographically overlaps with the Badlands FGV

Page (2008) Sample Points: n = 18 (samples comprised of a mix of subtypes, Appendix D, Table D.5)

Skinner Sample Points: n = 15 (all subtype A, Appendix D, Table D.2)

ORB Artifacts: n = 10 (Table 5.1)

As discussed above, the Deep Creek and Badlands FGV types are found largely overlapping to the northwest of the Deep Creek Range in western Tooele County, Utah, and southeast of White Horse Mountain in Elko County, Nevada. Crafford (2007) defines the region's low-lying, unnamed ridges as andesite or dacite flows from 30 to 45 Ma (*Ta1* in Figure 5.9). Aside from these volcanic flows, the area is largely comprised of more recent sedimentary deposits and alluvium.

Archaeologically and geologically, most of our understanding of this area and of the Deep Creek FGV geochemical type comes from the work by Page (2008) who classifies it as andesite and trachyandesite.

Two sets of sample points were available. Page (2008) provides 18 FGV samples in secondary context. Skinner (2021; Appendix D, Table D.2), who performed the XRF analysis for Page, provided 15 sample points, of which three (SO-65-1058, -1393, and -1397) were not provided by Page (2008). These points were combined (n = 21), buffered to 20 m, and the 15 × 15 flow is predicted in Figure 5.9.

The Deep Creek prediction (Figure 5.9) presents a discoverability exposure (E) signal of 108 km^2.

Flat Hills

Source Type: Fine-grained volcanic; andesite, dacite and trachydacite (Page, 2008)

Location: Tooele County, Utah

Alternative Names: None, but five subtypes (A, B, C, D, and E)

Page (2008) Sample Points: n = 26 (samples comprised of a mix of subtypes; Appendix D, Table D.5)

ORB Artifacts: n = 182 (Table 5.1)

The Flat Hills lie about 2 km south of the town of Dugway, Utah, at the southern end of the Cedar Mountains, within Tooele County.

The Flat Hills FGV source was extensively documented by Page (2008), who provides the most complete dataset of FGV samples. Page classifies the Flat Hills FGV into five subtypes (A, B, C, D, and E) but these cluster within the area. Types A, B, D, and E all fall in a northern cluster, while all the C types appear in a cluster about 3 km farther south.

At its height, Lake Bonneville inundated almost the entire area (Chen & Maloof, 2017a). As no FGV primary sources are present in the Flat Hills, which are sedimentary in origin, Page (2008) suggests the material in this area is the result of a tombolo, or sandbar, joining the Flat Hills with the Cedar Mountains during the Provo recession. FGV secondary material was then deposited on this tombolo as Lake Bonneville wave action entrained FGV nodules.

Archaeologically, as can be seen from Table 5.1, the Flat Hills were significantly exploited for toolstone by the people living in the Old River Bed delta across multiple temporal periods.

For the purposes of determining a discoverability signal, 20 m buffers of the complete set of Flat Hills subtypes were used to generate the flow predictions. While these samples do not appear to represent a primary source, the deposits should be eroding by alluvial/colluvial action to the east into the lower elevations of Skull Valley.

The Flat Hills prediction (Figure 5.10) presents a discoverability exposure (E) signal of 21 km^2.

Kane Springs Wash Caldera

Source Type: Obsidian; two subtypes (Variety 1 and Variety 2)

Location: Lincoln County, Nevada

Alternative Names: Kane Spring Wash (Nelson & Holmes, 1979; Sappington, 1981)

Variety 1: Delamar Mountains (Skinner, 2021), Kane Springs C (Johnson & Wagner, 2005);

Variety 2: Kane Spring, Kane Springs, Kane Springs A (Johnson & Wagner, 2005)

Skinner sample points: n = 25 (Appendix D, Table D.2)

ORB Paleoindian artifacts: n = 1 (Table 5.1)

The Kane Springs Wash Caldera (KSWC) obsidian is found in southeastern Nevada, in Lincoln County, and

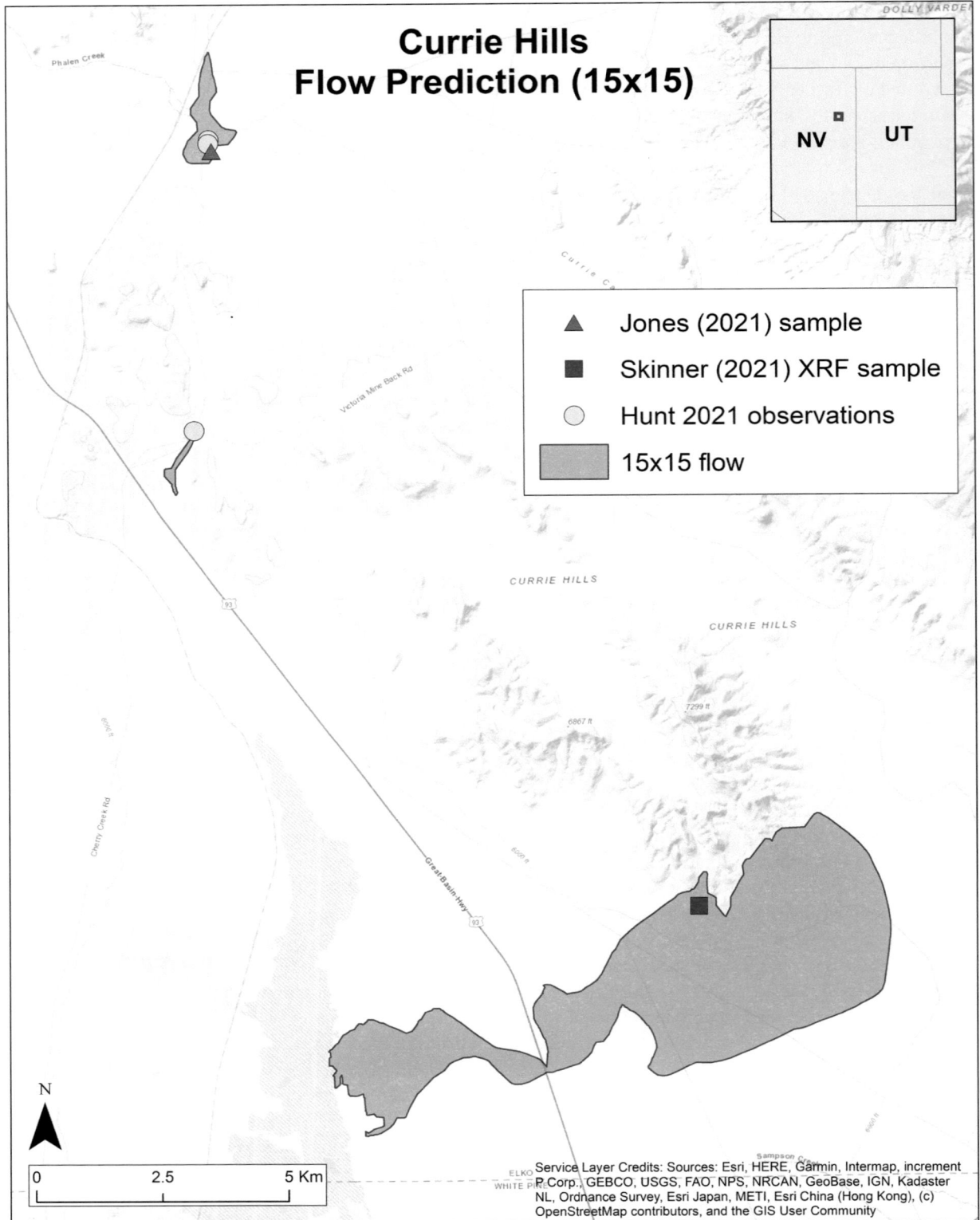

FIGURE 5.8. Currie Hills fine-grained volcanics (FGV) 15×15 flow prediction.

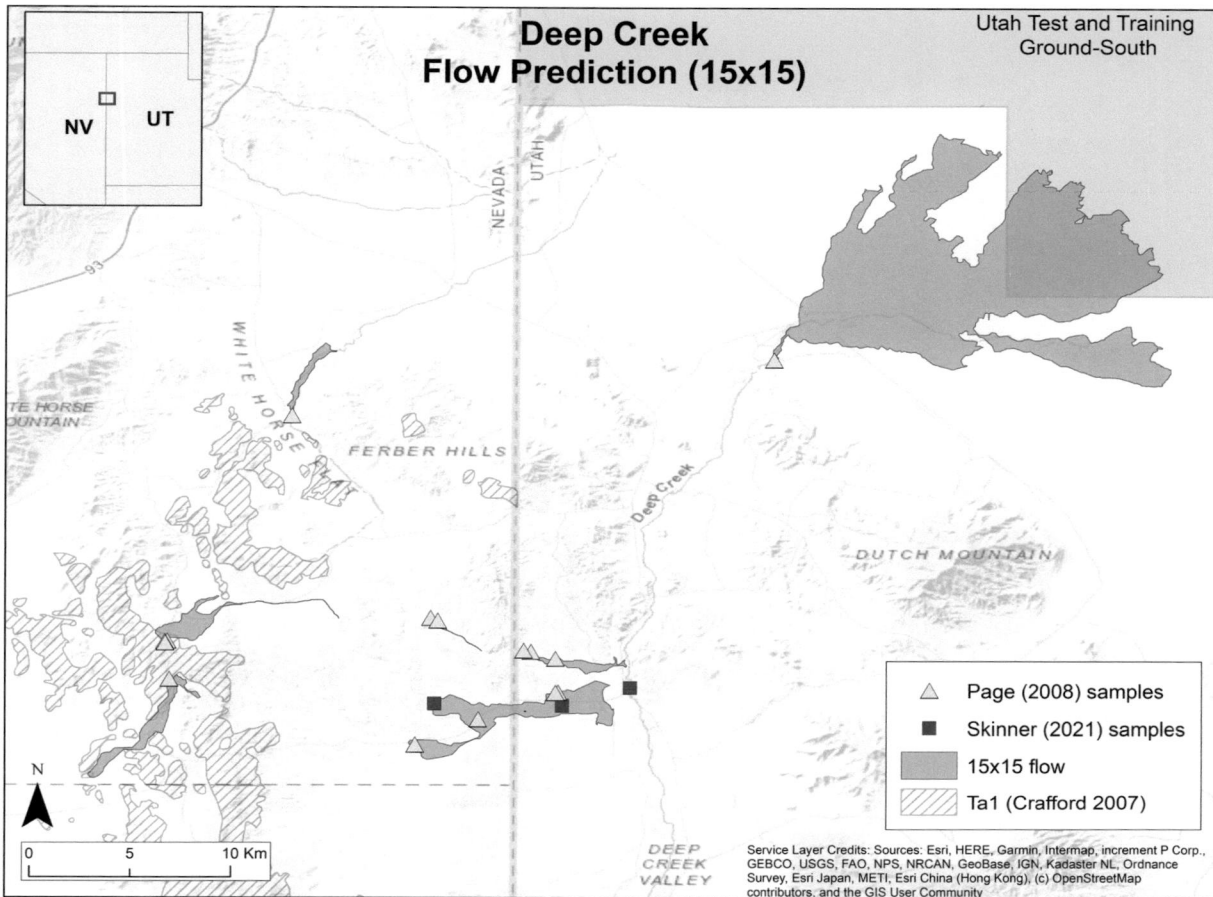

FIGURE 5.9. Deep Creek fine-grained volcanics (FGV) 15×15 flow prediction.

about 110 km north of Las Vegas. The source material appears in the Delamar and Meadow Valley Mountains, in and around the remnants of a collapsed Miocene-aged (23.3 to 5.3 Ma) volcanic caldera.

The caldera formed about 14.1 Ma ago with the eruption and collapse of a rhyolitic dome (Novak, 1984, 1985; Novak & Mahood, 1986). Two subsequent highly silicic, rhyolitic magma flows were then constrained within the rim of this caldera (Figure 5.11), forming obsidian as they were quenched. These intracaldera units are referred to as the "early moat rhyolite" (sometime between 14.1 and 13.3 Ma) and the "late moat rhyolite" (around 13.3 Ma). Obsidian from the early moat rhyolite now bears the label "KSWC Variety 1" and, due to its older age, largely manifests as marekanites (Apache tears; Johnson & Wagner, 2005; Shackley, 2021). Primary sources for Variety 1 occurred in both the Delamar and Meadow Valley mountain ranges at one time, but these sources are unknown or are now eroded and depleted. Obsidian from the late moat rhyolite is labelled "KSWC Variety 2," and primary exposures, yielding cobbles to 15 cm, are still present on the western rim of the caldera, with

secondary distributions within the Delamar Mountains, downslope into Kane Springs Wash, and as far southwest as Coyote Spring Valley.

The Kane Springs Wash Caldera obsidians (Varieties 1 and 2) are now geochemically well-characterized (Johnson & Wagner, 2005; Skinner & Thatcher, 2005). "Kane Spring Wash" obsidian was first analyzed and characterized by Nelson & Holmes (1979, as source #15), and corresponds with Variety 2. The township-range location for this sample places it near the southwesternmost sample in Figure 5.11, at the southern mouth of Kane Spring Canyon. Johnson & Wagner (2005; see also Appendix D, Table D.2) provide a large sample set ($n = 25$) that was used to distinguish the geochemical signatures and rough distributions of Varieties 1 and 2.

Prehistorically, the KSWC obsidian was widely used in the region (Hull, 2010), and some evidence suggests exploitation continued during the Paleoindian period, with Jensen (2004, 2005) reporting both a fluted point and stemmed points at a local site matched to KSWC obsidian.

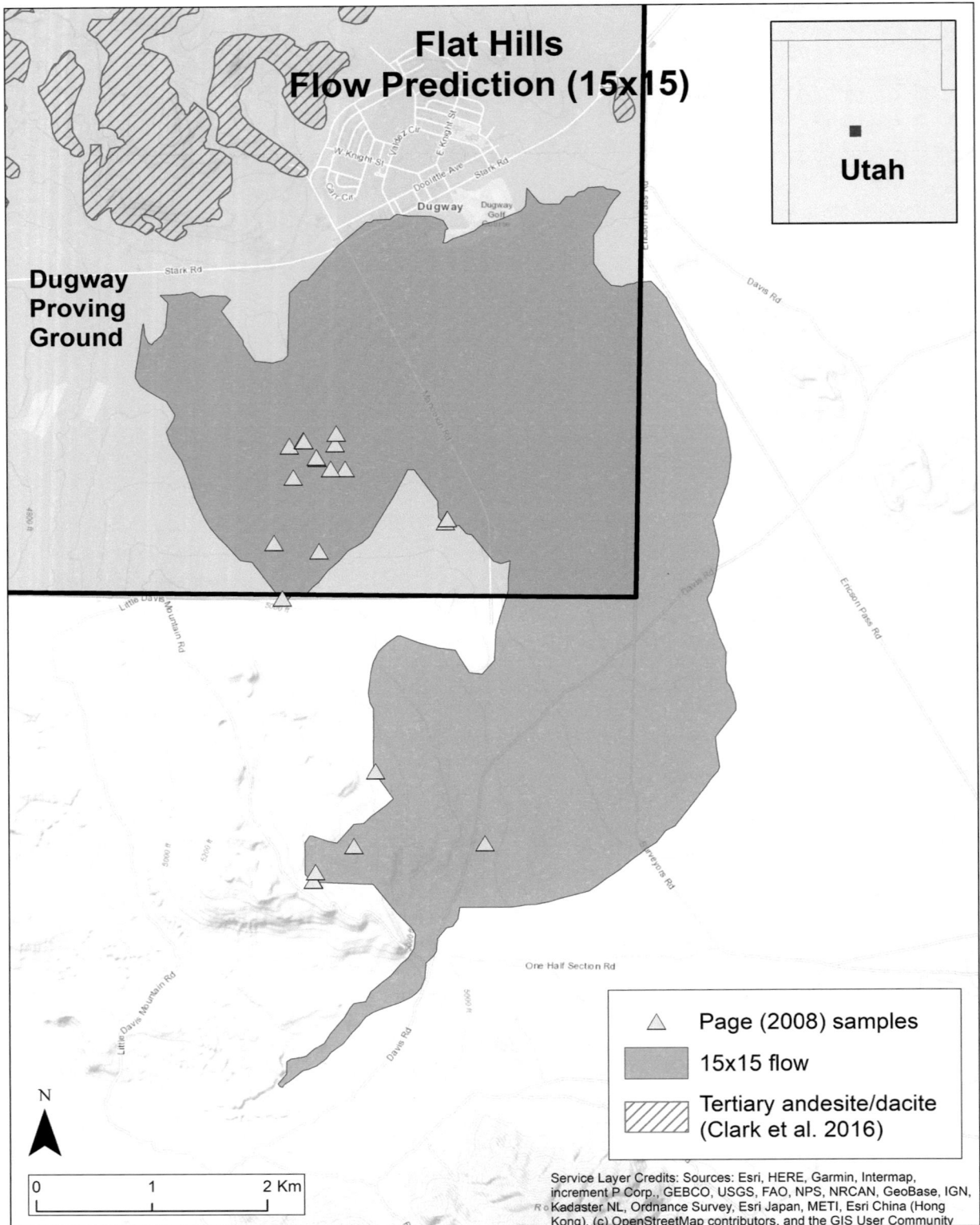

FIGURE 5.10. Flat Hills fine-grained volcanics (FGV) 15×15 flow prediction.

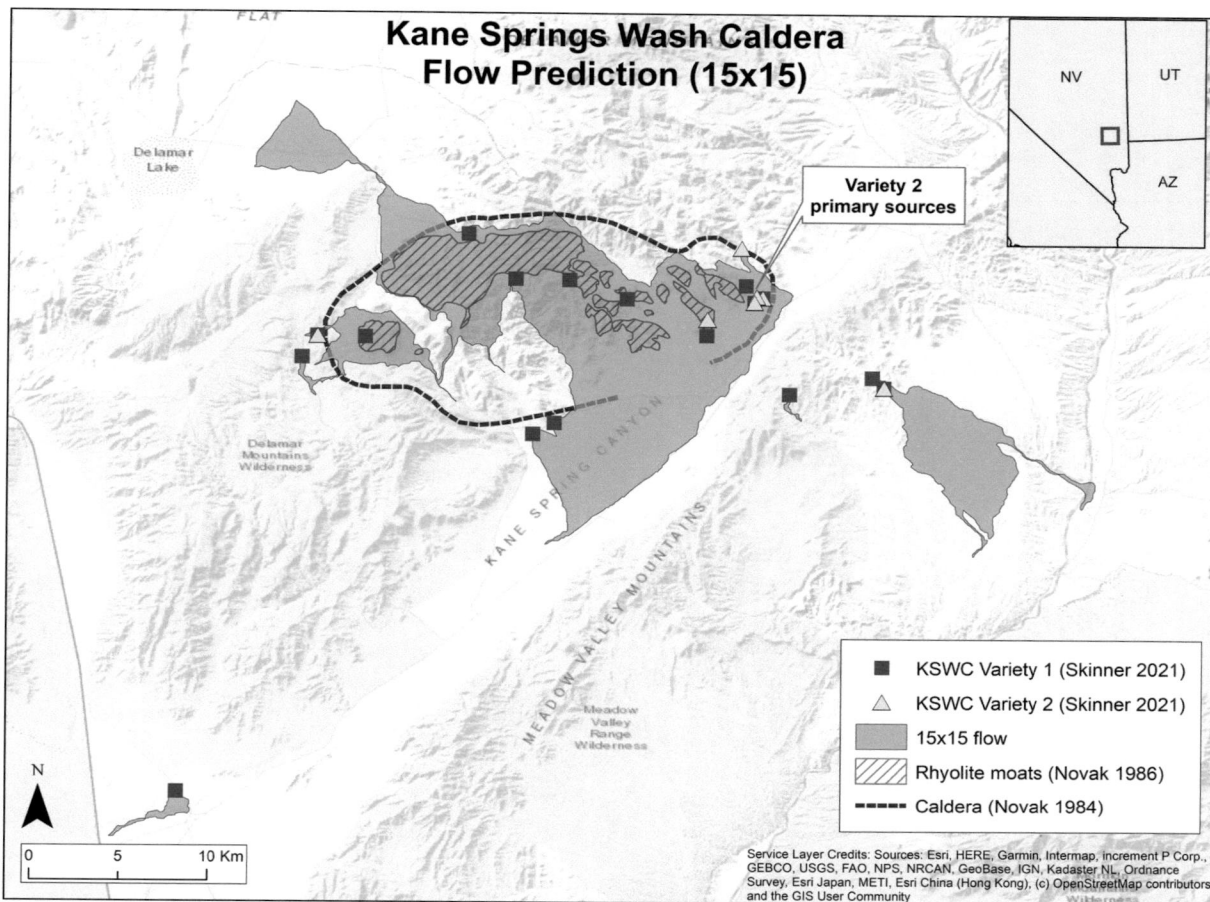

FIGURE 5.11. Kane Springs Wash Caldera obsidian 15×15 flow prediction.

To predict the secondary flow extent, the early and late moat rhyolites reported by Novak & Mahood (1986, Figure 1) provide the best description of the parental units for KSWC obsidian and are in good concordance with the known sample points. The outline of this extent was converted to polygons that served as the proxy primary sources to calculate the flow prediction. In addition, it is clear from the survey by Johnson & Wagner (2005) that primary sources, particularly those of Variety 1, occurred outside of these areas, most notably in the Meadow Valley Mountains. For this reason, 20 m buffers were also applied to the known sample points and merged with the rhyolite polygons to serve as the proxy primary sources when creating the weighted raster used for the flow prediction.

The Kane Springs Wash Caldera obsidian source has an exposure (*E*) value of 207 km².

Malad

Source Type: Obsidian
Location: Oneida and Bannock Counties, Idaho
Alternative Names: Dairy Creek, Garden Creek Gap,

Hawkins, Oneida, Wright Creek (Fowler, 2014; Gallagher, 1979; Holmer, 1997; Sappington, 1981)
Richard Holmer (Personal Communication, July 24, 2019): n = 1 (Appendix D, Table D.4)
Skinner Sample Points: n = 5 (Appendix D, Table D.2)
ORB Paleoindian Artifacts: n = 4 (Table 5.1)

The Malad obsidian is found in Oneida and Bannock Counties, Idaho, primarily in the fork between the confluence of Dairy and Wright Creeks, 8 km northwest of Elkhorn Peak. This region is just south of the Picabo eruptive center (Figure 5.3) described earlier; obsidian in the area manifests as high-quality cobbles, up to 25 cm, within a pyroclastic tuff (Ellis et al., 2012; Moore, 2009; Whitman, 2013). This tuff is currently commercially mined in the Wright Creek area for pumice used to manufacture high-grade industrial abrasives.

Malad obsidian was first analyzed and characterized by Nelson & Holmes (1979, see also Gallagher, 1979; Nelson, 1984). Since that time it has become recognized as one of the most commonly exploited obsidian sources in Idaho (Fowler, 2014; Holmer, 1997; Reid,

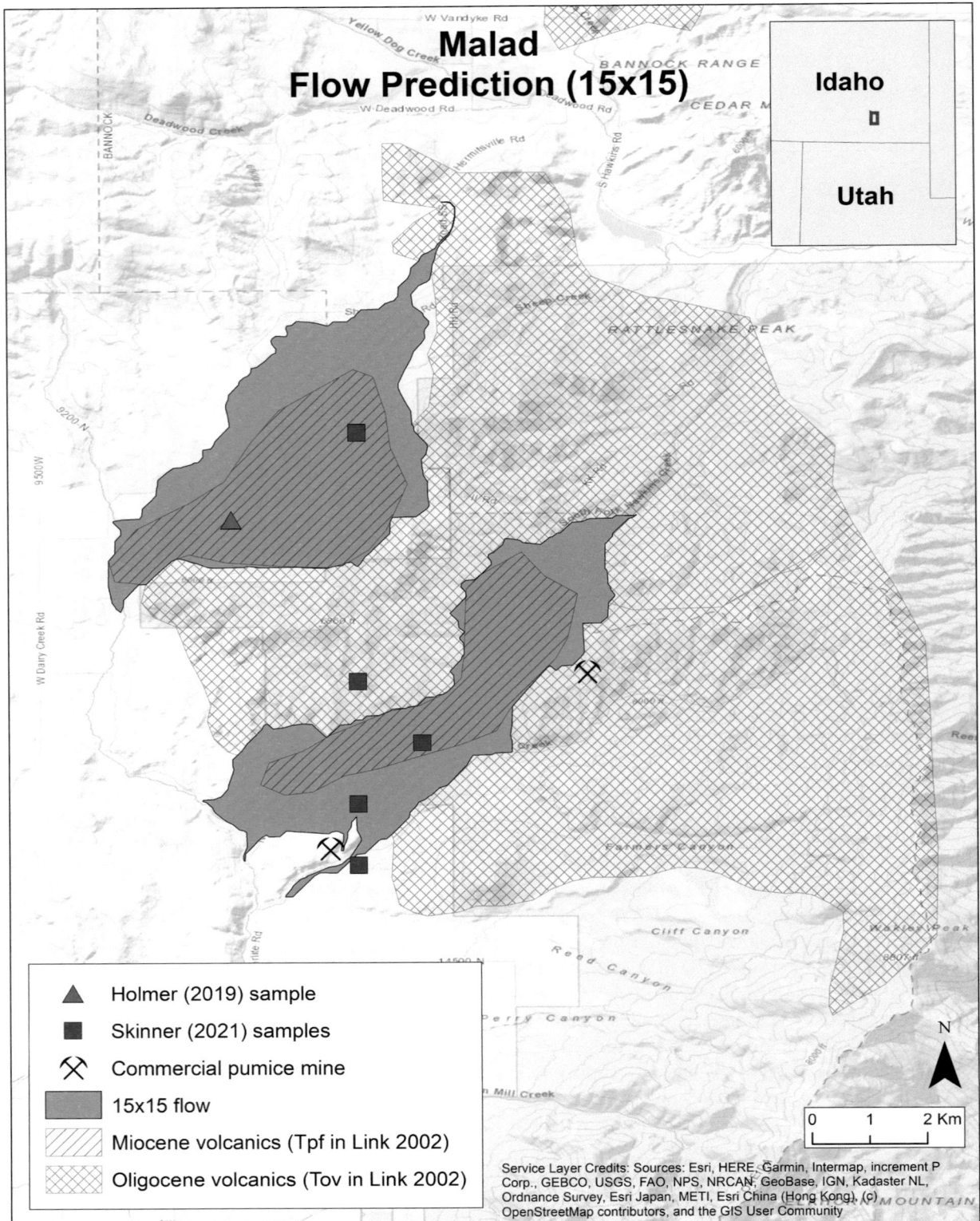

FIGURE 5.12. Malad obsidian 15×15 flow prediction.

2014; Whitman, 2013; Willson, 2007). Malad obsidian is also found in archaeological contexts at considerable distance (>1200 km), recorded at sites in Arkansas, Colorado, Iowa, Kansas, Nebraska, Nevada, North Dakota, Oklahoma, Texas, Utah, and Wyoming (Fowler, 2014; Holmer, 1997; Hughes, 2007a; Logan et al., 2001).

Our understanding of the extent of the Malad obsidian is limited, with only a few sample points using GPS coordinates reported by Holmer (Appendix D, Table D.4) and Skinner (Appendix D, Table D.2). There are no known primary source exposures, aside from the broad distribution of cobbles within the tuff. These appear to be emanating from Miocene-aged (23.3–5.3 Ma) volcanic deposits (*Tpf* in Figure 5.12), which overlay an older Oligocene (39.9–23.3 Ma) volcanic deposit (*Tov* in Figure 5.12).

The Miocene volcanic deposit recorded by Link (2002) provides the best description of this cobble-rich extent and finds good concordance with the known sample points. The outline of this extent was converted to polygons that served as the proxy primary sources to calculate the flow prediction. The prediction captures three of the five samples provided by Skinner (Appendix D, Table D.2), and the two exceptions are less than 600 m outside the prediction.

Also of note, Bailey (1992) reports the presence of Malad obsidian within the Hess Pumice Mine tailings. Marshall (1961) argues that, globally, obsidian is rarely older than the Miocene due to the instability of glass and the natural hydration, or devitrification, process that breaks down obsidian into marekanites and, eventually, perlite. Since the known samples fall within the same geochemical signature, it seems most likely the mines (indicated on Figure 5.12) are encroaching on the *Tpf* deposit as they work the Oligocene-aged *Tov* deposit.

The Malad obsidian source has an exposure (*E*) value of 24 km².

Owyhee

Source Type: Obsidian
Location: Owyhee County, Idaho, and Malheur County, Oregon
Alternative Names: Browns Castle, Oreana, Toy Pass (Holmer, 1997)
Richard Holmer (Personal Communication, July 24, 2019): n = 4 (Appendix D, Table D.4)
Skinner Sample Points: n = 53 (Appendix D, Table D.2)
ORB Artifacts: n = 2 (Table 5.1)

The Owyhee obsidian manifests as massive cobble distributions found in northern Owyhee County, Idaho, and into Malheur County, Oregon. Sappington (1981), one of the earliest obsidian researchers in the region,

suggested the distribution extends more than 1600 km². In Idaho, obsidian nodules are primarily clustered on the east slope of the Owyhee Mountains, though other samples are scattered northwest of this cluster. Over 100 km to the northwest, in Oregon, another smaller cluster appears near Grassy Mountain (Figure 5.14).

Both clusters are located north of the Owyhee eruptive centers (Figure 5.3) and in regions described by Bennett as "rhyolitic pyroclastic and lava flows" (1976, p. 7; see also Lewis et al., 2012; Walker & MacLeod, 1991). These appear to be emanating from Miocene-aged (23.3–5.3 Ma) volcanic deposits (*Tmr* and *Trh* in Figure 5.14) that erupted approximately 14 Ma ago (Bennett, 1976; Ellis et al., 2012; Lewis et al., 2012; Walker & MacLeod, 1991).

The Owyhee obsidian geochemical signature was first analyzed and characterized by Nelson (1984). Like Malad, Owyhee has become recognized as one of the most commonly exploited sources of toolstone in Idaho (Fowler, 2014; Holmer, 1997; Reid, 2014; Whitman, 2013; Willson, 2005, 2007). The distribution region is well researched and has been extensively sampled (Bailey, 1992; Holmer, 1997; Nelson & Holmes, 1979; Sappington, 1981; Skinner, 2021); however, the area has no known primary source outcrops, aside from the broad distributions of high-quality cobbles, up to 20 cm, within the tuff (Bailey, 1992; Ellis et al., 2012; Moore, 2009).

The Owyhee cobble fields are reminiscent of those on the east slope of the Panaca Summit/Modena source area (see Chapter 4). For this reason, a similar strategy was used to create the proxy source. Polygons were created that aggregated known sample points (n = 57) from Holmer (1997) and Skinner (2021; Appendix D, Table D.2; Figure 5.13) to represent the localized cobble fields. An aggregation of points within 15 km of each other seemed to provide the fewest tight clusters, and these were then used as the proxy sources for flow prediction (Figure 5.14).

The Owyhee obsidian source has an exposure (*E*) value of 829 km².

Paradise Valley

Source Type: Obsidian
Location: Humboldt County, Nevada
Alternative Names: Santa Rosa Mountain (Moore, 2009)
Skinner Sample Points: n = 3 (Appendix D, Table D.2)
ORB Artifacts: n = 3 (Table 5.1)

The Paradise Valley obsidian is found in the Santa Rosa Mountains in Humboldt County, Nevada (Figure 5.15). This region is less than 30 km southwest of the Owyhee eruptive center (Figure 5.3) described earlier.

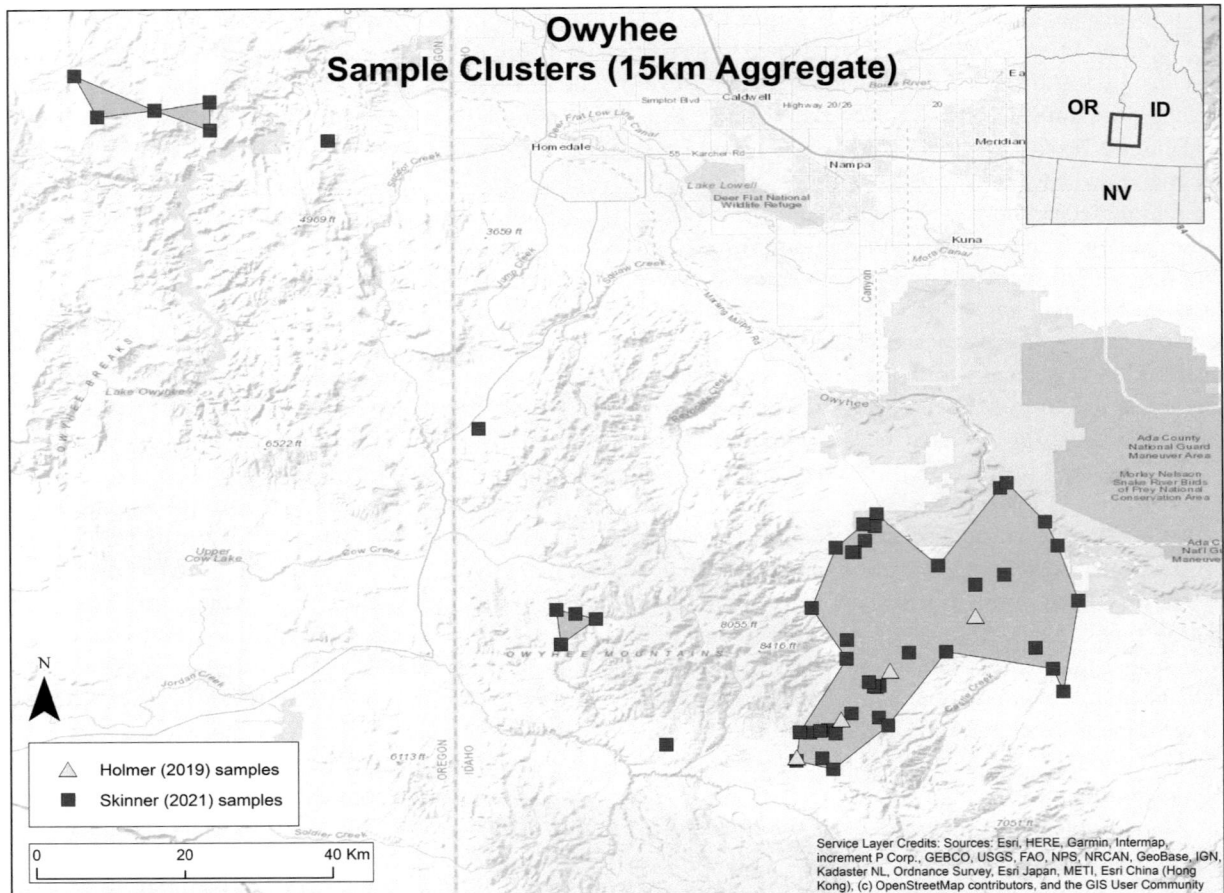

FIGURE 5.13. Proxy sources generated from sample clustering.

This region was subjected to silicic volcanism beginning around 16.6 Ma, continuing to about 12 Ma. As a result, middle- to late-Miocene rhyolitic flows dominate the western edge of the eruptive center (Brueseke & Hart, 2008; Ellis et al., 2012; *Geologic Map of Nevada—Data series 249*, 2021).

Archaeologically, the Paradise Valley obsidian is a prominent regional toolstone (Beck & Jones, 2011; Elston & Budy, 1990; Hughes, 1990; Hutchins & Simons, 2000; Jones et al., 2003; LaValley, 2013; Newlander, 2012; Stephenson & Wilkinson, 1969), but the source itself is poorly described. Sappington (1981) stated that it is geochemically well-characterized, but provided no references to support this claim. Nelson (1984, Figure 1) appeared to illustrate and enumerate the location for this source, as well as several other eastern Nevada sources, but these sources were then absent from his results (1984, Table 6). Skinner (2021; Appendix D, Table D.2) provides the current best characterization of this source.

Similarly, our understanding of the source extent is limited. Skinner (2021; Appendix D, Table D.2) reported three XRF sample points with GPS coordinates. Sap-

pington (1981) reported a single sample observation at T41N R43E, section 3, approximately 42 km southeast of the Santa Rosa Mountains, in the Little Humboldt River Valley, and close to the Chimney Dam. Moore (2009) reports this same location, and seven other locations, without attribution: six in sections within T43N R39E (sections 2, 11, 14, 15, 22, 23), and one in T42N R38E, section 17, all in the Santa Rosa Mountains (Figure 5.15). However, our precise understanding of the source location is limited to the three data points provided by Skinner.

To predict the Paradise Valley extent, the method described in the Panaca Summit/Modena section of Chapter 4 was utilized to form a proxy source polygon from the three points provided by Skinner. While this analysis produces a significant flow into the southern Paradise Valley, it does not capture the source regions suggested by Sappington or Moore. The secondary extent is probably considerably larger than this prediction, but without more definitive data the methodology must rely on these confirmed sample locations. Our understanding of Paradise Valley would benefit significantly from targeted fieldwork in this area.

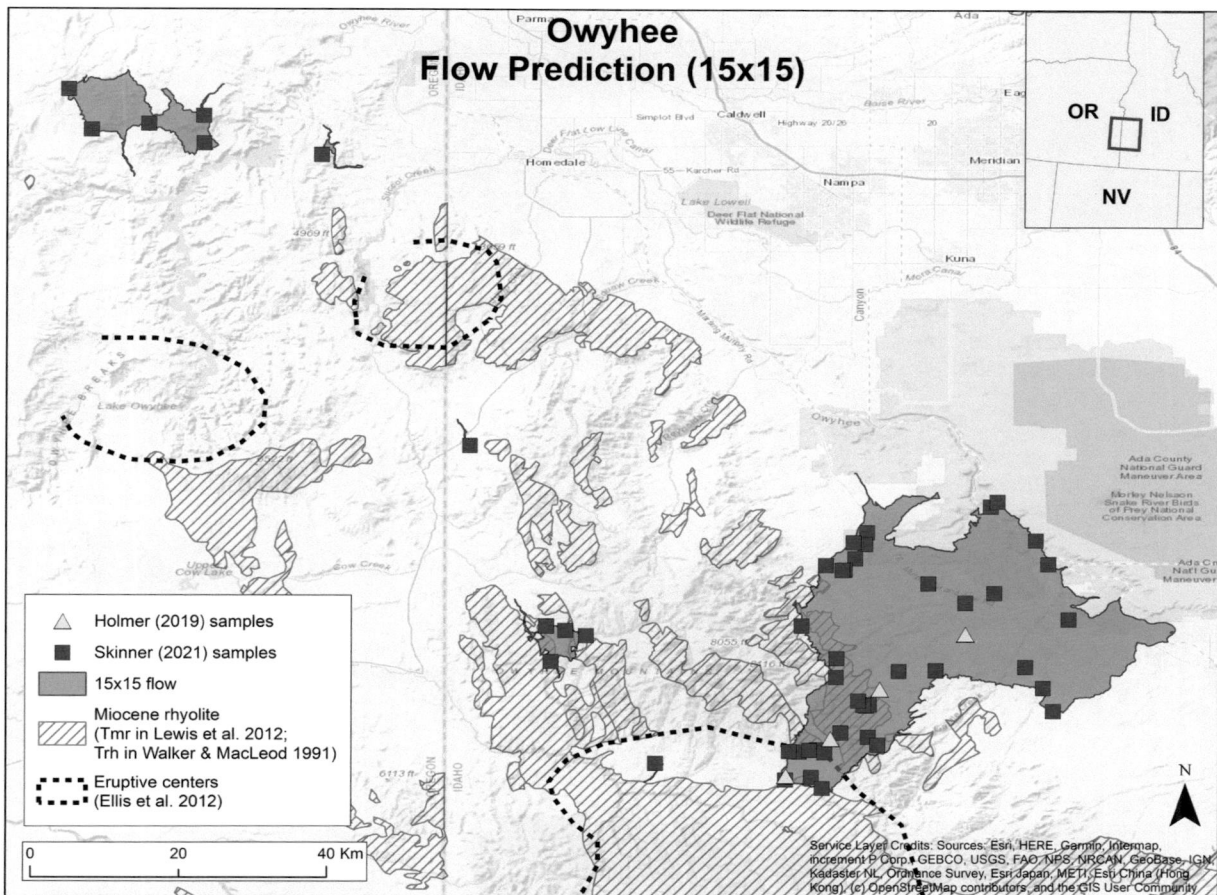

FIGURE 5.14. Owyhee obsidian 15×15 flow prediction.

The Paradise Valley obsidian source has an exposure (E) value of 134 km².

Pumice Hole Mine

Location: Beaver County, Utah
Alternative Names: n/a
Skinner Sample Points: $n = 3$ (Appendix D, Table D.2)
ORB Paleoindian Artifacts: $n = 1$ (Table 5.1)

The Pumice Hole Mine (PHM) obsidian type presents an enduring enigma in Great Basin obsidian research. The PHM type was originally recorded by Nelson and Holmes (1979, Table III, Source 3), using a single sample received from a second party (Hull, 1994). This party stated the sample was collected within T28S R9W sec 2, NE1/4 (Figure 5.16)—south of Wildhorse Canyon, near South Twin Fork Mountain, and close to Ranch Canyon. This information was repeated, with minor XRF data variations, in Nelson (1984, Table 4, Source #4).

During the Kern River Pipeline survey, Hull (1994, pp. 7–13) noted that obsidian found in the Ranch Canyon alluvium contained "abundant phenocrysts"

and knapped poorly, even crumbling when this activity was attempted. Within the report, Hull's personal communications with Nelson and others note the visual differences between the previously tested obsidian by Nelson and Holmes (1979) and the samples collected by Hull in Ranch Canyon. These differences suggested that the original sample may have come from another, unknown, location.

This suggestion gained support as a result of a regional survey by Jackson et al. (2009), who also surveyed the Wildhorse Canyon and Bailey Ridge areas to the north of Ranch Canyon. All 10 samples collected by the authors were XRF tested and classified as "Pumice Hole Mine Type B," which originates from pyroclastic deposits above Ranch Canyon. This finding led Jackson et al. (2009, p. 115) to assert that the "Pumice Hole Mine obsidian by Nelson and Holmes actually originated from a source outside the Mineral Mountains."

However, around 2006, University of California, Davis graduate student Clint Cole collected three samples that XRF-tested in the range of the original PHM type (Craig Skinner, personal communication, October 28, 2021). Two of the samples were located between

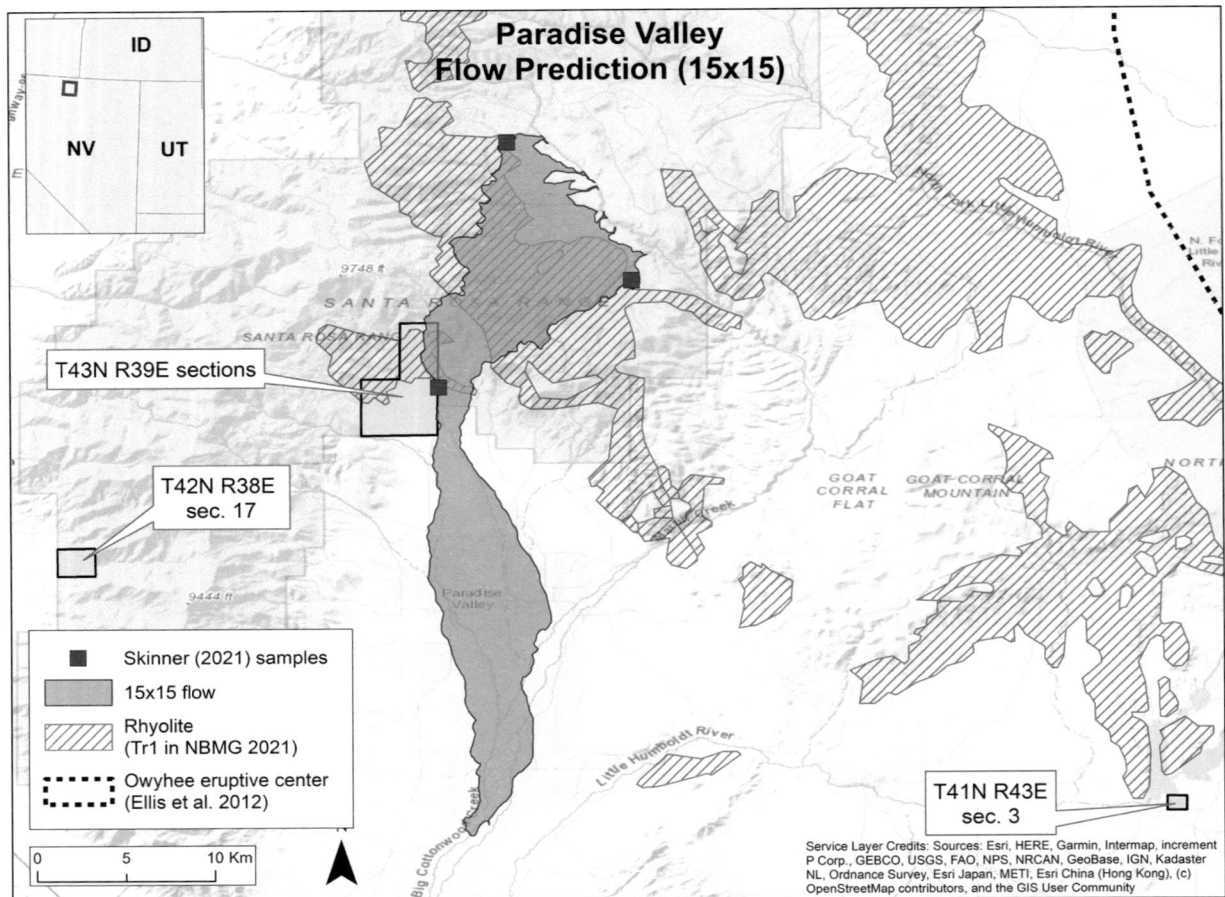

FIGURE 5.15. Paradise Valley obsidian 15×15 flow prediction.

Bailey Ridge and Wildhorse Canyon, above Big Cedar Cove, and one appears at the mouth of Wildhorse Canyon. As such, the secondary distribution from these points flows into the flows emanating from Bailey Ridge and Wildhorse Canyon. To a hunter-gatherer discovering these sources for the first time, these would appear as a single signal on the landscape.

For this reason, the Mineral Mountains (Bailey Ridge and Wildhorse Canyon) and PHM flows were combined into a single discoverability signal. The PHM flow was predicted by creating 20 m buffers around the three points by Cole. When this flow (Figure 5.16) is considered in relation to the actual flow results from the Mineral Mountains survey, it adds 10.1 km² of flow extent (gray hatched areas) to the overall actual MM survey (originally 160 km²).

The updated and combined Mineral Mountains (now including PHM) obsidian source has an exposure (E) value of 170 km².

SUMMARY

In this chapter, the secondary distribution extents (E) were predicted for 14 obsidian and FGV types used by people living in the Old River Bed delta. The Brown's Bench (BB), Brown's Bench Area (BBA) and the Butte Valley Group A (BVGA) types were combined into a single discoverability signal, as the extents of these distinct types overlap significantly. Similarly, the Pumice Hole Mine (PHM) type was merged into the Mineral Mountains extent. The final E values for all ORB types are summarized in Table 5.2 and these will be used in Chapter 6 as the discoverability hypothesis is tested.

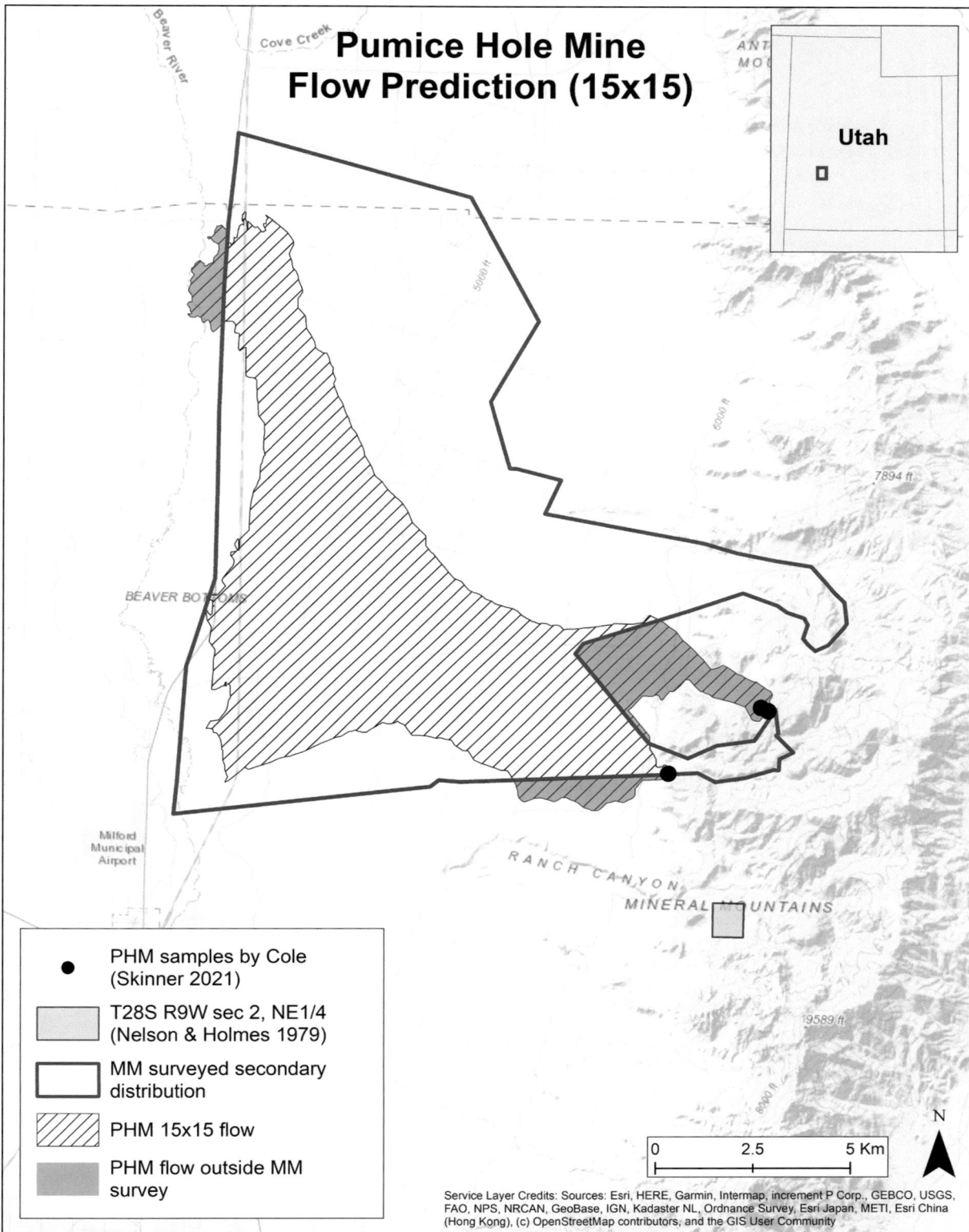

Figure 5.16. Pumice Hole Mine obsidian 15×15 flow in relation to the actual survey outline for Mineral Mountains sources.

TABLE 5.2. Old River Bed Delta Toolstone Sources and Their Resultant Exposure (*E*) Values.

Sources	ORB Artifacts	*E* (km²)
Badlands	18	66
Bear Gulch	1	129
Black Rock Area	10	**353**
Brown's Bench + Brown's Bench Area + Butte Valley Group A	46	5173
Cedar Mountain	8	37
Currie Hills	3	26
Deep Creek	10	108
Ferguson Wash	1	**4**
Flat Hills	182	21
Kane Springs Wash Caldera	1	207
Malad	4	24
Mineral Mountains + Pumice Hole Mine	10	**170**
Owyhee	2	829
Panaca Summit/Modena	1	**358**
Paradise Valley	3	134
Topaz Mountain	130	**309**
Totals	**430**	

Note: Bolded sources were surveyed and discussed in Chapter 4.

6 Testing the Discoverability Model

In this chapter, the discoverability model described in Chapter 3 will be tested. This analysis is accomplished using the toolstone source exposure (E) values surveyed and predicted in Chapters 4 and 5 in conjunction with temporal groupings of Paleoindian artifacts from the Old River Bed (ORB) delta in Utah (described in Appendix A, https://collections.lib.utah.edu/ark:/87278/s6mntfnx). Ranked according to their discoverability values, the expected toolstone proportions will be compared to their observed proportions using Spearman's rank-order correlation and other statistical tests. Finally, the landscape learning variable ($\%LL$) will be calculated from the coefficient of determination for various temporal groups and plotted over the time of the Paleoindian occupation of the ORB delta. The goal of these tests is to determine if, in fact, changes in landscape learning can be detected at the ORB delta using the proposed discoverability methodology.

ESTABLISHING TEMPORAL GROUPS OF PALEOINDIAN ARTIFACTS

Small sample sizes routinely pose difficulties in the statistical analysis of Paleoindian assemblages. To counter this issue, rather than group ORB Paleoindian artifacts by site (mean = 15.5 artifacts/site), artifacts were grouped into larger temporal clusters or assemblages, with the goal of creating the largest number of temporally distinct clusters with the highest counts of artifacts. The cleaned ORB Paleoindian database (Appendix A) with known toolstone sources (via X-ray fluorescence) are associated with the dated ORB channels listed in Table 6.1. For each channel, a midpoint age is determined, using the midpoint of the channel age ranges reported by Madsen et al. (2015).

These data will be examined in two ways. First, artifacts will be pooled within nonoverlapping date ranges, resulting in three discrete age groups, designated A1–A3 (Table 6.2). This consolidation creates the largest possible sample groups. Second, artifacts directly associated with the individually dated channels will be tested, offering the greatest available number of distinct temporal periods for comparison. In this latter case, only channels with a sample count of 20 or more sourced artifacts will be used. Five such groups emerged from this process, designated C1–C5 (Table 6.3). In each case, the groups were placed in order of midpoint channel age. However, it is important to note that for both the A and C groups, the time intervals between groups are uneven. This unevenness is an unavoidable attribute of the available data and will affect later analysis when attempting to gauge landscape learning over time.

These data are further broken out by toolstone source within each group. Tables 6.4 and 6.5 present the actual artifact counts (n) per toolstone source.

ESTABLISHING THE DISTANCES (d)

Figure 6.1 (full regional scale) and Figure 6.2 (smaller scale) illustrate the distribution of utilized toolstone source exposures ($n = 16$) in relation to the overall centroid of the ORB Paleoindian artifacts ($n = 430$).

To determine the discoverability of each toolstone source in relation to the artifact pools listed in Tables 6.2 and 6.3, the distance (d) of the artifacts from the originating source extents (E) must be determined. For each group of artifacts, a centroid was calculated using an average of the pooled artifact UTM coordinates (Tables 6.6 and 6.7).

TABLE 6.1. Paleoindian Artifacts Associated with Dated Old River Bed Delta Channels.

Channel Association	Paleoindian Artifacts w/XRF[a]	Channel Age (^{14}C yr BP)[b]	Midpoint Age (^{14}C yr BP)
Black	229	~11,000–10,300	10,650
Limestone	4	~10,500–10,000	10,250
Yellow	2	~10,300–10,100	10,200
Green	69	~10,300–9,800	10,050
Red	4	~9,860–9,740	9,800
Blue B	24	~10,000–9,500	9,750
Light Blue	78	~9,800–8,800	9,300
Lavender	20	~9,100–9,000	9,050
Total:	**430**		

[a] See Appendix A.
[b] Madsen et al., 2015.

TABLE 6.2. Grouping Artifacts by Discrete, Nonoverlapping Channel Age Spans.

Group	Channel Associations	Paleoindian Artifacts w/XRF[a]	Age Span (^{14}C yr BP)[b]	Midpoint Age (^{14}C yr BP/cal BP)[c]
A1	Black	229	~11,000–10,300	10,650/12,674
A2	Green and Yellow	71	~10,300–9,800	10,050/11,578
A3	Light Blue and Lavender	98	~9,800–8,800	9,300/10,444
	Total:	**398**		

TABLE 6.3. Grouping Artifacts by Individual Channels.

Group	Channel Association	Paleoindian Artifacts w/XRF[a]	Channel Age (^{14}C yr BP)[b]	Midpoint Age (^{14}C yr BP/cal BP)[c]
C1	Black	229	~11,000–10,300	10,650/12,674
C2	Green	69	~10,300–9,800	10,050/11,578
C3	Blue B	24	~10,000–9,500	9,750/11,167
C4	Light Blue	78	~9,800–8,800	~9,300/10,444
C5	Lavender	20	~9,100–9,000	~9,050/10,221
	Total:	**420**		

[a] See Appendix A.
[b] Madsen et al. 2015.
[c] Calendar dates calculated with OxCal 4.4.4 (Bronk Ramsey, 2021; Reimer et al., 2020), using the Midpoint Age radiocarbon date ± 50 years.

TABLE 6.4. A Groups Actual Artifact Counts (n).

Source	A1 n	A2 n	A3 n	Totals
Badlands	14	0	1	**15**
Bear Gulch	0	0	1	**1**
Black Rock Area	5	2	2	**9**
Brown's Bench	23	11	11	**45**
Cedar Mountain	6	0	2	**8**
Currie Hills	2	1	0	**3**
Deep Creek	7	1	1	**9**
Ferguson Wash	0	0	0	**0**
Flat Hills	117	20	38	**175**
Kane Springs Wash Caldera	0	0	0	**0**
Malad	3	0	0	**3**
Mineral Mountains	3	2	3	**8**
Owyhee	1	1	0	**2**
Panaca Summit/Modena	0	0	1	**1**
Paradise Valley	0	1	1	**2**
Topaz Mountain	48	32	37	**117**
Totals	**229**	**71**	**98**	**398**

TABLE 6.5. C Groups Actual Artifact Counts (n).

Source	C1 n	C2 n	C3 n	C4 n	C5 n	Totals
Badlands	14	0	2	1	0	**17**
Bear Gulch	0	0	0	1	0	**1**
Black Rock Area	5	2	1	2	0	**10**
Brown's Bench	23	11	1	8	3	**46**
Cedar Mountain	6	0	0	2	0	**8**
Currie Hills	2	1	0	0	0	**3**
Deep Creek	7	1	1	1	0	**10**
Ferguson Wash	0	0	1	0	0	**1**
Flat Hills	117	20	5	38	0	**180**
Kane Springs Wash Caldera	0	0	1	0	0	**1**
Malad	3	0	0	0	0	**3**
Mineral Mountains	3	2	1	2	1	**9**
Owyhee	1	1	0	0	0	**2**
Panaca Summit/Modena	0	0	0	1	0	**2**
Paradise Valley	0	1	0	1	0	**1**
Topaz Mountain	48	30	11	21	16	**126**
Totals	**229**	**69**	**24**	**78**	**20**	**420**

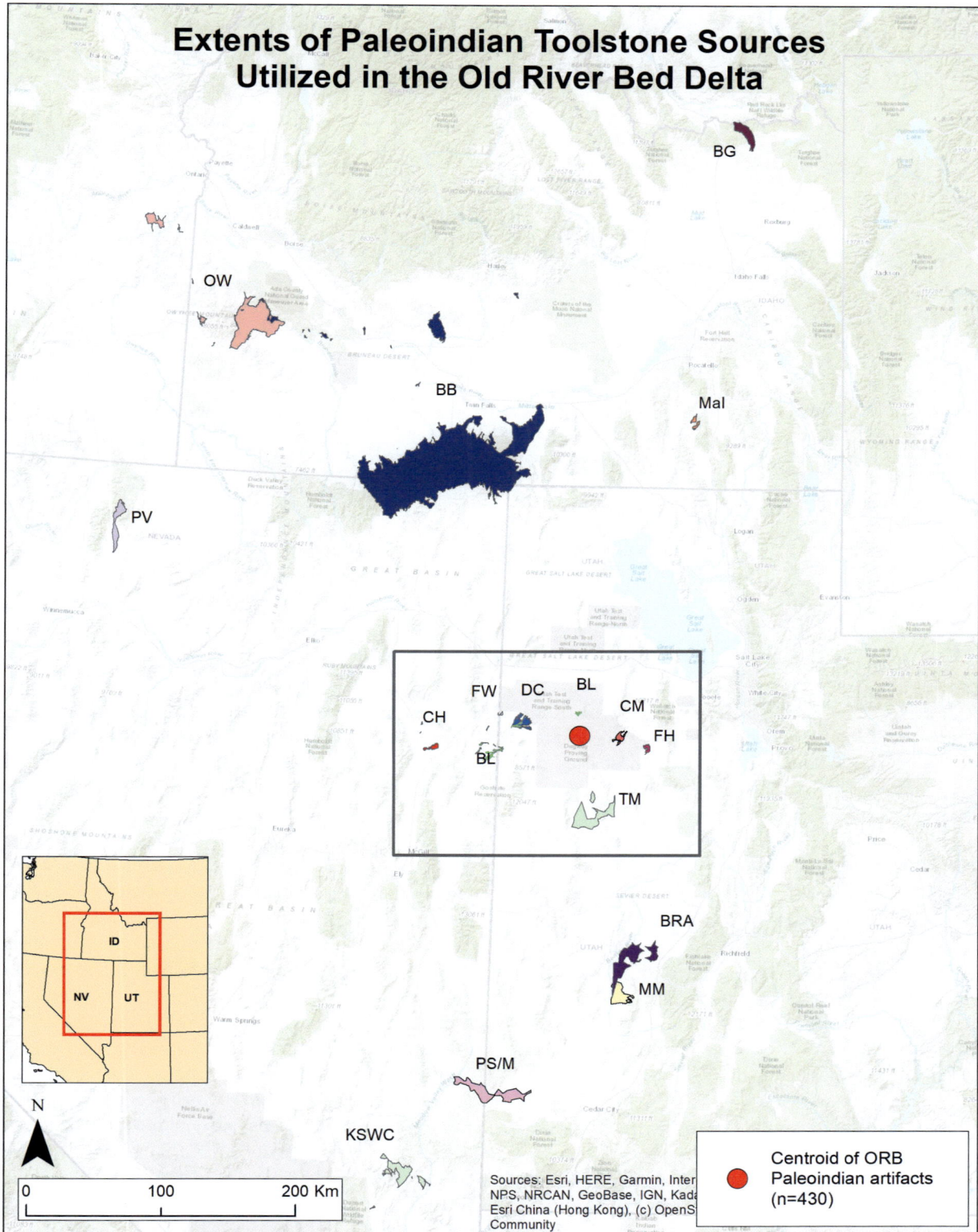

FIGURE 6.1. Extents of obsidian and fine-grained volcanic (FGV) toolstone sources utilized by Paleoindian people occupying the Old River Bed delta channels. Key: Badlands (BL), Brown's Bench (BB), Bear Gulch (BG), Black Rock Area (BRA), Currie Hills (CH), Cedar Mountain (CM), Deep Creek (DC), Ferguson Wash (FW), Flat Hills (FH), Kane Springs Wash Caldera (KSWC), Malad (Mal), Mineral Mountains (MM), Owyhee (OW), Panaca Summit/Modena (PS/M), Paradise Valley (PV), Topaz Mountain (TM). See Chapters 4 and 5 for individual source details. Box indicates extent of Figure 6.2.

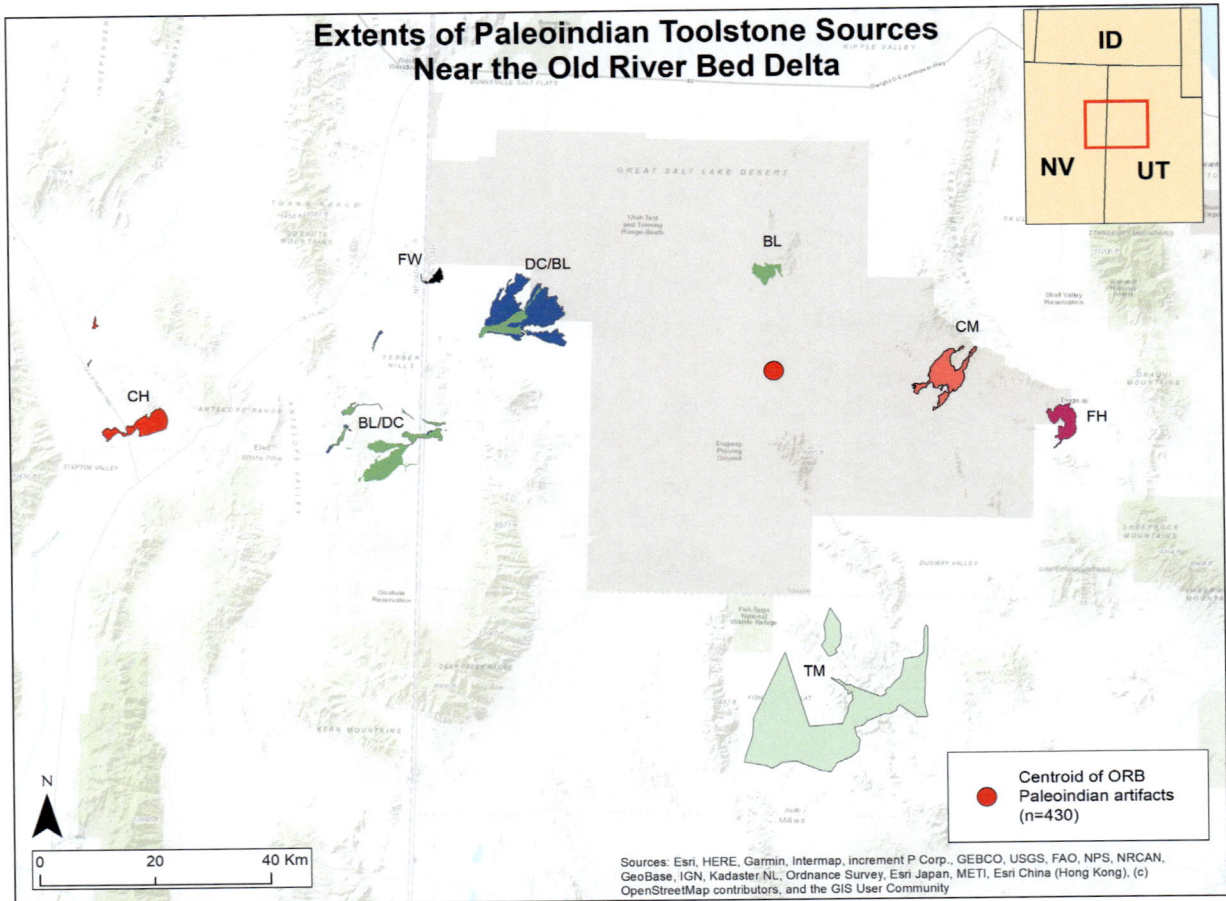

FIGURE 6.2. Extents of obsidian and fine-grained volcanics (FGV) toolstone sources utilized by Paleoindian people occupying the Old River Bed delta channels (smaller scale). Key: Badlands (BL), Currie Hills (CH), Cedar Mountain (CM), Deep Creek (DC), Ferguson Wash (FW), Flat Hills (FH), and Topaz Mountain (TM). See Chapters 4 and 5 for individual source details.

TABLE 6.6. A Groups Centroids.

Group Name	Channel Associations	Easting (UTM 12)	Northing
A1	Black	300899	4462256
A2	Green and Yellow	300546	4455275
A3	Light Blue and Lavender	306576	4457929

TABLE 6.7. C Groups Centroids.

Group Name	Channel Associations	Easting (UTM 12)	Northing
C1	Black	300899	4462256
C2	Green	300588	4455346
C3	Blue B	297658	4457739
C4	Light Blue	297903	4449522
C5	Lavender	308800	4460085

Using these centroids and the extents surveyed and predicted in Chapters 4 and 5, the least-cost path (LCP) distances from the centroid to the closest discoverable edge of each source extent were calculated. To calculate the LCP, an anisotropic (directionally-dependent) accumulated cost surface (ACS) is derived from a cost, or friction, surface using a cumulative cost algorithm. This calculation was accomplished by applying the ArcMap *Path Distance* (Esri 2022a) function to a regional digital elevation model (DEM), which acts as the friction surface, and using Tobler's (1993) hiking function to calculate travel time (provided in CSV file form by Tripcevich 2009). Tobler's hiking function calculates hiking velocity as it relates to slope; speed increases at slightly negative slopes and decreases when slope increases. The least cumulative cost distance is then generated from this anisotropic cost surface by using the ArcMap *Cost Distance* function (Esri 2022b). Finally, the resultant raster is converted to polylines which represent the most cost-effective travel path between each centroid and the

TABLE 6.8. Least-Cost Distances (*d*) of the A Groups Centroids to the Nearest Source Extent Edge.

Source	A1 (km)	A2 (km)	A3 (km)	Mean
Badlands	13.4	20.4	19.6	17.8
Bear Gulch	493.9	500.9	496.7	497.2
Black Rock Area	176.2	168.8	169.9	171.6
Brown's Bench	201.0	208.0	207.3	205.4
Cedar Mountain	26.3	26.4	19.4	24.0
Currie Hills	111.0	109.3	115.0	111.8
Deep Creek	35.4	38.1	42.7	38.7
Ferguson Wash	61.1	63.9	68.6	64.5
Flat Hills	51.1	48.6	43.8	47.8
Kane Springs Wash Caldera	375.8	368.8	374.3	373.0
Malad	265.5	273.8	269.6	269.6
Mineral Mountains	200.7	193.7	194.7	196.3
Owyhee	397.1	402.8	403.9	401.3
Panaca Summit/Modena	284.6	277.7	283.0	281.8
Paradise Valley	402.6	405.7	410.2	406.2
Topaz Mountain	48.9	41.9	42.5	44.4

TABLE 6.9. Least-Cost Distances (*d*) of the C Groups Centroids to the Nearest Source Extent Edge.

Source	C1 (km)	C2 (km)	C3 (km)	C4 (km)	C5 (km)	Mean
Badlands	13.4	19.9	18.5	26.6	18.4	19.4
Bear Gulch	493.9	503.3	552.1	510.1	495.6	511.0
Black Rock Area	176.2	168.2	171.1	162.8	169.3	169.5
Brown's Bench	201.0	207.4	203.9	212.2	206.1	206.1
Cedar Mountain	26.3	25.8	28.2	30.6	17.9	25.8
Currie Hills	111.0	109.8	106.0	106.1	116.2	109.8
Deep Creek	35.4	38.5	34.7	38.3	44.8	38.3
Ferguson Wash	61.1	64.3	60.4	64.0	70.5	64.1
Flat Hills	51.1	49.5	53.3	51.9	43.0	49.8
Kane Springs Wash Caldera	375.8	369.1	370.3	362.3	377.4	371.0
Malad	265.5	275.1	273.9	281.9	267.5	272.8
Mineral Mountains	200.7	193.4	196.6	188.4	196.1	195.0
Owyhee	397.1	407.2	403.5	411.4	407.5	405.3
Panaca Summit/Modena	284.6	280.6	281.9	273.9	290.2	282.2
Paradise Valley	402.6	406.4	452.7	407.3	411.9	416.2
Topaz Mountain	48.9	46.7	50.1	41.8	43.9	46.3

edges of the flow extents. Figure 6.3 illustrates the LCP distances for the A1 groups (12,674 cal BP). The least-cost path distances calculated for each source, dependent on group centroids, are shown in Tables 6.8 and 6.9. These distances are used in the subsequent discoverability calculations.

CREATING THE GROUP *DLISTS* AND *OLISTS*

Using the distance (*d*) and exposure (*E*) values for each toolstone source, the discoverability value (*D*) was calculated for each source using Equation 3.2:

$$D = E * \frac{1}{d^2} \qquad (Eq. 3.2)$$

Within each group, the *D* values were normalized to a percentage that represents the "expected" proportion of source use within that pooled group. These percentages were then ranked, with any tied ranks receiving an average of the tied scores. This ranked list is the group's discoverability list, or *Dlist*, the expected ranked order of toolstone source use in an unknown/unlearned landscape. Similarly, the observed list, or *Olist*, is calculated by determining the proportion of the actual number of artifacts belonging to each known source. These proportions are then ranked, creating the *Olist*.

Table 6.10 presents the calculations of the *Dlist* and the *Olist* for the A1 group. The Group A and Group C *Dlists* and *Olists* are shown in Tables 6.11 and 6.12, respectively. The large number of ties shown in these tables reflects the unfortunately small samples of

sourced ORB Paleoindian artifacts available for the analyses presented here. Those small samples, and resultant large number of tied ranks (most notable for group C5 in Table 6.12), decrease the potential accuracy and precision of statistical analyses applied to them. I return to this issue in the summary.

A GROUPS ANALYSIS

The A groups represent the largest available sample clusters of ORB Paleoindian artifacts within nonoverlapping temporal ranges (see Table 6.2).

If the utilization of toolstone is deterministic, driven only by its discoverability variables, I expect to see a strongly positive monotonic relationship between the *Dlist* and *Olist* for each group; that is, a significant positive correlation between the two sets. The *Dlist* and *Olist* ranked lists are, by definition, ordinal data, and Spearman's rank-order correlation test is a nonparametric monotonicity test appropriate for such a comparison. For 100 percent positive monotonic results, Spearman's should return an r_s of +1, (*Dlist* = *Olist*) and decrease toward zero (increasingly non-monotonic) as landscape learning affects the *Olist*.

A Groups Correlation Statistics

For each A group, the Spearman's rank order correlation coefficient for the relationship between the *Dlist* and *Olist* was calculated (Table 6.13) and the *p* values for

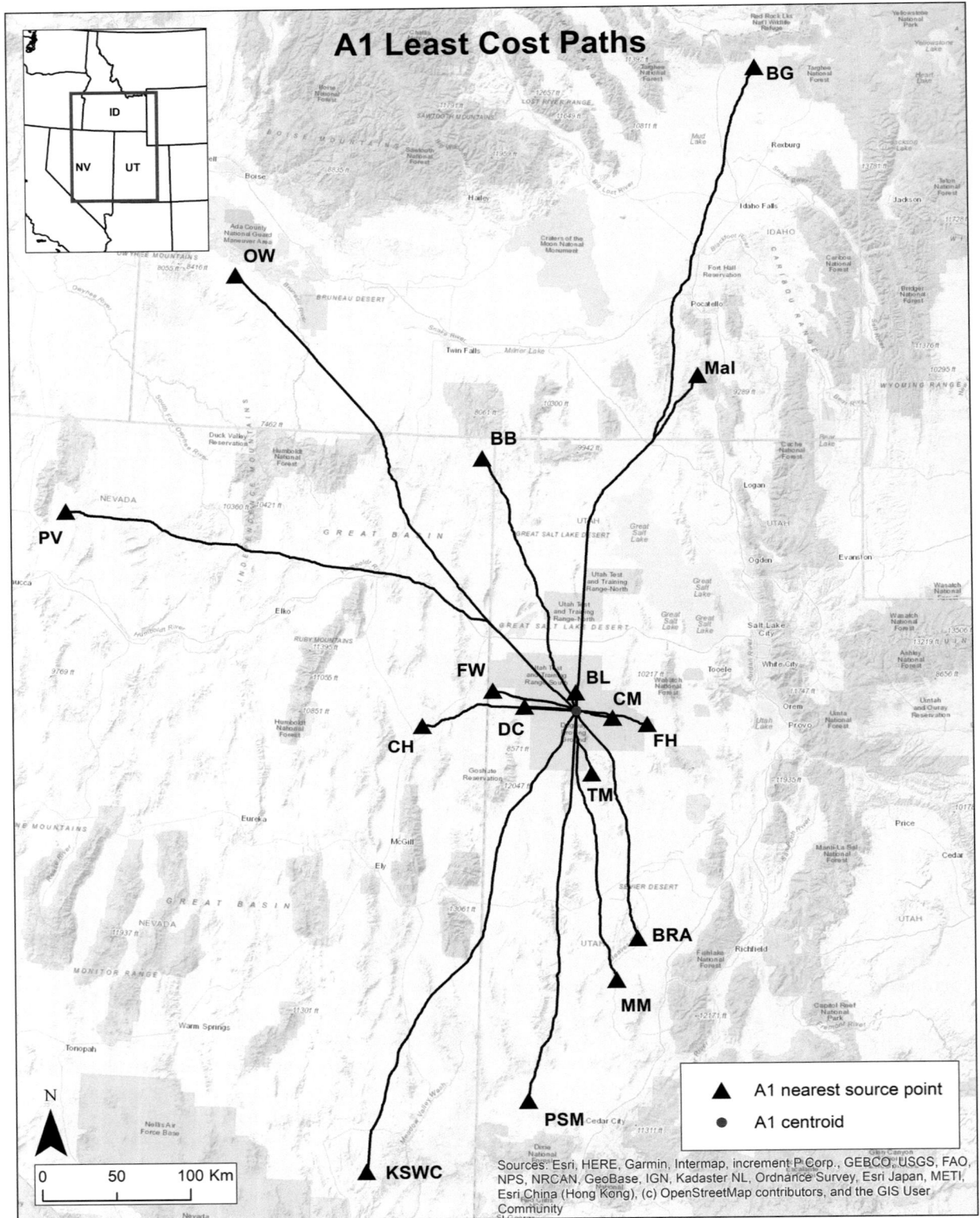

FIGURE 6.3. Least-cost paths from the A1 centroid to nearest source extents.

TABLE 6.10. Calculation of Discoverability (*D*) Values, the *Dlist* Ranks, and the *Olist* Ranks for the A1 Pool.

Source	d (km)	E (km²)	D	Expected Proportions (100×D/ΣD)	Dlist Rank	Artifact Counts (N=229)	Observed Proportions (100×n/N)	Olist rank
Badlands	13.4	66	0.369566	45.86%	1	14	6.1%	4
Bear Gulch	493.9	128.8	0.000528	0.07%	15	0	0.0%	14
Black Rock Area	176.2	353	0.011370	1.41%	6	5	2.2%	7
Brown's Bench	201.0	5173	0.128041	15.89%	2	23	10.0%	3
Cedar Mountain	26.3	37	0.053356	6.62%	5	6	2.6%	6
Currie Hills	111.0	26.1	0.002117	0.26%	11	2	0.9%	10
Deep Creek	35.4	107.6	0.086040	10.68%	4	7	3.1%	5
Ferguson Wash	61.1	4	0.001072	0.13%	13	0	0.0%	14
Flat Hills	51.1	21	0.008049	1.00%	7	117	51.1%	1
Kane Springs Wash Caldera	375.8	207	0.001466	0.18%	12	0	0.0%	14
Malad	265.5	23.8	0.000338	0.04%	16	3	1.3%	8.5
Mineral Mountains	200.7	170	0.004221	0.52%	10	3	1.3%	8.5
Owyhee	397.1	829.4	0.005260	0.65%	8	1	0.4%	11
Panaca Summit/Modena	284.6	358	0.004419	0.55%	9	0	0.0%	14
Paradise Valley	402.6	134.2	0.000828	0.10%	14	0	0.0%	14
Topaz Mountain	48.9	309	0.129164	16.03%	3	48	21.0%	2

TABLE 6.11. *Dlist* and *Olist* Ranked List Pairs for the A Groups.

Source	A1 Dlist	A1 Olist	A2 Dlist	A2 Olist	A3 Dlist	A3 Olist
Badlands	1	4	2	13	1	9
Bear Gulch	15	14	15	13	15	9
Black Rock Area	6	7	6	4.5	6	5.5
Brown's Bench	2	3	3	3	3	3
Cedar Mountain	5	6	5	13	4	5.5
Currie Hills	11	10	11	7.5	11	14
Deep Creek	4	5	4	7.5	5	9
Ferguson Wash	13	14	13	13	13	14
Flat Hills	7	1	7	2	7	1
Kane Springs Wash Caldera	12	14	12	13	12	14
Malad	16	8.5	16	13	16	14
Mineral Mountains	10	8.5	9	4.5	10	4
Owyhee	8	11	8	7.5	8	14
Panaca Summit/Modena	9	14	10	13	9	9
Paradise Valley	14	14	14	7.5	14	9
Topaz Mountain	3	2	1	1	2	2

Note: Calculations are the same as in Table 6.10, but all columns are not shown.

all A groups are significant (α = 0.05). For the A groups, the correlation coefficients indicate an initially high correlation, declining to moderately correlated data as time on the landscape increases.

A Groups Descriptive Statistics

The *Dlists* and *Olists* are ordinal lists with potentially unequal intervals between each rank and thus cannot be appropriately assessed using linear regression analysis. Here, I subjectively assess the outliers by calculating the absolute difference between the expected rank

for a given source versus the actual observed rank (Table 6.14) and by review of scatter plots presenting the bivariate relationships between the temporal group *Dlists* and *Olists* (Figures 6.3–6.5).

For the A groups, I focus on extreme values that are patterned across all temporal groups. For the A1 (12,674 cal BP) group, Malad and Flat Hills have the most extreme rank differences and are potential outliers (see also Figure 6.4). For Malad, this finding is simply a case of a source with a very low discoverability rank (16th) which is elevated by three artifacts appearing in the

TABLE 6.12. *Dlist* and *Olist* Ranked List Pairs for the C Groups.

Source	C1 Dlist	C1 Olist	C2 Dlist	C2 Olist	C3 Dlist	C3 Olist	C4 Dlist	C4 Olist	C5 Dlist	C5 Olist
Badlands	1	4	2	13	1	3	3	9	3	10
Bear Gulch	15	14	15	13	15	13	15	9	15	10
Black Rock Area	6	7	6	4.5	6	6.5	6	5	6	10
Brown's Bench	2	3	3	3	3	6.5	2	3	2	2
Cedar Mountain	5	6	5	13	5	13	5	5	5	10
Currie Hills	11	10	11	7.5	11	13	11	14	11	10
Deep Creek	4	5	4	7.5	4	6.5	4	9	4	10
Ferguson Wash	13	14	13	13	13	6.5	13	14	13	10
Flat Hills	7	1	7	2	7	2	7	1	7	10
Kane Springs Wash Caldera	12	14	12	13	12	6.5	12	14	12	10
Malad	16	8.5	16	13	16	13	16	14	16	10
Mineral Mountains	10	8.5	9	4.5	10	6.5	9	5	9	3
Owyhee	8	11	8	7.5	8	13	8	14	8	10
Panaca Summit/Modena	9	14	10	13	9	13	10	9	10	10
Paradise Valley	14	14	14	7.5	14	13	14	9	14	10
Topaz Mountain	3	2	1	1	2	1	1	2	1	1

Note: Calculations are the same as in Table 6.10, but all columns are not shown.

TABLE 6.13. A Groups Spearman's r_s Results.

Group	Spearman's r_s	p Value
A1	0.777	0.0004
A2	0.502	0.048
A3	0.592	0.016

TABLE 6.14. A Groups Rank Differences with Potential Outliers Highlighted.

Source	A1 Diffs	A2 Diffs	A3 Diffs
Badlands	3	**11**	8
Bear Gulch	1	2	6
Black Rock Area	1	1.5	0.5
Brown's Bench	1	0	0
Cedar Mountain	1	**8**	1.5
Currie Hills	1	3.5	3
Deep Creek	1	3.5	4
Ferguson Wash	1	0	1
Flat Hills	**6**	5	6
Kane Springs Wash Caldera	2	1	2
Malad	**7.5**	3	2
Mineral Mountains	1.5	4.5	6
Owyhee	3	0.5	6
Panaca Summit/Modena	5	3	0
Paradise Valley	0	6.5	5
Topaz Mountain	1	0	0

assemblage. However, the case with Flat Hills is remarkable. As shown in Table 6.4, the artifact counts for Flat Hills are extremely high relative to all other source counts. This raises Flat Hills to the first rank of the A1 *Olist*, and a marked difference from its expected *Dlist* rank (seventh). In fact, Table 6.4 establishes that Flat Hills is a highly utilized source across all the A groups (discussed further below).

The Cedar Mountain source is quite close to the ORB but is absent from the pooled A2 (11,578 cal BP) assemblage. As a result, the expected (fifth) and the observed (thirteenth) ranks for this source differ substantially.

The Badlands source appears exceptionally underutilized in the A2 (11,578 cal BP) and A3 (10,444 cal BP) groups, where it is expected to command the second and first ranks, respectively. This result is anomalous to its utilization in A1 (12,674 cal BP), where its expected rank was first and it appears in the fourth rank. The Badlands source is, on average, only about 18 km (Table 6.8) from the A groups clusters, while the highly utilized Flat Hills source is about 48 km away. Page's (2008) classification of the Badlands source as a high-quality fine-grained volcanic (FGV) suggests that adaptive factors other than distance, exposure, and quality might be at play here. Those factors might also explain the virtual abandonment of this source in later temporal periods. This interpretation becomes even more evident when evaluating the C groups (below).

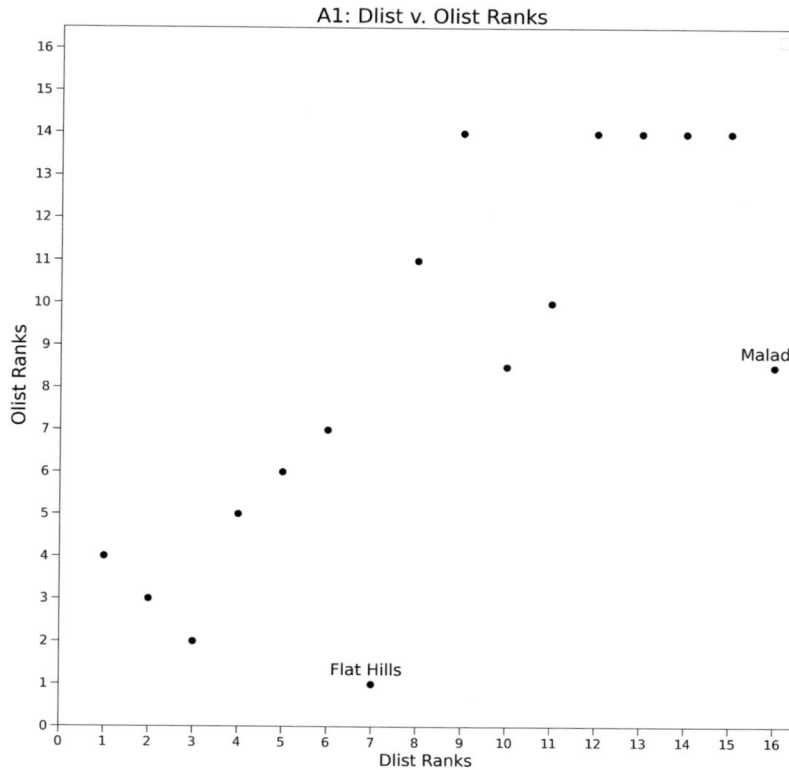

FIGURE 6.4. A1 scatter plot with Flat Hills and Malad outliers noted.

TABLE 6.15. A Groups *%LL* Calculation.

Group	Spearman's r_s	r_s^2	%LL
A1	0.777	0.603	39.7%
A2	0.502	0.252	74.8%
A3	0.592	0.350	65.0%

TABLE 6.16. A Groups *%LL* and Mean Ages.

Group	%LL	Midpoint Age (^{14}C yr BP/cal BP)
A1	39.6	10,650/12,674
A2	74.8	10,050/11,578
A3	65.0	9,300/10,444

Figures 6.4, 6.5, and 6.6 illustrate the scatter plots for the A groups, with possible outliers labeled.

A Groups Landscape Learning

The level of landscape learning for each A group was calculated using Equation 3.3:

$$\%LL = (1 - r_s^2) * 100 \qquad (Eq.\ 3.3)$$

The A groups *%LL* and midpoint ages are presented in Table 6.16 and plotted in Figure 6.7 (using calibrated years BP).

The fitted line returns a Pearson's *r* of 0.692 (*p* = 0.514) and a coefficient of determination (R^2) of 0.479, suggesting that ~48% of the variance of *%LL* over time is explained by this model. While *%LL* appears to present an upward trend over time, not much more can be concluded with statistical rigor from only these three

sample points. Using radiocarbon rather than calibrated dates in this analysis produces slightly lower results ($R^2 = 0.425$).

A Groups Outliers Discussion

The descriptive statistics reveal a few instances of possible outliers, which are highlighted in Table 6.14. In the Flat Hills case, there are many more samples than expected (*n* = 117 or 51% of the entire A1 [12,674 cal BP] group sample set). As noted previously in this chapter, Flat Hills presents more samples than expected in all three A groups.

Flat Hills FGV may also stand out as a geological and logistical outlier when considering all the toolstone sources utilized in the ORB. Flat Hills FGV manifests as cobbles of high quality that are large enough for tools, mixed within a sandbar (tombolo) on the basin

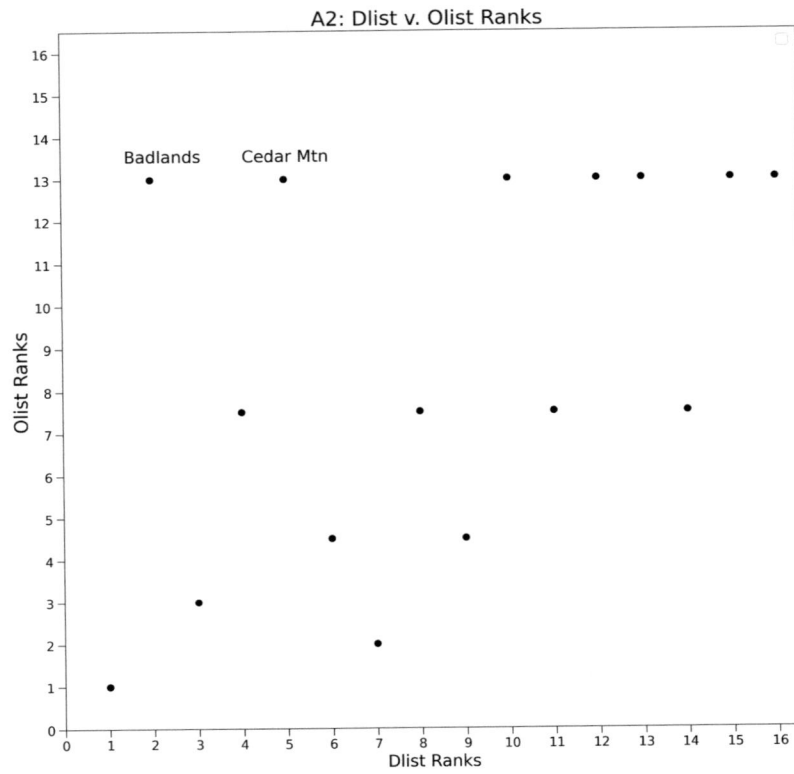

Figure 6.5. A2 scatter plot with Badlands and Cedar Mountain outliers noted.

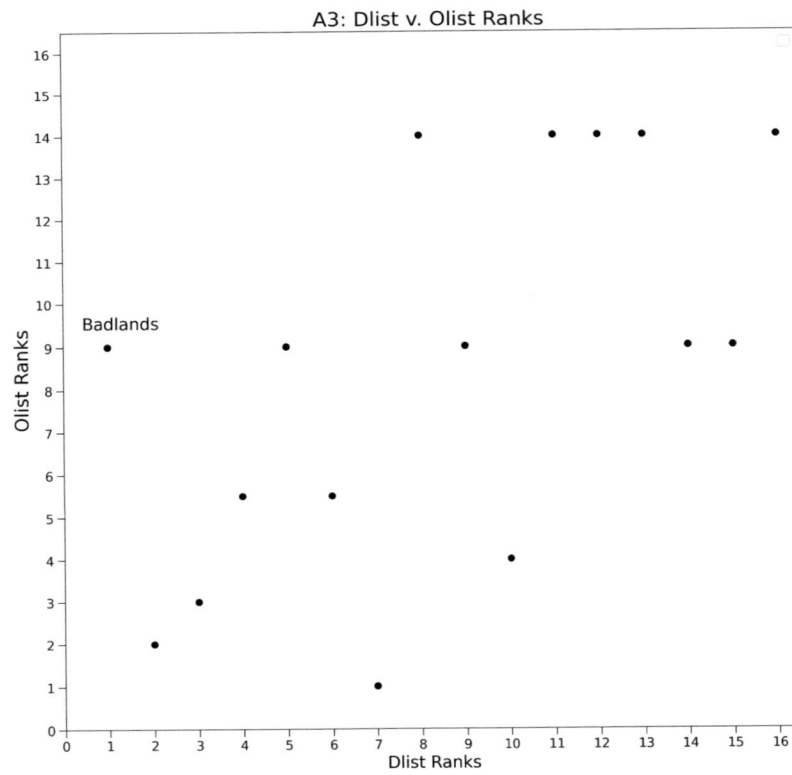

Figure 6.6. A3 scatter plot with Badlands outlier noted.

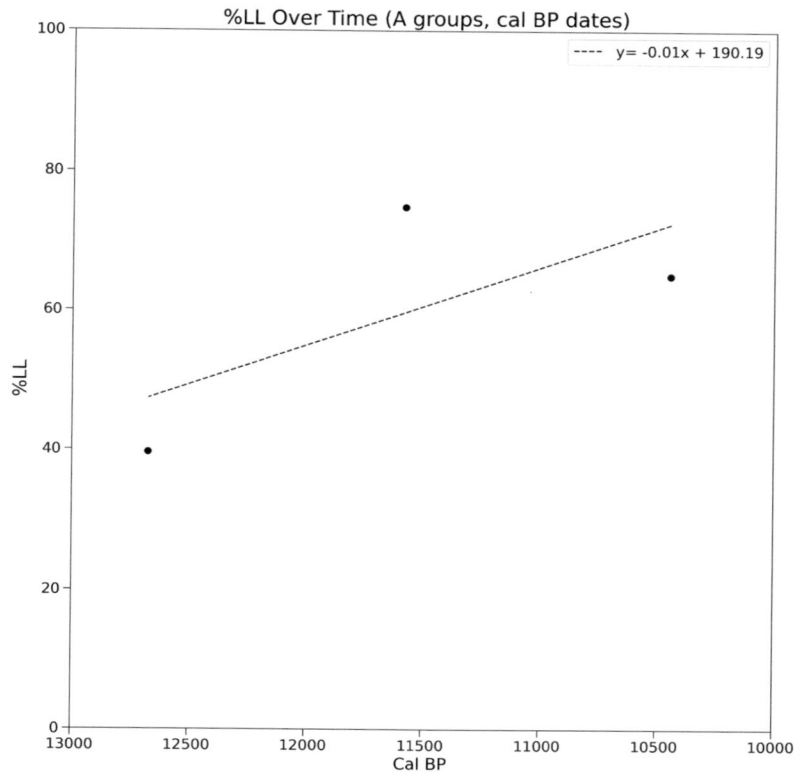

FIGURE 6.7. Regression of *%LL* across A groups using calibrated years BP.

TABLE 6.17. C Groups Spearman's r_s Results.

Group	Spearman's r_s	p Value
C1 (Black Channel)	0.777	0.0004
C2 (Green)	0.502	0.048
C3 (Blue B)	0.597	0.015
C4 (Light Blue)	0.648	0.007
C5 (Lavender)	0.500	0.048

bottom, and are remnants of material transported and deposited by receding Lake Bonneville (Page, 2008; see also Chapter 5). This exposure differs significantly from the alluvial fan patterns seen in basin bottoms during my survey work, described in Chapter 4, where only pebbles, usually too small for tools, reach the basin bottom. These small pebbles may present a discoverability signal but rarely offer a quarrying opportunity. The geologic phenomenon of Flat Hills FGV, its high quality, and easy accessibility at low elevation may have resulted in a greater attractiveness upon discovery, fueling higher utilization early in the occupation of the ORB. Possibly, this explains why Flat Hills is consistently very highly ranked across all groups, when its discoverability index suggests it should rank much lower. This source was clearly "learned" at the earliest dated periods of the ORB occupation and well-utilized across all occupation periods, exceeding the predictions derived from

the model presented here. On the other hand, given that a significance level of $\alpha = 0.05$ is used here, one outlier is not unexpected by chance within a set of 16 samples, and it is possible, though unlikely, that this has occurred by chance.

C GROUPS ANALYSIS

The C groups divide the ORB Paleoindian artifacts into the largest number of distinct temporal groups while maintaining statistically meaningful assemblage sizes.

C Groups Correlation Statistics

For each C group, the Spearman's rank order correlation coefficient was calculated and the *p* values for all C groups are significant ($\alpha = 0.05$). For the C groups, the correlation coefficients indicate an initially high correlation, declining, over time, to moderately correlated data.

C Groups Descriptive Statistics

As with the A groups, among the C groups, outliers may be detected by calculating the absolute difference between the expected rank for a given source versus the actual observed rank (Table 6.18) and by review of scatter plots presenting the bivariate relationships between the C group *Dlists* and *Olists* (Figures 6.8–6.12).

The C1 (12,674 cal BP) group (the Black channel) is the same as the A1 group (see above) with the same

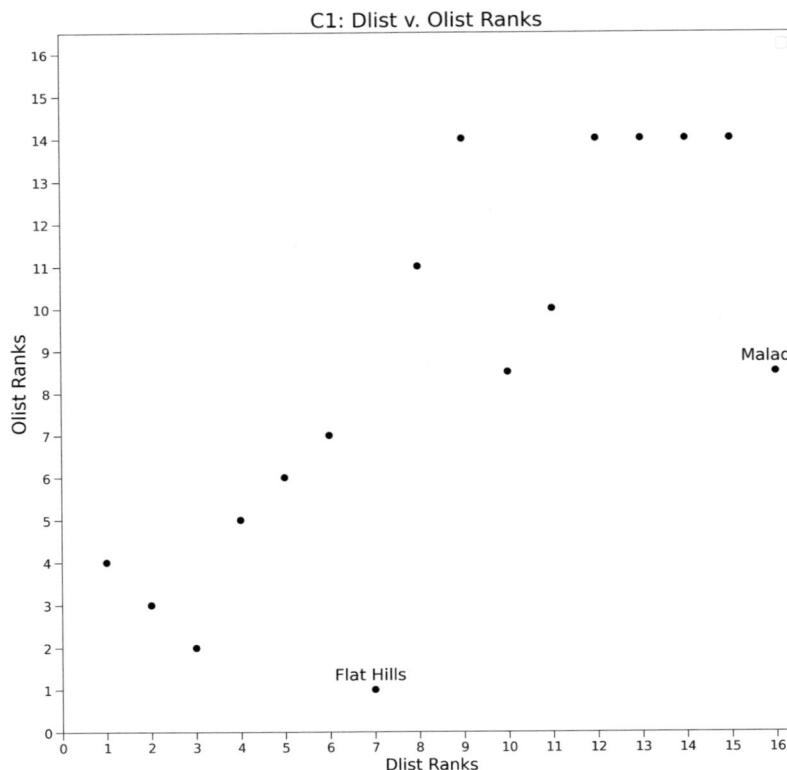

FIGURE 6.8. C1 scatter plot with Flat Hills and Malad outliers indicated. Note: the C1 group is identical to the A1 group.

potential outliers; Malad and Flat Hills have the most extreme rank differences (see also Figure 6.8).

As in the A2 (11,578 cal BP) group, the Cedar Mountain source is absent from the C2 (11,578 cal BP) pooled assemblage (the Green channel). As a result, the expected (fifth) and the observed (thirteenth) ranks for this source differ substantially. The C3 (11,167 cal BP) group comprises a smaller set of artifacts (n = 24) from the Blue B channel. Cedar Mountain is absent from this assemblage, resulting in the largest rank difference. A single sample from Ferguson Wash creates the second largest rank difference.

As in the A groups, the Badlands source appears remarkably underutilized in groups C2, C4, and C5, where it is expected to occupy one of the top three ranks in each group. This position is anomalous to its utilization in A1/C1, where its expected rank was first and it appears in the fourth rank, resulting in an unremarkable difference. As noted above, the Badlands FGV appears to be almost abandoned in later temporal groups, superseded by Flat Hills FGV as the dominant toolstone.

In the C5 (10,221 cal BP) group, it is important to note that this group has the lowest sample size (n = 20) and exhibits the lowest toolstone source richness (n = 3) of all the groups. This lack of diversity results in 13 tied ranks where source samples are absent, a prime

example of the sample size problem I noted above and to which I return in the summary.

Figures 6.8 through 6.12 present the plots for the C groups, with possible outliers labeled.

C Groups Landscape Learning

The level of landscape learning for each C group was calculated using Equation 3.3:

$$\%LL = (1 - r_s^2) * 100 \qquad \text{(Eq. 3.3)}$$

The C groups %LL and midpoint ages are presented in Table 6.20 and plotted in Figure 6.13 (using calibrated years BP).

Using calibrated year dates, the fitted line returns a Pearson's r of 0.662 (p = 0.224) and a coefficient of determination (R^2) of 0.438, suggesting that ~44% of the variance of %LL over time is explained by my model. Using radiocarbon dates in this analysis produces slightly lower results (R^2 = 0.409).

SUMMARY

In this chapter, the discoverability model was tested. This model hypothesizes that landscape learning can be detected over time by analyzing the utilization of known toolstone resources and the relation of those resources

TABLE 6.18. C Groups Rank Differences with Potential Outliers Highlighted.

Source	C1 Diff	C2 Diff	C3 Diff	C4 diff	C5 Diff
Badlands	3	**11**	2	**6**	**7**
Bear Gulch	1	2	2	**6**	5
Black Rock Area	1	1.5	0.5	1	4
Brown's Bench	1	0	3.5	1	0
Cedar Mountain	1	**8**	**8**	0	5
Currie Hills	1	3.5	2	3	1
Deep Creek	1	3.5	2.5	5	6
Ferguson Wash	1	0	**6.5**	1	3
Flat Hills	**6**	5	5	**6**	3
Kane Springs Wash Caldera	2	1	5.5	2	2
Malad	**7.5**	3	3	2	6
Mineral Mountains	1.5	4.5	3.5	4	6
Owyhee	3	0.5	5	**6**	2
Panaca Summit/Modena	5	3	4	1	0
Paradise Valley	0	6.5	1	5	4
Topaz Mountain	1	0	1	1	0

to a given assemblage in terms of exposure size (E) and distance (d).

Using the Paleoindian artifact data recorded at the ORB delta (Appendix A), artifacts were divided into nonoverlapping, discrete temporal ranges. The A groups ($n = 3$) emphasized grouping the largest available sample sizes per temporal group while the C groups ($n = 5$) emphasized creating the largest number of distinct temporal groups. These groupings provided the best possibilities for analyzing landscape learning despite the small sample sizes available. The discoverability equation (Equation 3.2) and the %LL equation (Equation 3.3) were then applied to each of these discrete assemblages in conjunction with the source extents surveyed and predicted in Chapters 4 and 5.

For both the A and C groups, the oldest assemblages (A1 and C1 were identical) presented very strong correlations ($r_s = 0.777$) with their expected, and deterministic, *Dlists*. This analysis, in turn, returned the lowest level of landscape learning of any of the temporal groups (%LL = 39.7%), as the model predicts. Importantly, the magnitude of difference in %LL ($\delta = 35.1\%$) between the oldest and next oldest assemblages (A1:A2 and C1:C2) is significantly greater than any differences between any other subsequent temporal steps for either the A or C groups. Even the differences between the A1/C1 values and the next lowest %LL values in each group were 25.3% (A1:A3) and 18.3% (C1:C4), greater than any differences between any subsequent time periods (the next greatest difference is C4:C5 at 17%). These results seem to indicate a significant step in landscape learning between the earliest assemblages and the next temporally discrete assemblages.

TABLE 6.19. C Groups *%LL* Results.

Group	Spearman's r	r_s^2	%LL
C1	0.777	0.603	39.7%
C2	0.502	0.252	74.8%
C3	0.597	0.357	64.3%
C4	0.648	0.420	58.0%
C5	0.500	0.250	75.0%

TABLE 6.20. C Groups *%LL* and Mean Ages.

Group	%LL	Midpoint Age (^{14}C yr BP/cal BP)
C1	39.7	10,650/12,674
C2	74.8	10,050/11,578
C3	64.3	9,750/11,167
C4	58.0	9,300/10,444
C5	75.0	9,050/10,221

There are multiple reasons why we may not see greater discrimination between the later temporal assemblages. The most obvious is the limitations of the available sample sizes, particularly in the C groups (C3 and C5 are especially small; see Table 6.5). The small sample sizes are further affected by the large number of available obsidian/FGV sources ($n = 16$) which dilute the rank values within the *Dlists* and increase the number of ties for those groups.

By the time of the "next oldest" temporal group, the landscape also likely had been largely learned. The age step between A1:A2 and C1:C2 is ~1096 cal years (see Tables 6.2 and 6.3). While a significant %LL step can be seen, no significant change occurs in toolstone source

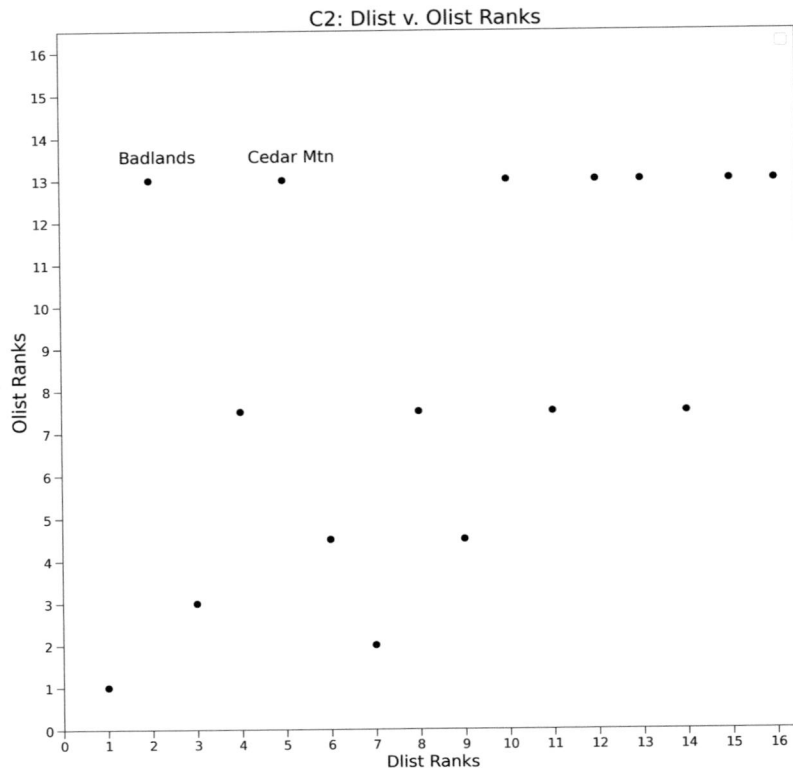

FIGURE 6.9. C2 scatter plot with Badlands and Cedar Mountain outliers indicated.

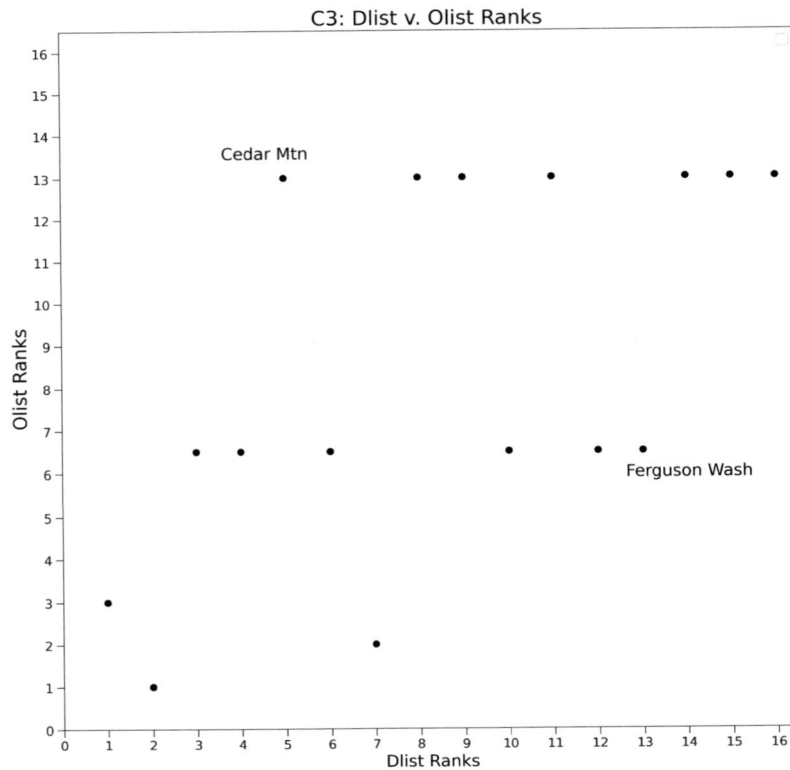

FIGURE 6.10. C3 scatter plot with Cedar Mountain and Ferguson Wash outliers indicated.

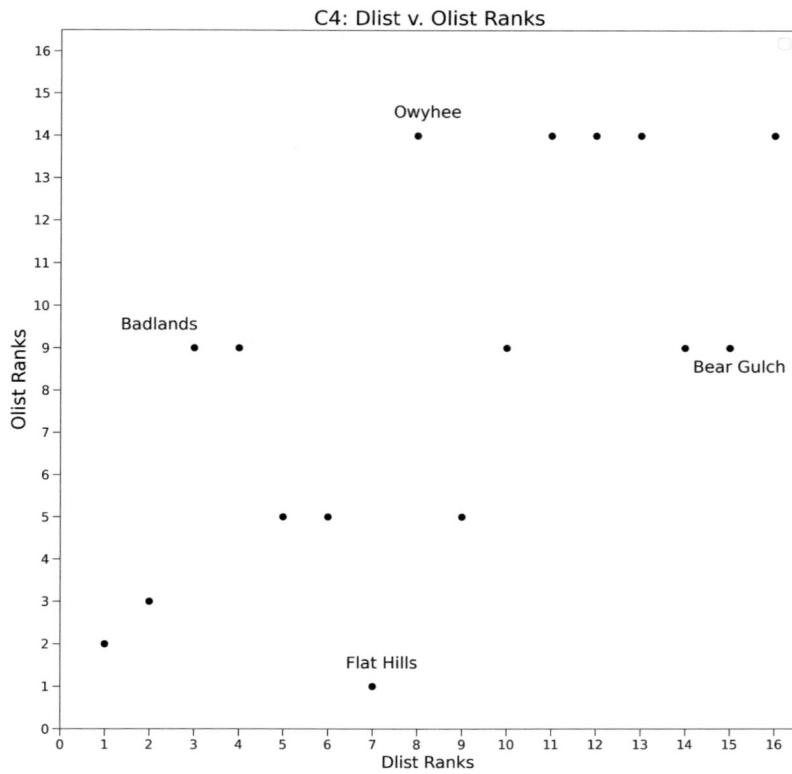

FIGURE 6.11. C4 scatter plot with outliers indicated.

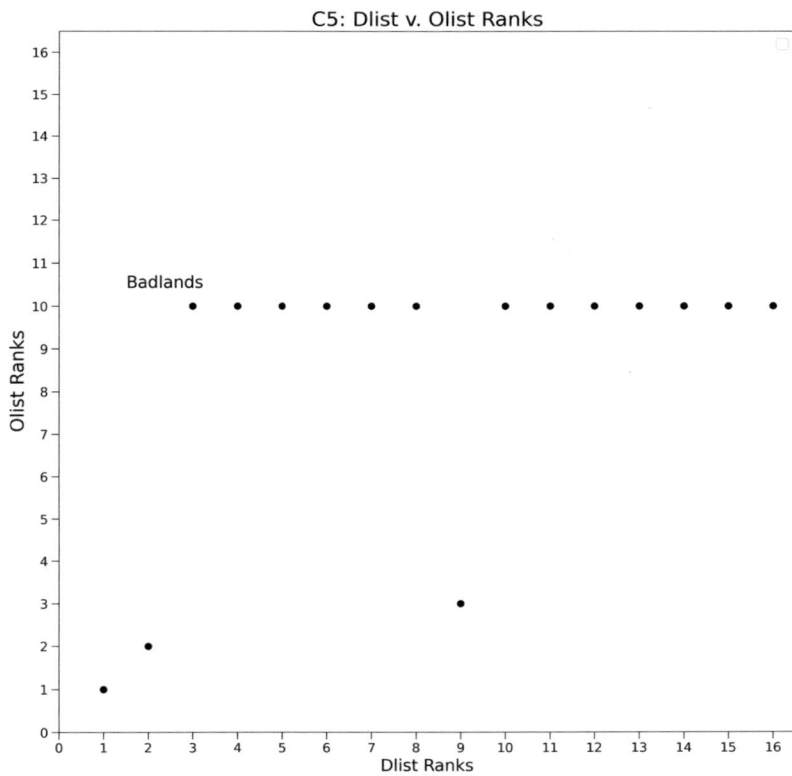

FIGURE 6.12. C5 scatter plot with Badlands outlier indicated.

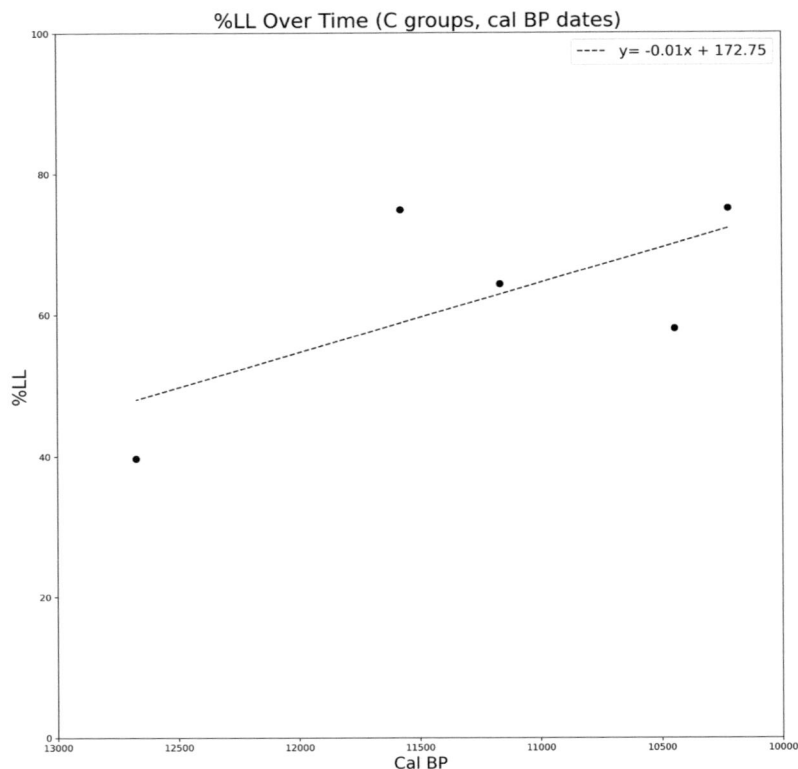

FIGURE 6.13. Regression of *%LL* across C groups using calibrated years BP.

richness (Table 6.21) between the earliest and later temporal assemblages. In fact, A1/C1 have the highest level of source richness (*n* = 11) of the temporal groups. This finding seems to imply that the ORB delta lithic universe was "learned" within that first temporal step. The variation in *%LL* we see beyond this first step then may be due to random variations or variations dependent on other human behaviors (perhaps the rise of exchange or territoriality) that this model does not quantify.

Finally, both the A and C groups provide similar R^2 values, 0.479 and 0.438 respectively, suggesting that up to 48 percent of the variance in landscape learning over time is explained by my discoverability model.

TABLE 6.21. Toolstone Source Richness by Temporal Group.

Temporal Group	Toolstone Richness *n*
A1	11
A2	9
A3	11
C1	11
C2	9
C3	9
C4	11
C5	3

REPOSITORY AND SOFTWARE

GitHub repository (*GitHub*, 2021). All Jupyter notebooks, spreadsheets, and source extent shapefiles used for the calculations in this chapter are available in GitHub repository DOI: 10.5281/zenodo.6544114. These are also available directly at GitHub: https://github.com/davehuntoo/dhuntoo_dissertation

The following software tools were used to create the programs described in this chapter:

Anaconda Navigator, v. 1.9.12 (Anaconda Software Distribution, 2021). The versions of all installs and libraries encapsulated in this aggregation are listed in the environment.yml file in the repository referenced below.

Jupyter Notebook, v. 6.0.3 (*Project Jupyter*, 2021). Jupyter notebooks were created to run the regression analysis, graph and analyze the resultant data, and to replicate various figures that appear in this chapter.

Python v. 3.7.6 (64-bit; Python Software Foundation, 2021). The Jupyter notebooks utilize this Python version.

ArcGIS Desktop 10.8.1 (Esri, 2021a). The toolstone source extent shapefiles were created using this software and are available in the GitHub repository.

7 Conclusions

In this volume, I proposed new methodologies for measuring landscape learning and gauging residence time on a landscape. I used the landscape learning model to set expectations and proposed testable hypotheses utilizing these methods. The model and methodologies were then tested against data in the context of a Paleoindian colonizing event within the Old River Bed (ORB) delta in Utah.

At the conclusion of Chapter 1, I asked:

Can landscape learning be detected in the archaeological record and then be used to place assemblages in relative chronological order?

In Chapter 3, I developed and demonstrated the discoverability model, a model to predict the order in which a random walker will discover patchy resources found on a neutral landscape, dependent only on distance and patch size. The simulation results for the model positively supported the hypothesis that patch size affects encounter rate and that the model could be used to create a deterministic baseline for patch discovery on an otherwise "unknown landscape"—in other words, a baseline against which to measure the accumulation of landscape knowledge over time.

The discoverability model requires knowing the size of the resource patches on the landscape. In the Great Basin, most prehistorically utilized lithic sources are geographically known as point samples and in general locational terms. However, the size of the secondary distributions—the flow of obsidian or fine-grained volcanic (FGV) sediments by alluvial or colluvial action—are unknown. This data is important because I argue that

these secondary distributions likely acted as signals to hunter-gatherers as they foraged, directing them to primary sources.

In Chapter 4, an original methodology to quantitatively determine these toolstone patch sizes, or exposure extents (E), was presented. This methodology uses hydrographic algorithms along with known primary source locations or, in their absence, proxy sources as algorithm seeds, to predict the primary and secondary distribution signals on the landscape.

Testing this methodology involved extensive fieldwork at 5 of the 16 toolstone sources used by Paleoindians residing in the ORB delta. The results (Tables 4.8 and 4.9) demonstrate that, on average, the methodologies predicted 66 percent of the actual downslope flow of obsidian sediments. From these tests, the optimal digital elevation model (DEM) smoothing (smoothing index) was determined, and when this level of smoothing was applied to the hydrographic models for all sources (less Ferguson Wash, excluded by exception), the methodology successfully returned an average scaled prediction of 89 percent of the area of the actual surveyed flow extents. The success of these tests validates this method to then predict patch size of many sources at a consistent scale without the need for extensive field work. These methodologies, however, have room for improvement. They are reliant on some knowledge of upslope toolstone sources, though the examples presented here demonstrate how a few point samples can provide a proxy for the primary source. Also, while the flow predictions conformed well in steeper areas, they suffered in the very flat basin bottoms typical of the Great Basin. Increased resolution of digital elevation data, such as that of LiDAR datasets, may help increase the predictive performance of these methods in the future.

In Chapter 5, the optimal smoothing index, established in Chapter 4, was used to predict the secondary distributions of the remaining 11 toolstone sources that were not surveyed. Together with the five surveyed sources, these calculations provided the exposure (E) variable inputs for the discoverability model.

In Chapter 6, the discoverability model was tested using the exposure (E) values derived from the ORB toolstone sources in Chapters 4 and 5. The ORB Paleoindian assemblages were divided into temporal groups, and centroids for each assemblage were determined. Using these centroids and the nearest exposure edge of the 16 toolstone sources, the distances (d) were calculated. For each assemblage, the discoverability values (D) were calculated using the E and d values (Eq. 3.2) for each toolstone source, and the *Dlists* of expected rank-order usage of toolstone sources were created. The corresponding *Olists* were generated using the observed toolstone proportions in each assemblage. The *Dlists* and *Olists* were then compared using Spearman's rank order correlation. From these results, the landscape learning variable (%LL) was calculated (Equation 3.3) for each temporal group/assemblage.

The oldest temporal group's *Olist* returned a very strong correlation (r_s = 0.777) with its expected *Dlist*. This analysis, in turn, returned the lowest level of landscape learning of any of the temporal groups (%LL = 39.7%), as my model predicts. Importantly, the magnitude of difference in %LL (δ = 35.2%) between the oldest and next oldest assemblage (~1,096 cal years later) is significantly greater than the differences between any other subsequent temporal steps between the assemblages. These results indicate a significant step in landscape learning between the earliest assemblage and the next temporally discrete assemblages.

While multiple reasons may explain why we may not see greater discrimination in %LL between the later temporal groups, in this case study, the most obvious is the limitation of available sample sizes. The small sample sizes are further affected by the large number of regionally utilized toolstone sources (n = 16) which dilute the rank values and negatively affect the strength of the rank correlation tests. The landscape also is likely to have been fully learned between the first temporal assemblage and the next, a span of ~1,096 cal years. This finding is not out of line with expectations set in Chapter 2, though it seems to occur more quickly than Tolan-Smith (2003) predicts (one to two millennia) at this regional scale, albeit in a very different geographic setting. At the ORB delta, landscape learning appears to have happened quickly relative to the resolution of the archaeological record, perhaps culminating within ~1,100 years. Variation in landscape learning (%LL) between later assemblages is likely the result of small sample sizes and human behavioral variations not quantified by this model. Overall, the results suggest that up to 48 percent of the variance in landscape learning over time at the ORB delta is explained by the discoverability model.

The answer, then, to the opening question is "yes, with limitations." The methods introduced here do appear to effectively measure the accumulation of landscape knowledge and therefore act as a proxy for residence on the landscape. With this information, the methods show promise as a means to place assemblages in relative order, based on increasing landscape knowledge. However, two primary limitations seem to be present. Given the speed at which landscape learning appears to occur, even at this large regional scale, the archaeological record under examination must provide sufficient temporal resolution in proportion to the regional scale. Second, the methods are limited by adequate sample sizes, a common problem with Paleoindian data, which itself is subject to further dilution depending on the number of resource patches that exist within the resource universe. If these two conditions can be overcome, the model and resultant methods show promise as a means to quantify and rank the level of landscape learning in a set of assemblages and therefore place them in relative chronological order.

Prior to this study, no methods have been offered to effectively capture and measure this important aspect of human adaptation to new, unknown landscapes. I have proposed and tested original methods to set a baseline against which to measure landscape learning, tools to quantify landscape learning based on resource usage, methods to predict lithic resource patch size inclusive of secondary distributions and signals on the landscape, and approaches to compare these predictions with surveyed results. These techniques have shown success, despite limitations in the available test data, in gauging this important aspect of human adaption.

Investigations continue at the ORB delta, and I hope to see more extensive X-ray fluorescence (XRF) analyses released in the future. These will provide an even better dataset for further investigations of this model and these methodologies. Further research avenues include improvements, as noted in Chapters 4 and 5, in flow predictions, perhaps with the addition of algorithms that factor in particle size. Other primary sources, such as clay or temper sources in ceramic studies, may similarly benefit from these means to quantify landscape learning.

References Cited

Abuzaid, A. H., El-hanjouri, M. M., & Kulab, M. M. (2015). On discordance tests for the wrapped Cauchy distribution. *Open Journal of Statistics, 5*, 245–253. https://doi.org/10.4236/ojs.2015.54026.

Amsden, C. A. (1937). The Lake Mohave artifacts. In E. W. C. Campbell, W. H. Campbell, E. Antevs, C. A. Amsden, J. A. Barbieri, & F. D. Bode (Eds.), *The archaeology of Pleistocene Lake Mohave* (pp. 51–97). Southwest Museum Papers 11.

Anaconda Software Distribution. (2021). In *Anaconda Documentation* (Version 1.9) [computer software]. Anaconda. https://docs.anaconda.com.

Anthony, D. W. (1997). Prehistoric migration as social pattern. In J. Chapman & H. Hamerow (Eds.), *Migrations and invasions in archaeological explanation* (pp. 21–32). Archaeopress.

Archuleta, C.-A. M., Constance, E. W., Arundel, S. T., Lowe, A. J., Mantey, K. S., & Phillips, L. A. (2017). The National Map seamless digital elevation model specifications. *U.S. Geological Survey, Techniques and Methods 11-B9,* 39. https://doi.org/10.3133/tm11B9.

Argialas, D., & Tzotsos, A. (2006). Automatic extraction of physiographic features and alluvial fans in Nevada, USA from digital elevation models and satellite imagery through multiresolution segmentation and object-oriented classification. *American Society for Photogrammetry and Remote Sensing—Annual Conference of the American Society for Photogrammetry and Remote Sensing 2006: Prospecting for Geospatial Information Integration, 1,* 68–77.

Arkush, B. S., & Pitblado, B. L. (2000). Paleoarchaic surface assemblages in the Great Salt Lake Desert, northwestern Utah. *Journal of California and Great Basin Anthropology, 22,* 12–42.

Armstrong, R. L. (1970). Geochronology of Tertiary igneous rocks, eastern Basin and Range Province, western Utah, eastern Nevada, and vicinity, U.S.A. *Geochimica et Cosmochimica Acta, 34,* 203–232. https://doi.org/10.1016/0016-7037(70)90007-4.

Atwood, G., Wambeam, T. J., & Anderson, N. J. (2016). The present as a key to the past: Paleoshoreline correlation insights from Great Salt Lake. In C. G. Oviatt & J. F. Shroder (Eds.), *Lake Bonneville, a scientific update* (pp. 1–27). Developments in Earth Surface Processes 20. Elsevier. https://doi.org/10.1016/B978-0-444-63590-7.00001-9.

Auger-Méthé, M., Derocher, A. E., Plank, M. J., Codling, E. A., & Lewis, M. A. (2015). Differentiating the Lévy walk from a composite correlated random walk. *Methods in Ecology and Evolution, 6,* 1179–1189. https://doi.org/10.1111/2041-210X.12412.

Bailey, J. (1992). *X-ray fluorescence characterization of volcanic glass artifacts from Wilson Butte Cave, Idaho* (Publication No. 304029237)[Master's thesis, University of Alberta]. ProQuest Dissertations & Theses Global.

Bartumeus, F., Da Luz, M. G. E., Viswanathan, G. M., & Catalan, J. (2005). Animal search strategies: A quantitative random-walk analysis. *Ecology, 86,* 3078–3087.

Batschelet, E. (1965). *Statistical methods for the analysis of problems in animal orientation and certain biological rhythms (AIBS monograph).* American Institute of Biological Sciences.

Batschelet, E. (1981). *Circular statistics in biology.* Academic Press.

Beaton, J. M. (1991). Colonizing continents: Some problems from Australia and the Americas. In T. D. Dillehay & D. J. Meltzer (Eds.), *The first Americans: Search and research* (pp. 209–230). CRC Press.

Beck, C., & Jones, G. T. (1990). Toolstone selection and lithic technology in early Great Basin prehistory. *Journal of Field Archaeology, 17,* 283–299. https://doi.org/10.2307/530023.

Beck, C., & Jones, G. T. (1994). Dating surface asssemblages using obsidian hydration. In C. Beck (Ed.), *Dating in Exposed and Surface Contexts* (pp. 47–76). University of New Mexico Press.

Beck, C., & Jones, G. T. (1997). The Terminal Pleistocene/Early Holocene archaeology of the Great Basin. *Journal of World Prehistory, 11,* 161–236. http://link.springer.com/article/10.1007/BF02221204.

Beck, C., & Jones, G. T. (2009). *The archaeology of the eastern Nevada Paleolithic, part 1: The Sunshine Locality.* University of Utah Press.

Beck, C., & Jones, G. T. (2010). Clovis and Western Stemmed: Population migration and the meeting of two technologies in the Intermountain West. *American Antiquity, 75,* 81–116.

Beck, C., & Jones, G. T. (2011). The role of mobility and exchange in the conveyance of toolstone during the Great Basin Paleoarchaic. In R. E. Hughes (Ed.), *Perspectives on prehistoric trade and exchange in California and the Great Basin* (pp. 55–82). University of Utah Press.

Beck, C., & Jones, G. T. (2015). Lithic analysis. In D. B. Madsen, D. N. Schmitt, & D. Page (Eds.), *The Paleoarchaic occupation of the Old River Bed delta* (pp. 97–208). University of Utah Press.

Beck, C., Taylor, A. K., Jones, G. T., Fadem, C. M., Cook, C. R., & Millward, S. A. (2002). Rocks are heavy: Transport costs and Paleoarchaic quarry behavior in the Great Basin. *Journal of Anthropological Archaeology, 21,* 481–507. https://doi.org/10.1016/S0278-4165(02)00007-7.

Bell, W. J. (1990). *Searching behavior, Chapman and Hall animal behavior series.* Springer Netherlands. http://link.springer.com/10.1007/978-94-011-3098-1_12.

Benhamou, S. (2006). Detecting an orientation component in animal paths when the preferred direction is individual-dependent. *Ecology, 87,* 518–528.

Benhamou, S. (2007). How many animals really do the Lévy walk? *Ecology, 88,* 1962–1969.

Ben-Israel, A. (2013). A concentrated Cauchy distribution with finite moments. *Annals of Operations Research, 208,* 147–153. https://doi.org/10.1007/s10479-011-0995-z.

Bennett, E. H. (1976). *Reconnaissance geology and geochemistry of the South Mountain—Juniper Mountain region, Owyhee County, Idaho,* Pamphlet No. 166. Idaho Bureau of Mines and Geology.

Best, M. G., Christiansen, E. H., Deino, A. L., Gromme, S., Hart, G. L., & Tingey, D. G. (2013). The 36-18 Ma Indian Peak-Caliente ignimbrite field and calderas, southeastern Great Basin, USA: Multicyclic super-eruptions. *Geosphere, 9,* 864–950. https://doi.org/10.1130/GES00902.1.

Bettinger, R. L., & Eerkens, J. (2004). Evolutionary implications of metrical variation in Great Basin projectile points. *Archeological Papers of the American Anthropological Association, 7,* 177–191. https://doi.org/10.1525/ap3a.1997.7.1.177.

Binford, L. (1979). Organization and formation processes: Looking at curated technologies. *Journal of Anthropological Research, 35,* 255–273.

Blurton Jones, N., & Konner, M. J. (1976). !Kung knowledge of animal behavior (or: The proper study of mankind is animals). In R. B. Lee & I. DeVore (Eds.), *Kalahari Hunter-Gatherers: Studies of the !Kung San and Their Neighbors* (pp. 325–348). Harvard University Press.

Bonnichsen, B., Leeman, W. P., Honjo, N., McIntosh, W. C., & Godchaux, M. M. (2008). Miocene silicic volcanism in southwestern Idaho: Geochronology, geochemistry, and evolution of the central Snake River Plain. *Bulletin of Volcanology, 70,* 315–342. https://doi.org/10.1007/s00445-007-0141-6.

Bonnichsen, B., Leeman, W. P., Jenks, M. D., & Honjo, N. (1988). Geologic field trip guide to the Central and Western Snake River Plain, Idaho, emphasizing the silicic volcanic rocks. In P. K. Link & W. Hackett (Eds.), *Guidebook to the Geology of Central and Southern Idaho* (pp. 247–282). Idaho Geological Survey.

Bovet, P., & Benhamou, S. (1988). Spatial analysis of animals' movements using a correlated random walk model. *Journal of Theoretical Biology, 131,* 419–433. https://doi.org/10.1016/S0022-5193(88)80038-9.

Bowers, A. W., & Savage, C. N. (1962). *Primitive man on Browns Bench.* Idaho Bureau of Mines and Geology.

Brantingham, P. J. (2003). A neutral model of stone raw material procurement. *American Antiquity, 68,* 487–509.

Brantingham, P. J. (2006). Measuring forager mobility. *Current Anthropology, 47,* 435–459. https://doi.org/10.1086/503062.

Bronk Ramsey, C. (2021). *OxCal* (Version 4.4) [computer software]. https://c14.arch.ox.ac.uk/oxcal.html.

Bruce, P., & Bruce, A. (2017). *Practical statistics for data scientists: 50 essential concepts.* O'Reilly Media.

Brueseke, M. E., & Hart, W. K. (2008). *Geology and petrology of the Mid-Miocene Santa Rosa-Calico Volcanic Field, northern Nevada.* Nevada Bureau of Mines and Geology Bulletin 113.

Bryan, A. (1980). The stemmed point tradition: An early technological tradition in western North America. In L. B. Harten, C. N. Warren, & D. R. Tuohy (Eds.), *Anthropological Papers in Memory of Earl H. Swanson Jr.* (pp. 77–107). Idaho State Museum of Natural History.

Cann, J. R., & Renfrew, C. (1964). The characterization of obsidian and its application to the Mediterranean region. *Proceedings of the Prehistoric Society, 30,* 111–133. https://doi.org/10.1017/S0079497X00015097.

Cartwright, C. (1981). *Utah Antiquities Site Form: 42JB275.* Utah Department of Heritage and Arts.

Cathey, H. E., & Nash, B. P. (2004). The Cougar Point Tuff: Implications for thermochemical zonation and longevity of high-temperature, large-volume silicic magmas of the Miocene Yellowstone hotspot. *Journal of Petrology, 45,* 27–58. https://doi.org/10.1093/petrology/egg081.

Chapman, R., & Wylie, A. (2016). *Evidential Reasoning in Archaeology.* Bloomsbury Academic Publishing.

Chen, C. Y., & Maloof, A. C. (2017a). Dataset: Revisiting the deformed high shoreline of Lake Bonneville: Datasets and supplementary materials. *Quaternary Science Reviews.* https://doi.org/http://dx.doi.org/10.17632/fhvsfjx7j6.1#file-5ebe6271-3670-4e38-817c-1dd719f6348b.

Chen, C. Y., & Maloof, A. C. (2017b). Revisiting the deformed high shoreline of Lake Bonneville. *Quaternary Science Reviews, 159,* 169–189. https://doi.org/10.1016/j.quascirev.2016.12.019.

Christiansen, E. H., Bikun, J. V., Sheridan, M. F., & Burt, D. M. (1984). Geochemical evolution of topaz rhyolites from the Thomas Range and Spor Mountain, Utah. *American Mineralogist, 69,* 223–236.

Christiansen, E. H., Burt, D. M., & Sheridan, M. F. (1986). *The geology and geochemistry of Cenozoic topaz rhyolites from the western United States.* Geological Society of America Special Paper 205.

Christiansen, R. L., & Lipman, P. W. (1972). Cenozoic volcanism and plate-tectonic evolution of the western United States. II. Late Cenozoic. *Philosophical Transactions of the Royal Society of London, 271,* 249–284.

Clark, D. L., Oviatt, C. G., & Page, D. (2016). *Geologic map of Dugway Proving Ground and adjacent areas, Tooele County, Utah.* Utah Geologic Survey.

Coats, R. R. (1987). *Geology of Elko County, Nevada.* Nevada Bureau of Mines and Geology Bulletin 101.

Codling, E. A., Plank, M. J., & Benhamou, S. (2008). Random walk models in biology. *Interface: Journal of*

the Royal Society, 5, 813–834. https://doi.org/10.1098/rsif
.2008.0014.

Connolly, T. J. (1999). *Newberry Crater: A ten-thousand-year record of human occupation and environmental change in the basin-plateau borderlands.* University of Utah Anthropological Paper 121. University of Utah Press.

Conrad, O., Bechtel, B., Bock, M., Dietrich, H., Fischer, E., Gerlitz, L., Wehberg, J., Wichmann, V., & Boehner, J. (2015). System for Automated Geoscientific Analyses (SAGA) v. 7.4.0. *Geoscientific Model Development*, 8, 1991–2007. https://doi.org/doi:10.5194/gmd-8-1991-2015.

Costa-Cabral, M. C., & Burges, S. J. (1994). Digital Elevation Model Networks (DEMON): A model of flow over hillslopes for computation of contributing and dispersal areas. *Water Resources Research*, 30, 1681–1692. https://doi.org/10.1029/93WR03512.

Crafford, A. E. J. (2007). *Geologic Map of Nevada: U.S. Geological Survey Data Series 249* (pp. 1–46). U.S. Geological Survey.

Crecraft, H. R., Nash, W. P., & Evans, Jr., S. H. (1981). Late Cenozoic volcanism at Twin Peaks, Utah: Geology and petrology. *Journal of Geophysical Research*, 86, 10303–10320.

Crist, T. O., & Haefner, J. W. (1994). Spatial model of movement and foraging in harvester ants (*Pogonomyrmex*) (II): The roles of environment and seed dispersion. In *Journal of Theoretical Biology, 166*, 315–323. https://doi.org/10.1006/jtbi.1994.1028.

Currey, D. R., Atwood, G., & Mabey, D. R. (1984). *Major levels of Great Salt Lake and Lake Bonneville.* Utah Geological and Mineral Survey Map 73.

D'Avello, T., Brennan, J., & Loomis, L. (2016). *Modifying digital elevation models to develop more realistic wetness index layers for soil survey applications.* National Resources Conservation Service. https://www.nrcs.usda.gov/sites/default/files/2022-12/DEM-Wetness-Index.pdf.

Davis, L. G., Madsen, D. B., Becerra-Valdivia, L., Higham, T., Sisson, D. A., Skinner, S. M., Stueber, D., Nyers, A. J., Keen-Zebert, A., Neudorf, C., Cheyney, M., Izuho, M., Iizuka, F., Burns, S. R., Epps, C. W., Willis, S. C., & Buvit, I. (2019). Late Upper Paleolithic occupation at Cooper's Ferry, Idaho, USA, ~16,000 years ago. *Science, 365*, 891–897. https://doi.org/10.1126/science.aax9830.

Davis, L. G., Madsen, D. B., Sisson, D. A., Valdivia-Becerra, L., Higham, T., Stueber, D., Bean, D. W., Nyers, A. J., Carroll, A., Ryder, C., Sponheimer, M., Izuho, M., Iizuka, F., Li, G., Epps, C. W., & Halford, F. K. (2022). Dating of a large tool assemblage at the Cooper's Ferry site (Idaho, USA) to ~15,785 cal yr BP extends the age of stemmed points in the Americas. *Science Advances, 8*(51), eade1248. https://doi.org/10.1126/sciadv.ade1248.

Davis, L. G., Willis, S. C., & MacFarlan, S.J.. (2012). Lithic technology, cultural transmission, and the nature of the Far Western Paleoarchaic/Paleoindian Co-Tradition. In D. Rhode (Ed.), *Meeting at the margins* (pp. 47–64). University of Utah Press.

DeChambre, D. J. (1979). *Site survey form: 26EK1976.* Bureau of Land Management, Elko District.

Duke, D. G. (2011). *If the desert blooms: A technological perspective on Paleoindian ecology in the Great Basin from the Old River Bed, Utah* (Publication No. 894264178) [Doctoral dissertation, University of Nevada, Reno]. ProQuest Dissertations & Theses Global.

Duke, D. G. (2013). The exploded fine-grained volcanic sources of the desert west and the primacy of tool function in material selection. *North American Archaeologist, 34*, 323–354. https://doi.org/10.2190/NA.34.4.c.

Duke, D. G., & Young, D. C. (2007). Episodic permanence in Paleoarchaic basin selection and settlement. In K. E. Graf & D. N. Schmitt (Eds.), *Paleoindian or Paleoarchaic? Great Basin human ecology at the Pleistocene/ Holocene transition* (pp. 123–138). University of Utah Press.

Dyson-Hudson, R., & Smith, E. A. (1978). Human territoriality: An ecological reassessment. *American Anthropologist, 80*, 21–41.

Ellis, B. S., Branney, M. J., Barry, T. L., Barfod, D., Bindeman, I., Wolff, J. A., & Bonnichsen, B. (2012). Geochemical correlation of three large-volume ignimbrites from the Yellowstone hotspot track, Idaho, USA. *Bulletin of Volcanology, 74*, 261–277. https://doi.org/10.1007/s00445-011-0510-z.

Elston, R. G., & Budy, E. E. (Eds.). (1990). *The Archaeology of James Creek Shelter.* University of Utah Anthropological Papers 115. University of Utah Press.

Erlandson, J. M., Rick, T. C., Braje, T. J., Casperson, M., Culleton, B., Fulfrost, B., Garcia, T., Guthrie, D. A., Jew, N., Kennett, D. J., Moss, M. L., Reeder, L., Skinner, C., Watts, J., & Willis, L. (2011). Paleoindian seafaring, maritime technologies, and coastal foraging on California's Channel Islands. *Science, 331*, 1181–1185. https://doi.org/10.1126/science.1201477.

Esri. (2021a). *ArcGIS Desktop* (Version 10.8) [computer software]. Environmental Systems Research Institute.

Esri. (2021b). *Fill.* Retrieved November 1, 2021, from https://desktop.arcgis.com/en/arcmap/latest/tools/spatial-analyst-toolbox/fill.htm.

Esri. (2021c). *How Focal Statistics works.* Retrieved November 1, 2021, from https://desktop.arcgis.com/en/arcmap/latest/tools/spatial-analyst-toolbox/how-focal-statistics-works.htm.

Esri. (2021d). *How Sink works.* Retrieved November 1, 2021, from https://desktop.arcgis.com/en/arcmap/latest/tools/spatial-analyst-toolbox/how-sink-works.htm.

Esri. (2022a). *Path distance (spatial analyst).* Retrieved May 2, 2022, from https://pro.arcgis.com/en/pro-app/2.8/tool-reference/spatial-analyst/path-distance.htm.

Esri. (2022b). *Cost distance.* Retrieved May 2, 2022, from https://pro.arcgis.com/en/pro-app/2.8/tool-reference/spatial-analyst/cost-distance.htm.

Estes, M. B. (2009). *Paleoindian occupations in the Great Basin: A comparative study of lithic technological organization, mobility, and landscape use from Jakes Valley, Nevada* (Publication No.304943187) [Master's thesis, University of Nevada, Reno]. ProQuest Dissertations & Theses Global.

Evans, Jr., S. H., Nash, W. P., & University of Utah, Department of Geology and Geography. (1978). *Quaternary rhyolite from the Mineral Mountains, Utah, USA*. All U.S. Government Documents (Utah Regional Depository).

Everts, M. L. (1991). *Cudahy Mine*. Mineral Resources Data System (MRDS), U.S. Geological Survey. https://mrdata.usgs.gov/mrds/show.php?labno=10101543.

Fairfield, J., & Leymarie, P. (1991). Drainage networks from grid digital elevation models. *Water Resources Research*, 27, 709–717. https://doi.org/10.1029/90WR02658.

Fike, R. E. (1974). *Antiquities site inventory: 42BE88*. Bureau of Land Management.

Fisher, N. I. (1993). *Statistical Analysis of Circular Data*. Cambridge University Press.

Fitzhugh, B. (2004). Colonizing the Kodiak Archipelago: Trends in raw material use and lithic technologies at the Tanginak Spring site. *Arctic Anthropology*, 41, 14–40. https://doi.org/10.1353/arc.2011.0076.

Fitzhugh, B., & Trusler, A. K. (2009). Experimentation and innovation in the archaeological record: A case study in technological evolution from Kodiak, Alaska. In S. Shennan (Ed.), *Pattern and Process in Cultural Evolution* (pp. 203–220). University of California Press.

Ford, A. (2011). Learning the lithic landscape: using raw material sources to investigate Pleistocene colonisation in the Ivane Valley, Papua New Guinea. *Archaeology in Oceania*, 46, 42–53.

Foster, C., & Foster, D. (2000). *The Great Dance: A Hunter's Story*. Aardvark Pictures/Earthrise. https://www.cultureunplugged.com/documentary/watch-online/filmedia/play/2419/The-Great-Dance.

Fowler, B. L. (2014). *Obsidian toolstone conveyance: Southern Idaho forager mobility* (Publication No. 1659783206) [Master's thesis, Utah State University]. ProQuest Dissertations & Theses Global.

Freeman, T. G. (1991). Calculating catchment area with divergent flow based on a regular grid. *Computers and Geosciences*, 17, 413–422. https://doi.org/10.1016/0098-3004(91)90048-I.

Freund, K. P., Johnson, L. R. M., & Duke, D. (2021, April 30–May 2). *The character and use of Ferguson Wash obsidian in Eastern Great Basin prehistory* [Poster presentation]. International Obsidian Conference 2021, virtual. http://arf.berkeley.edu/files/attachments/pages/IOC_Posters2021.pdf.

Gallagher, J. G. (1979). *The archaeology of the Sheepeater Battleground and Redfish Overhang sites*. U.S.D.A Forest Service, Intermountain Region.

Geologic Map of Nevada—Data series 249. (2021). Nevada Bureau of Mines and Geology Open Data, University of Nevada. https://data-nbmg.opendata.arcgis.com/.

GitHub. (2021). GitHub [computer software repository platform], https://github.com/about.

Goebel, T., Holmes, A., Keene, J. L., & Coe, M. M. (2018). Technological change from the Terminal Pleistocene through Early Holocene in the eastern Great Basin, USA: The record from Bonneville Estates Rockshelter. In E. Robinson, & F. Sellet (Eds.), *Lithic technological organization and paleoenvironmental changes. Global and diachronic perspectives, studies in human ecology and adaptation 9* (pp. 235–261). Springer. https://doi.org/10.1007/978-3-319-64407-3_11.

Goebel, T., and Keene, Joshua L. (2013). Are Great Basin stemmed points as old as Clovis in the Intermountain West? In N. J. Parezo and J. C. Janetski (Eds.), *Archaeology in the Great Basin and Southwest: Papers in honor of Don D. Fowler*, (35–60). University of Utah Press.

Golledge, R. G. (2003). Human wayfinding and cognitive maps. In M. Rockman & J. Steele (Eds.), *Colonization of unfamiliar landscapes: The archaeology of adaptation* (pp. 25–43). Routledge.

Google Earth Pro. (2020). Google LLC. https://www.google.com/earth/.

Graf, K. E. (1995). *Paleoindian technological provisioning in the northwestern Great Basin* (Publication No. 205436522) [Master's thesis, University of Nevada, Reno]. ProQuest Dissertations & Theses Global.

Graf, K. E. (2007). Stratigraphy and chronology of the Pleistocene to Holocene transition at Bonneville Estates Rockshelter, eastern Great Basin. In K. E. Graf & D. N. Schmitt (Eds.), *Paleoindian or Paleoarchaic? Great Basin human ecology at the Pleistocene/Holocene transition* (pp. 82–104). University of Utah Press.

Grayson, D. K. (1993). *The desert's past: A natural prehistory of the Great Basin*. Smithsonian Institution Press.

Grayson, D. K. (2011). *The Great Basin: A natural prehistory*. University of California Press.

Griffin, J. B., Gordus, A. A., & Wright, G. A. (1969). Identification of the sources of Hopewellian obsidian in the Middle West. *American Antiquity*, 34, 1–14.

Haarklau, L., Johnson, L., & Wagner, D. L. (2005). *Fingerprints in the Great Basin: The Nellis Air Force Base Regional Obsidian Sourcing Study*. Prewitt and Associates, Austin. Submitted to Nellis Air Force Base, Nevada.

Hart, W. S., Quade, J., Madsen, D. B., Kaufman, D. S., & Oviatt, C. G. (2004). The $^{87}Sr/^{86}Sr$ ratios of lacustrine carbonates and lake-level history of the Bonneville paleolake system. *Bulletin of the Geological Society of America*, 116, 1107–1119. https://doi.org/10.1130/B25330.1.

Haynes, G. (2007). Paleoindian or Paleoarchaic? In K. E. Graf & D. N. Schmitt (Eds.), *Paleoindian or Paleoarchaic? Great Basin human ecology at the Pleistocene/Holocene transition* (pp. 251–258). University of Utah Press.

Heizer, R. F., & Hester, T. R. (1978). *Great Basin projectile points: Forms and chronology*. Ballena Press Publications in Archaeology, Ethnology and History, No. 10.

Hildebrandt, W. R., Colligan, K., & Bloomer, W. (2016). Flaked stone production patterns. In W. Hildebrandt, K. McGuire, K., J. King, A. Ruby, & D. C. Young (Eds.), *Prehistory of Nevada's Northern Tier: Archaeological investigations along the Ruby Pipeline* (pp. 237–260). American Museum of Natural History Anthropological Papers 101.

Hintze, L. F. (1988). *Geologic history of Utah*. Brigham Young University Geology Studies Special Publication 7.

Hintze, L. F., Davis, F. D., Rowley, P. D., Cunningham, C. G.,

Steven, T. A., Willis, G. C., Hintze, L. F., Davis, F. D., Rowley, P. D., Cunningham, C. G., Steven, T. A., & Willis, G. C. (2003). *Geologic map of the Richfield 30' x 60' quadrangle, southeast Millard County and parts of Beaver, Piute, and Sevier Counties.* Utah Geological Survey Map 195. https://doi.org/10.34191/m-195dm.

Hintze, L. F., Willis, G. C., Laes, D. Y. M., Sprinkel, D. A., & Brown, K. D. (2000). *Digital geologic map of Utah.* Utah Geological Survey. https://geology.utah.gov/apps/int geomap/.

Hockett, B. S. (1995). Chronology of Elko Series and split stemmed points from Northeastern Nevada. *Journal of California and Great Basin Anthropology, 17,* 41–53.

Hockett, B. S. (2015). The zooarchaeology of Bonneville Estates Rockshelter: 13,000 years of Great Basin hunting strategies. *Journal of Archaeological Science: Reports, 2,* 291–301. https://doi.org/10.1016/j.jasrep.2015.02.011.

Holmer, R. N. (1997). Volcanic glass utilization in Eastern Idaho. *Tebiwa, 26,* 186–204.

Hughes, R. E. (1986). *Diachronic variability in obsidian procurement patterns in Northeastern California and South-central Oregon.* University of California Press.

Hughes, R. E. (1990). Obsidian sources at James Creek Shelter, and trace element geochemistry of some northeastern Nevada volcanic glass. In R. G. Elston & E. E. Budy (Eds.), *The archaeology of James Creek Shelter* (pp. 297–305). University of Utah Anthropological Papers 115.

Hughes, R. E. (2007a). Provenance analysis of obsidian. In G. C. Frison, D. N. Walker, & D. R. Bach (Eds.), *Medicine Lodge Creek: Holocene archaeology of the Eastern Big Horn Basin, Wyoming* (Vol. 1). Clovis Press.

Hughes, R. E. (2007b). The geologic sources for obsidian artifacts from Minnesota archaeological sites. *Minnesota Archaeologist, 66,* 53–68.

Hughes, R. E. (2013). Long-term continuity and change in obsidian conveyance at Danger Cave, Utah. In N. J. Parezo & J. C. Janetski (Eds.), *Archaeology in the Great Basin and Southwest: Papers in honor of Don D. Fowler* (pp. 210–225). University of Utah Press.

Hughes, R. E., & Nelson, F. W. (1987). New findings on obsidian source utilization in Iowa. *Plains Anthropologist, 32,* 313–316.

Hughes, R. E., & Smith, R. L. (1993). Archaeology, geology, and geochemistry in obsidian provenance studies. *Special Paper of the Geological Society of America, 283,* 79–91. https://doi.org/10.1130/SPE283-p79.

Hull, K. L. (1994). Obsidian studies. In *Kern River Pipeline Cultural Resources Data Recovery Report: Utah* (Vol. 1, pp. 7-1-7-63). Dames & Moore. Report Submitted to the Federal Regulatory Commission, Washington, DC.

Hull, K. L. (2010). *Research design for obsidian hydration chronology-building in Lincoln County, Nevada.* USDI Bureau of Land Management.

Hunt, C. B. (1967). *Physiography of the United States.* W. H. Freeman.

Hutchins, J., & Simons, D. D. (2000). Obsidian studies in the Truckee Meadows, Nevada. *Journal of California and Great Basin Anthropology, 22,* 151–163.

Jack, R. N., & Heizer, R. F. (1968). "Finger-printing" of some Mesoamerican obsidian artifacts. *Contributions of the University of California Archaeological Research Facility, 5,* 81–100.

Jackson, R., Spidell, J., Kennelly-Spidell, D., & Kovak, A. (2009). *A historic context for Native American procurement of obsidian in the state of Utah.* Pacific Legacy, Cameron Park, California. Submitted to Logan Simpson Design, Salt Lake City, Utah.

Jammalamadaka, S. R., & SenGupta, A. (1996). *Topics in circular statistics.* World Scientific Publishing Company.

Jander, R. (1957). Die optische Richtungsorientierung der roten Waldameise (Formica rufa L.). *Zeitschrift Fur Vergleichende Physiologie, 40,* 162–238.

Jenkins, D. L., Davis, L. G., Stafford, T. W., Campos, P. F., Connolly, T. J., Cummings, L. S., Hofreiter, M., Hockett, B. S., Mcdonough, K., Luthe, I., Grady, P. W. O., Swisher, M. E., White, F., Yates, B., Ii, R. M. Y., Yost, C., & Willerslev, E. (2013). Geochronology, archaeological context, and DNA at the Paisley Caves. In K. E. Graf, C. V. Ketron, & M. R. Waters (Eds.), *Paleoamerican odyssey* (pp. 485–510). Texas A & M University Press.

Jenkins, D. L., Davis, L. G., Stafford, T. W., Campos, P. F., Hockett, B. S., Jones, G. T., Cummings, L. S., Yost, C., Connolly, T. J., Yohe, R. M., Gibbons, S. C., Raghavan, M., Rasmussen, M., Paijmans, J. L. A., Hofreiter, M., Kemp, B. M., Barta, J. L., Monroe, C., Gilbert, M. T. P., & Willerslev, E. (2012). Clovis age Western Stemmed projectile points and human coprolites at the Paisley Caves. *Science, 337,* 223–228. https://doi.org/10.1126 /science.1218443.

Jennings, J. D. (1957). *Danger Cave.* University of Utah Anthropological Papers 27. University of Utah Press.

Jensen, E. (2004). Kane Springs fluted point and a short literary digression. *In Situ: Newsletter of the Nevada Archaeological Association, 8*(4), 12–16.

Jensen, E. (2005). Flutes and glyphs and life lessons. *In Situ: Newsletter of the Nevada Archaeological Association, 9*(2), 10–13.

Jenson, S. K., & Domingue, J. O. (1988). Extracting topographic structure from digital elevation data for geographic information system analysis. *Photogrammetric Engineering and Remote Sensing, 54,* 1593–1600.

Johnson, L., & Wagner, D. L. (2005). Obsidian source characterization study. In L. Haarklau, L. Johnson, & D. L. Wagner (Eds.), *Fingerprints in the Great Basin: The Nellis Air Force Base Regional Obsidian Sourcing Study* (pp. 25–50). U.S. Army Corps of Engineers, Fort Worth District.

Jones, G. T., Bailey, D. G., & Beck, C. (1997). Source provenance of andesite artefacts using non-destructive XRF analysis. *Journal of Archaeological Science, 24,* 929–943. https://doi.org/10.1006/jasc.1996.0172.

Jones, G. T., & Beck, C. (1990). An obsidian hydration chronology of Late Pleistocene-Early Holocene surface assemblages from Butte Valley, Nevada. *Journal of California and Great Basin Anthropology, 12,* 84–100.

Jones, G. T., Beck, C., Jones, E. E., & Hughes, R. E. (2003). Lithic source use and Paleoarchaic foraging territories in the Great Basin. *American Antiquity, 68,* 5–38. https://doi.org/10.2307/3557031.

Kareiva, P. M., & Shigesada, N. (1983). Analyzing insect movement as a correlated random walk. *Oecologia, 56*(2), 234–238.

Kato, S., & Jones, M. C. (2013). An extended family of circular distributions related to wrapped Cauchy distributions via Brownian motion. *Bernoulli, 19,* 154–171. https://doi.org/10.3150/11-BEJ397.

Kellner, P. (2022). *England.* Britannica. https://www.britannica.com/place/England.

Kelly, R. L. (1978). *Paleo-Indian Settlement Patterns at Pleistocene Lake Tonopah, Nevada.* [Unpublished bachelor of arts thesis]. Cornell University.

Kelly, R. L. (1995). *The foraging spectrum: Diversity in hunter-gatherer lifeways.* Smithsonian Institution Press.

Kelly, R. L. (2003a). Colonization of new land by hunter-gatherers: Expectations and implications based on ethnographic data. In M. Rockman & J. Steele (Eds.), *Colonization of unfamiliar landscapes: The archaeology of adaptation* (pp. 44–58). Routledge.

Kelly, R. L. (2003b). Maybe we do know when people first came to North America; and what does it mean if we do? *Quaternary International, 109,* 133–145. https://doi.org/10.1016/S1040-6182(02)00209-4.

Kelly, R. L., & Todd, L. C. (1988). Coming into the country: Early Paleoindian hunting and mobility. *American Antiquity, 53,* 231–244.

Kent, J. T., & Tyler, D. E. (1988). Maximum likelihood estimation for the wrapped Cauchy distribution. *Journal of Applied Statistics, 15,* 247–254.

King, J. (2016). Obsidian conveyance patterns. In W. Hildebrant, K. McGuire, J. King, A. Ruby, & D. C. Young (Eds.), *Prehistory of Nevada's Northern Tier: Archaeological investigations along the Ruby Pipeline* (pp. 303–327). American Museum of Natural History Anthropological Papers No. 101.

Kirchhoff, M. D. (2009). Material agency: A theoretical framework for ascribing agency to material culture. *Techne: Research in Philosophy & Technology, 13,* 206–220.

Kitchel, N. R. (2018). Questioning the visibility of the landscape learning process during the Paleoindian colonization of northeastern North America. *Journal of Archaeological Science: Reports, 17,* 871–878. https://doi.org/10.1016/j.jasrep.2016.10.009.

Kulkarni, A., Chong, D., & Batarseh, F. A. (2020). Foundations of data imbalance and solutions for a data democracy. In Feras A. Batarseh & Ruixin Yang (Eds.), *Data democracy: At the nexus of artificial intelligence, software development, and knowledge engineering* (pp. 83–106). Academic Press. https://doi.org/10.1016/B978-0-12-818366-3.00005-8.

Latham, T. S., Sutton, P. A., & Verosub, K. L. (1992). Nondestructive XRF characterization of basaltic artifacts from Truckee, California. *Geoarchaeology, 7,* 81–101. https://doi.org/10.1002/gea.3340070202.

LaValley, S. J. (2013). *Late Holocene toolstone procurement and land-use strategies in the Black Rock Desert and High Rock Country of northwest Nevada* (Publication No. 1416355237) [Master's thesis, University of Nevada, Reno]. ProQuest Dissertations & Theses Global.

Le Bas, M. J. (1986). A chemical classification of volcanic rocks based on the total alkali-silica diagram. *Journal of Petrology, 27,* 745–750.

Le Bas, M. J., & Streckeisen, A. L. (1991). The IUGS systematics of igneous rocks. *Journal of the Geological Society, 148,* 825–833. https://doi.org/10.1144/gsjgs.148.5.0825.

Lehoczky, J. P. (2015). Distributions, statistical: Special and continuous. In *International encyclopedia of the social & behavioral sciences* (Vol. 6, 2nd ed., pp. 575–579). Elsevier. https://doi.org/10.1016/B978-0-08-097086-8.42115-X.

Lewis, R. S., Link, P. K., Stanford, L. R., & Long, S. P. (2012). *Geologic map of Idaho.* Idaho Geological Survey. https://www.idahogeology.org/Product/M-9.

Lindsey, D. A. (1979). *Geologic map and cross-section of Tertiary rocks in the Thomas Range and northern Drum Mountains, Juab Country, Utah.* U.S. Geological Survey Miscellaneous Investigation Map I-1176, scale 1:62,500. U.S. Geological Survey.

Lindsey, D. A. (1982). Tertiary volcanic rocks and uranium in the Thomas Range and northern Drum Mountains, Juab County, Utah. *U.S. Geological Survey Professional Papers, 1221.* https://doi.org/10.3133/pp1221.

Lindsey, D. A. (1998). *Slides of the fluorspar, beryllium, and uranium deposits at Spor Mountain, Utah.* U.S. Geological Survey. https://pubs.usgs.gov/of/1998/ofr-98-0524/HOME.HTM.

Link, Paul K. (2002). *Geology of Oneida County, Idaho.* Idaho State University, Geosciences Dept. https://digitalatlas.cose.isu.edu/counties/geomaps/geomap.htm.

Lipman, P. W., Rowley, P. D., Mehnert, H. H., Evans, Jr., S. H., Nash, W. P., Brown, F. H., Izett, G. A., Naeser, C. W., & Friedman, I. (1978). Pleistocene rhyolite of the Mineral Mountains, Utah—Geothermal and archaeological significance. *Journal of Research of the U.S. Geological Society, 6*(1), 133–147.

Llobera, M. (2001). Building past landscape perception with GIS: Understanding topographic prominence. *Journal of Archaeological Science, 28,* 1005–1014. https://doi.org/10.1006/jasc.2001.0720.

Logan, B., Hughes, R. E., & Henning, D. R. (2001). Western Oneota obsidian: Sources and implications. *Plains Anthropologist, 46,* 55–64. https://doi.org/10.1080/2052546.2001.11932057.

Louderback, L. A., Grayson, D. K., & Llobera, M. (2011). Middle-Holocene climates and human population densities in the Great Basin, western USA. *The Holocene, 21*(2), 366–373. https://doi.org/10.1177/0959683610374888.

Madsen, D. B. (2007). The Paleoarchaic to Archaic transition in the Great Basin. In K. E. Graf & D. N. Schmitt (Eds.), *Paleoindian or Paleoarchaic? Great Basin human ecology at the Pleistocene/Holocene transition* (pp. 3–20). University of Utah Press.

Madsen, D. B. (2016). The early human occupation of the Bonneville Basin. In C. G. Oviatt & J. F. Shroder (Eds.), *Lake Bonneville, a scientific update* (pp. 504–525). Developments in Earth Surface Processes 20. Elsevier. https://doi.org/10.1016/B978-0-444-63590-7.00018-4.

Madsen, D. B., Oviatt, C. G., & Young, D. C. (2015). Old River Bed Delta Geomorphology and Chronology. In D. B. Madsen, D. N. Schmitt, & D. Page (Eds.), *The Paleoarchaic occupation of the Old River Bed delta* (pp. 30–60). University of Utah Press.

Madsen, D. B., & Schmitt, D. N. (2005). *Buzz-cut Dune and Fremont foraging at the margin of horticulture.* University of Utah Press.

Madsen, D. B., Schmitt, D. N., & Page, D. (Eds.). (2015). *The Paleoarchaic Occupation of the Old River Bed delta.* University of Utah Press.

Mandryk, C. A. S. (2003). Forward. In M. Rockman & J. Steele (Eds.), *Colonization of unfamiliar landscapes: The archaeology of adaptation* (pp. xiii–xv). Routledge.

Mardia, K. V., & Jupp, P. E. (2000). *Directional Statistics.* Wiley.

Mark, D. M. (1988). *Modelling in geomorphological systems.* John Wiley.

Marshall, R. R. (1961). Devitrification of natural glass. *Geological Society of America Bulletin, 72,* 1493–1520.

Maurer, R. E. (1970). *Geology of the Cedar Mountains, Tooele County, Utah* (Publication No. 288081513) [Doctoral dissertation, University of Utah]. ProQuest Dissertations & Theses Global.

McDonough, K. N., R. L. Rosencrance, & J. E. Pratt (Eds.). (2024). *Current perspectives on stemmed and fluted technologies in the American Far West.* University of Utah Press.

Meltzer, D. J. (2002). What do you do when no one's been there before? Thoughts on the exploration and colonization of new lands. In N. G. Jablonski (Ed.), *The first Americans: the Pleistocene colonization of the New World* (pp. 27–58). Memoirs of the California Academy of Sciences No. 27.

Meltzer, D. J. (2003). Lessons in landscape learning. In M. Rockman & J. Steele (Eds.), *Colonization of unfamiliar landscapes: The archaeology of adaptation* (pp. 222–239). Routledge.

Meltzer, D. J. (2021). *First Peoples in a New World: Populating Ice Age America* (2nd ed.). Cambridge University Press.

Miliaresis, G. C., & Argialas, D. P. (2000). Extraction and delineation of alluvial fans from digital elevation models and Landsat Thematic Mapper images. *Photogrammetric Engineering and Remote Sensing, 66,* 1093–1101.

Miller, B. A., & Juilleret, J. (2020). The colluvium and alluvium problem: Historical review and current state of definitions. *Earth-Science Reviews, 209,* 103316. https://doi.org/10.1016/j.earscirev.2020.103316.

Monnereau, L. R., Ellis, B. S., Szymanowski, D., Bachmann, O., & Guillong, M. (2021). Obsidian pyroclasts in the Yellowstone-Snake River Plain ignimbrites are dominantly juvenile in origin. *Bulletin of Volcanology, 83*(4), 1–13. https://doi.org/10.1007/s00445-021-01448-1.

Montgomery, J. (1981). *Utah Antiquities Site Form: 42JB296.* Utah Department of Heritage and Arts.

Moore, J. (2009). *Great Basin tool-stone sources.* NDOT Obsidian and Tool-Stone Sourcing Project: 2002 Progress Report. Report on file, Nevada Department of Transportation, Environmental Services Division, Cultural Resources Section, Carson City.

Moore, W. J., & Sorensen, M. L. (1979). *Geologic map of the Tooele 1° x 2° quadrangle, Utah.* U.S. Geological Survey Miscellaneous Investigations Series Map I-1132, scale 1:250,000.

Morgan, L. A., & McIntosh, W. C. (2005). Timing and development of the Heise volcanic field, Snake River Plain, Idaho, western USA. *Bulletin of the Geological Society of America, 117,* 288–306. https://doi.org/10.1130/B25519.1.

Mullins, D., Karpinski, M., Adams, J., Karpinski, E., & Grimes, A. (2009). *A cultural resources survey of 6,202 acres within the Black Rock Obsidian Source Area of the Milford Flat ESR Project, Millard County, Utah.* Logan Simpson Design, Salt Lake City. On file with Utah Division of State History, State Project No. U-07-Ll-1266b,i,s.

Murphy, T. (1981). *Cultural Resources Inventory Record: Site 26EK3870.* U.S. Department of the Interior, Bureau of Land Management.

Nangia, V. (2010). Evaluation of a GIS-based watershed modeling approach for sediment transport. *International Journal of Agricultural and Biological Engineering, 3,* 43–53. https://doi.org/10.3965/j.issn.1934-6344.2010.03.043-053.

Nelson, F. W. (1984). X-ray fluorescence analysis of some western North American obsidians. In R. E. Hughes (Ed.), *Obsidian Studies in the Great Basin* (pp. 27–62). Archaeological Research Center, University of California, Berkeley.

Nelson, F. W., & Holmes, R. D. (1979). *Trace element analysis of obsidian sources and artifacts from western Utah.* Antiquities Section, Utah Division of State History.

Newlander, K. (2012). *Exchange, embedded procurement, and hunter-gatherer mobility: A case study from the North American Great Basin.* (Publication No. 1026968975). [Doctoral dissertation, University of Michigan]. ProQuest Dissertations & Theses Global.

Nielsen, G. (1990). *Intermountain Antiquities Computer System: 42JB440.* Utah Department of Heritage and Arts.

Nielson, A. (1990). *Intermountain Antiquities Computer System: 42JB450.* Utah Department of Heritage and Arts.

Norini, G., Clara, M., Jill, I., Aquino, D. T., Mahar, A., & Lagmay, F. (2016). Delineation of alluvial fans from Digital Elevation Models with a GIS algorithm for the geomorphological mapping of the Earth and Mars. *Geomorphology, 273,* 134–149. https://doi.org/10.1016/j.geomorph.2016.08.010.

Novak, S. W. (1984). Eruptive history of the rhyolitic Kane Springs Wash volcanic center, Nevada. *Journal of Geophysical Research, 89,* 8603–8615. https://doi.org/10.1029/JB089iB10p08603.

Novak, S. W. (1985). *Geology and geochemical evolution of the Kane Springs Wash volcanic center, Lincoln County,*

Nevada (Publication No. 303400246) [Doctoral dissertation, Stanford University]. ProQuest Dissertations & Theses Global.

Novak, S. W., & Mahood, G. A. (1986). Rise and fall of a basalt-trachyte-rhyolite magma system at the Kane Springs Wash Caldera, Nevada. *Contribution to Mineralogy and Petrology, 94,* 352–373.

O'Callaghan, J. F., & Mark, D. M. (1984). The extraction of ordered vector drainage networks from elevation data. *Computer Vision, Graphics, and Image Processing, 28,* 323–344.

O'Connor, J. (2016). The Bonneville Flood—A veritable débâcle. In C. G. Oviatt & J. F. Shroder (Eds.), *Lake Bonneville, a scientific update* (pp. 105–126). Developments in Earth Surface Processes 20. Elsevier. https://doi.org/10.1016/B978-0-444-63590-7.00006-8.

Oviatt, C. G., & Jewell, P. W. (2016). The Bonneville shoreline: Reconsidering Gilbert's interpretation. In C. G. Oviatt & J. F. Shroder (Eds.), *Lake Bonneville, a scientific update* (pp. 88–104). Developments in Earth Surface Processes 20. Elsevier. https://doi.org/10.1016/B978-0-444-63590-7.00005-6.

Oviatt, C. G., Madsen, D. B., & Schmitt, D. N. (2003). Late Pleistocene and early Holocene rivers and wetlands in the Bonneville basin of western North America. *Quaternary Research, 60,* 200–210. https://doi.org/10.1016/S0033-5894(03)00084-X.

Oviatt, C. G., & Shroder, J. F. (2016). Introduction. In C. G. Oviatt & J. F. Shroder (Eds.), *Lake Bonneville, a scientific update* (pp. xxv–xxxvi). Developments in Earth Surface Processes 20. Elsevier. https://doi.org/10.1016/B978-0-444-63590-7.09993-5.

Page, D. (2008). *Fine-grained volcanic toolstone sources and early use in the Bonneville Basin of Western Utah and Eastern Nevada* (Publication No. 304536340) [Doctoral dissertation, University of Nevada, Reno]. ProQuest Dissertations & Theses Global.

Page, D. (2015a). Results of XRF and pXRF analysis, supplemental digital material. In D. B. Madsen, D. N. Schmitt, & D. Page (Eds.), *The Paleoarchaic occupation of the Old River Bed delta.* University of Utah Press. https://uofupress.lib.utah.edu/wp-content/uploads/sites/21/2018/01/Chapter-6-SDM-Results-of-XRF-and-PXRF-Analysis.pdf.

Page, D. (2015b). Source assignment tables, supplemental digital material. In D. B. Madsen, D. N. Schmitt, & D. Page (Eds.), *The Paleoarchaic occupation of the Old River Bed delta.* University of Utah Press. https://uofupress.lib.utah.edu/wp-content/uploads/sites/21/2018/01/Chapter-6-SDM-Source-Assignment-Tables.pdf.

Page, D., & Bacon, S. (2016). *Browns Bench predictive modeling, resampling, and geochemical characterization across portions of Idaho, Nevada, and Utah.* Desert Research Institute, Reno, Nevada.

Page, D., & Duke, D. G. (2015). Toolstone sourcing, lithic resource use, and Paleoarchaic mobility in the western Bonneville Basin. In D. B. Madsen, D. N. Schmitt, &

D. Page (Eds.), *The Paleoarchaic occupation of the Old River Bed delta* (pp. 209–236). University of Utah Press.

Page, D., & Skinner, C. E. (2008, October 8–11). *Obsidian source use at Danger Cave* [Poster presentation]. The 31st Biennial Great Basin Anthropological Conference, Portland, Oregon.

Patlak, C. S. (1953). Random walk with persistence and external bias. *Bulletin of Mathematical Biophysics, 15,* 311–338. https://doi.org/10.1007/BF02476407.

Pendleton, L. S. (1979). *Lithic technology in early Nevada assemblages* (Publication No. 303019230) [Master's thesis, California State University, Long Beach]. ProQuest Dissertations & Theses Global.

Pontzer, H., Raichlen, D. A., Mabulla, A. Z. P., Wood, B. M., Gordon, A. D., & Marlowe, F. W. (2014). Evidence of Lévy walk foraging patterns in human hunter-gatherers. *Proceedings of the National Academy of Sciences, 111,* 728–733. https://doi.org/10.1073/pnas.1318616111.

Project Jupyter. (2021). https://jupyter.org/.

Python Software Foundation. (2021). *Python computer language* (Version 3.7.6) [computer software]. https://www.python.org/.

Qin, C. Z., Zhu, A. X., Pei, T., Li, B. L., Scholten, T., Behrens, T., & Zhou, C. H. (2011). An approach to computing topographic wetness index based on maximum downslope gradient. *Precision Agriculture, 12,* 32–43. https://doi.org/10.1007/s11119-009-9152-y.

Quinn, P., Beven, K., Chevallier, P., & Planchon, O. (1991). The prediction of hillslope flow paths for distributed hydrological modelling using digital terrain models. *Hydrological Processes, 5,* 59–79.

Raymond, A. W. (1981a). *Utah Antiquities Site Form: 42JB276.* Utah Department of Heritage and Arts.

Raymond, A. W. (1981b). *Utah Antiquities Site Form: 42JB277.* Utah Department of Heritage and Arts.

Regnier, J. (1960). Cenozoic geology in the vicinity of Carlin, Nevada. *Bulletin of the Geological Society of America, 71,* 1180–1210.

Reid, K. C. (2014). Through the glass, darkly: Patterns of obsidian and fine grained volcanic toolstone acquisition on the Southern Plateau. In D. H. MacDonald, W. Andrefsky Jr., & P.-L. Yu (Eds.), *Lithics in the West: Using lithic analysis to solve archaeological problems in western North America* (pp. 97–119). University of Montana Press.

Reid, K. C., Hughes, R. E., Root, M. J., & Rondeau, M. F. (2015). Clovis in Idaho: An update on its distribution, technology, and chronology. In A. M. Smallwood & T. A. Jennings (Eds.), *Clovis: On the edge of a new understanding* (pp. 53–81). Texas A&M University Press.

Reimer, P. J., Austin, W. E. N., Bard, E., Bayliss, A., Blackwell, P. G., Bronk Ramsey, C., Butzin, M., Cheng, H., Edwards, R. L., Friedrich, M., Grootes, P. M., Guilderson, T. P., Hajdas, I., Heaton, T. J., Hogg, A. G., Hughen, K. A., Kromer, B., Manning, S. W., Muscheler, R., … Talamo, S. (2020). The IntCal20 Northern Hemisphere Radiocarbon Age Calibration Curve

(0–55 cal kBP). *Radiocarbon, 62*, 725–757. https://doi.org/10.1017/RDC.2020.41.

Reynolds, A. M. (2010). Bridging the gulf between correlated random walks and Lévy walks: Autocorrelation as a source of Lévy walk movement patterns. *Interface: Journal of the Royal Society, 7*, 1753–1758. https://doi.org/10.1098/rsif.2010.0292.

Rhode, D., Goebel, T., Graf, K. E., Hockett, B. S., Jones, K. T., Madsen, D. B., Oviatt, C. G., & Schmitt, D. N. (2005). Latest Pleistocene–early Holocene human occupation and paleoenvironmental change in the Bonneville Basin, Utah–Nevada. In J. L. Pederson & C. M. Dehler (Eds.), *Field Guide 6: Interior Western United States* (pp. 211–230). Geological Society of America.

Rice, D. G. (1972). *The Windust phase in lower Snake River region prehistory* (Publication No. 302641955) [Doctoral dissertation, Washington State University]. ProQuest Dissertations & Theses Global.

Rockman, M. (2003). Knowledge and learning in the archaeology of colonization. In M. Rockman & J. Steele (Eds.), *Colonization of unfamiliar landscapes: The archaeology of adaptation* (pp. 3–24). Routledge.

Rockman, M. (2009). Landscape learning in relation to evolutionary theory. In A. M. Prentiss, I. Kuijt, & J. C. Chatters (Eds.), *Macroevolution in human prehistory: Evolutionary theory and processual archaeology* (pp. 51–71). Springer. https://doi.org/10.1007/978-1-4419-0682-3.

Rockman, M. (2013). Apprentice to the environment: Hunter-gatherers and landscape learning. In W. Wendrich (Ed.), *Archaeology and apprenticeship: Body knowledge, identity, and communities of practice* (pp. 99–118). University of Arizona Press.

Rockman, M., & Steele, J. (Eds.). (2003). *Colonization of unfamiliar landscapes: The archaeology of adaptation.* Routledge.

Roebroeks, W. (2003). Landscape learning and the earliest peopling of Europe. In M. Rockman & J. Steele (Eds.), *Colonization of unfamiliar landscapes: The archaeology of adaptation* (pp. 99–115). Routledge.

Rogers, M. J. (1939). *Early lithic industries of the Lower Basin of the Colorado River and adjacent desert areas.* San Diego Museum Papers 3.

Rosencrance, R. L. (2019). *Assessing the chronological variation within Western Stemmed Tradition projectile points* (Publication No. 2280627007) [Master's thesis, University of Nevada, Reno]. ProQuest Dissertations & Theses Global.

Rosencrance, Richard L., Daron Duke, Amanda J. Hartman, and Andrew Hoskins (2024). Western Stemmed Tradition projectile point chronology in the Intermountain West. In K. N. McDonough, R. L. Rosencrance, and J. E. Pratt (Eds.), *Current perspectives on stemmed and fluted technologies of the American Far West* (pp. 21–58). University of Utah Press.

Rowley, P. D., Lytle, F. W., Lytle, M. B., & Stever, K. R. (2002). *Geology of the Modena obsidian source, Prohibition Flat area, Lincoln County, Nevada.* Report on file at Bureau of Land Management, Ely Field Office.

Rowley, P. D., Vice, G. S., McDonald, R. E., Anderson, J. J., Machette, M. N., Maxwell, D. J., Ekren, E. B., Cunningham, C. G., Steven, T. A., & Wardlaw, B. R. (2005). *Interim geologic map of the Beaver 30' x 60' quadrangle, Beaver, Piute, Iron, and Garfield counties, Utah.* Utah Geologic Society. https://ugspub.nr.utah.gov/publications/open_file_reports/ofr-454.pdf.

Sappington, R. L. (1981). A progress report on the obsidian and vitrophyre sourcing project. *Idaho Archaeologist, 4*, 4–17.

Sargeant, K. E. (1973). *The Haskett tradition: A view from Redfish Overhang.* [Unpublished Master's thesis]. Idaho State University.

Scheiber, L. L., & Finley, J. B. (2011). Obsidian source use in the Greater Yellowstone area, Wyoming Basin, and central Rocky Mountains. *American Antiquity, 76*(2), 372–394.

Schmitt, D. N., Madsen, D. B., Oviatt, C. G., & Quist, R. (2007). Late Pleistocene/early Holocene geomorphology and human occupation of the Old River Bed delta, western Utah. In K. E. Graf & D. N. Schmitt (Eds.), *Paleoindian or Paleoarchaic? Great Basin human ecology at the Pleistocene/Holocene transition* (pp. 105–119). University of Utah Press.

Seibert, J., & McGlynn, B. L. (2007). A new triangular multiple flow direction algorithm for computing upslope areas from gridded digital elevation models. *Water Resources Research, 43*(4), 1–8. https://doi.org/10.1029/2006WR005128.

Shackley, M. S. (Ed.). (2010). *X-ray fluorescence spectrometry (XRF) in geoarchaeology.* Springer.

Shackley, M. S. (2021). *Source provenance of obsidian artifacts from five sites in southwest Utah.* Geoarchaeological XRF Laboratory. https://cloudfront.escholarship.org/dist/prd/content/qt9312n4wj/qt9312n4wj.pdf.

Shroder, J. F., Cornwell, K., Oviatt, C. G., & Lowndes, T. C. (2016). Landslides, alluvial fans, and dam failure at Red Rock Pass: The outlet of Lake Bonneville. In C. G. Oviatt & J. F. Shroder (Eds.), *Lake Bonneville, a scientific update* (pp. 75–87). Developments in Earth Surface Processes 20. Elsevier. https://doi.org/10.1016/B978-0-444-63590-7.00004-4.

Siegrist, K. (2020). *The Cauchy distribution.* LibreTexts: Statistics. https://stats.libretexts.org/@go/page/10372.

Siniff, D. B. (1967). *A simulation model of animal movement behaviors.* [Unpublished doctoral thesis]. University of Minnesota.

Skinner, C. E. (2021). *Northwest Research Obsidian Source Reference Database.* Northwest Research Obsidian Studies Laboratory. http://www.obsidianlab.com/universe.html.

Skinner, C. E., & Thatcher, J. J. (2005). X-ray fluorescence trace element provenance analysis of geologic sources of obsidian from the Nevada Test and Training Range and surrounding region, Nevada and California. In

L. Haarklau, L. Johnson, & D. L. Wagner (Eds.), *Fingerprints in the Great Basin: The Nellis Air Force Base Regional Obsidian Sourcing Study*. U.S. Army Corps of Engineers, Fort Worth District.

Smith, G. M., & Barker, P. (2017). The Terminal Pleistocene/Early Holocene record in the northwestern Great Basin: What we know, what we don't know, and how we may be wrong. *PaleoAmerica*, 3(1), 13–47. https://doi.org/10.1080/20555563.2016.1272395.

Smith, G. M., Duke, D., Jenkins, D. L., Goebel, T., Davis, L. G., O'Grady, P., Stueber, D., Pratt, J. E., & Smith, H. L. (2019). The Western Stemmed Tradition: Problems and prospects in Paleoindian archaeology in the Intermountain West. *PaleoAmerica*, 6, 23–42. https://doi.org/10.1080/20555563.2019.1653153.

Smith Jr., J. F., & Ketner, K. B. (1976). *Stratigraphy of post-Paleozoic rocks and summary of resources in the Carlin-Pinon Range Area, Nevada*. United States Geological Survey Professional Paper 867-B. https://doi.org/10.3133/pp867B.

Speth, J. D., Newlander, K., White, A. A., Lemke, A. K., & Anderson, L. E. (2013). Early Paleoindian big-game hunting in North America: Provisioning or politics? *Quaternary International*, 285, 111–139. https://doi.org/10.1016/j.quaint.2010.10.027.

Spiess, A., Wilson, D., & Bradley, J. W. (1998). Paleoindian occupation in the New England maritime region: Beyond cultural ecology. *Archaeology of Eastern North America*, 26, 201–264.

Staatz, M., & Carr, W. (1964). Geology and mineral deposits of the Thomas and Dugway Ranges, Juab and Tooele Counties, Utah. *Professional Papers of the U.S. Geological Survey 415*.

Stephenson, R. L., & Wilkinson, K. (1969). *Archaeological reconnaissance of the Winnemucca-Battle Mountain area of Nevada*. Nevada Archaeological Survey Research Papers No. 1. University of Nevada, Reno.

Swanson, E. H., Powers, R., & Bryan, A. L. (1964). The material culture of the 1959 southwestern Idaho survey. *Tebiwa*, 7(2), 1–27.

Talbot, R. K., Richens, L. D., Searcy, M. T., Christiansen, E. H., & Ure, S. M. (2015). *Obsidian crossroads: An archaeological investigation of the Panaca Summit/Modena obsidian source in Lincoln County, Nevada*. Brigham Young University.

Tarboton, D. G. (1997). A new method for the determination of flow directions and upslope areas in grid digital elevation models. *Water Resources Research*, 33, 309–319.

Tarboton, D. G., Bras, R. L., & Rodriguez-Iturbe, I. (1991). On the extraction of channel networks from digital elevation data. *Hydrological Processes*, 5, 81–100. https://doi.org/10.1002/hyp.3360050107.

Tobler, W. R. (1970). A computer movie simulating urban growth in the Detroit region. *Economic Geography*, 46, 234–240.

Tobler, W. R. (1993). Three presentations on geographical analysis and modeling: Non-isotropic geographic modeling speculations on the geometry of geography global spatial analysis. *Technical Report 93-1*. National Center for Geographic Information and Analysis, University of California, Santa Barbara.

Tolan-Smith, C. (2003). The social context of landscape learning and the Lateglacial: Early Postglacial recolonization of the British Isles. In M. Rockman & J. Steele (Eds.), *Colonization of unfamiliar landscapes: The archaeology of adaptation* (pp. 116–129). Routledge.

Tripcevich, N. (2009). *Cost-distance analysis*. Retrieved May 2, 2022, from http://mapaspects.org/node/3744/.

Tripp, B. T. (2000). The Basin Perlite Company Mine and Mill, Beaver County, Southwest Utah. *Utah Geological Survey Notes*, 32(3), 6–7.

Tuohy, D. R. (1968). Some early lithic sites in Western Nevada. In C. Irwin-Williams (Ed.), *Early man in western North America, Symposium of the Southwestern Anthropological Association* (Vol. 1, Issue 4, pp. 27–38). Eastern New Mexico University Paleo-Indian Institute.

Tuohy, D. R. (1974). A comparative study of late Paleo-Indian manifestations of the western Great Basin. In R. Elston (Ed.), *Collected Papers on Great Basin Archaeology* (pp. 91–116). Nevada Archaeological Survey Research Paper 5, University of Nevada, Reno.

Tuohy, D. R., & Layton, T. N. (1977). Towards the establishment of a new series of Great Basin projectile points. *Nevada Archaeological Survey Reporter*, 10(6), 1–5.

Turchin, P. (1996). Fractal analyses of animal movement: A critique. *Ecology*, 77, 2086–2090.

Turchin, P. (2006). Comment. In J. P. Brantingham, "Measuring forager mobility." *Current Anthropology*, 47, 453–454.

Umshler, D. B. (1975). *Source of the Evan's Mound obsidian*. New Mexico Institute of Mining and Technology, Socorro.

U.S. Geological Survey. (2020a). *3D Elevation Program (3DEP)*. https://www.usgs.gov/core-science-systems/ngp/3dep/about-3dep-products-services.

U.S. Geological Survey. (2020b). *NHD 20200615 for Utah State or Territory* (FileGDB 10.1 Model Version 2.2.1) [Data set]. ScienceBase-Catalog. https://www.sciencebase.gov/catalog/item/4f5545cce4b018de15819ca9.

U.S. Geological Survey. (2020c). *The National Map Viewer*. Department of the Interior, U.S. Geological Survey. https://www.usgs.gov/tools/national-map-viewer.

Utah Department of Heritage and Arts. (2020). *Archaeology Report Records*. J. Willard Marriott Digital Library, University of Utah.

Utah Division of State History. (2020). *SEGO*.

Utah Geospatial Reference Center. (2017). *Historic Lake Bonneville*. https://gis.utah.gov/data/water/historic-lake-bonneville/.

Virtanen, P., Gommers, R., Oliphant, T. E., Haberland, M., Reddy, T., Cournapeau, D., Burovski, E., Peterson, P., Weckesser, W., Bright, J., van der Walt, S. J., Brett, M., Wilson, J., Millman, K. J., Mayorov, N., Nelson, A. R. J., Jones, E., Kern, R., Larson, E.,… Vázquez-Baeza, Y. (2020). SciPy 1.0: Fundamental algorithms for scientific computing in Python. *Nature Methods, 17*(3), 261–272. https://doi.org/10.1038/s41592-019-0686-2.

Viswanathan, G. M., Bartumeus, F., Buldyrev, S. V., Catalan, J., Fulco, U. L., Havlin, S., Da Luz, M. G. E., Lyra, M. L., Raposo, E. P., & Stanley, H. E. (2002). Lévy flight random searches in biological phenomena. *Physica A: Statistical Mechanics and Its Applications, 314*, 208–213. https://doi.org/10.1016/S0378-4371(02)01157-3.

Viswanathan, G. M., Da Luz, M. G. E., Raposo, E. P., & Stanley, H. E. (2011). *The physics of foraging: An introduction to random searches and biological encounters.* Cambridge University Press.

Walker, G. W., & MacLeod, N. S. (1991). *Geologic map of Oregon.* U.S. Geological Survey. https://ngmdb.usgs.gov/Prodesc/proddesc_16259.htm.

Wallace, B. N. (2017). *MU505, TG506, OD508 munitions response sites, Tooele County, Utah: Results of a cultural resources inventory* (Final report, Vol. 1). On file with Utah Division of State History, State Project No. U-15-UI-0799b.

Wallace, B. N. (2018). *Remedial investigations for MU505 and TG506 munitions response sites, Tooele County, Utah: Cultural resource monitoring results* (Final report, Vol. 2). On file with Utah Division of State History, State Project No. U-18-OM-0118.

Warren, C. N. (1967). The San Dieguito complex: A review and hypothesis. *American Antiquity, 32*, 168–185.

Waters, M. R., & Stafford, T. W. (2007). Redefining the age of Clovis: Implications for the peopling of the Americas. *Science, 315*(5815), 1122–1126. https://doi.org/10.1126/science.1137166.

Weide, D. L. (1964). *Site survey sheet: 42BE52.* Department of Anthropology, University of Utah.

Weisler, M. I., & Woodhead, J. D. (1995). Basalt Pb isotope analysis and the prehistoric settlement of Polynesia. *Proceedings of the National Academy of Sciences of the United States of America, 92*(6), 1881–1885. https://doi.org/10.1073/pnas.92.6.1881.

Wentworth, C. K. (1922). A scale of grade and class terms for clastic sediments. *Journal of Geology, 30*, 377–392. https://doi.org/10.1086/622910.

Whitman, S. J. (2013). *Near or far: An analysis of prehistoric obsidian procurement behavior in the greater Yellowstone area* (Publication No. 1368239131) [Master's thesis, Northern Arizona University]. ProQuest Dissertations & Theses Global.

Williams, V. S., Best, M. G., & Keith, J. D. (1997). *Geologic map of the Ursine-Panaca Summit—Deer Lodge area, Lincoln County, Nevada, and Iron County, Utah.* U.S. Geological Survey.

Willig, J. A., & Aikens, C. M. (1988). The Clovis-Archaic interface in far western North America. In J. A. Willig, C. M. Aikens, & J. L. Fagan (Eds.), *Early human occupation in far western North America: The Clovis-Archaic interface* (pp. 1–40). Nevada State Museum Anthropological Papers 21.

Willingham, C. (1995). Big Table Mountain: An obsidian source in the Centennial Mountains of Eastern Idaho. *Idaho Archaeologist, 18*, 3–7.

Willson, C. A. (2005). *X-ray fluorescence analysis of obsidian associated with Late Archaic sites in Southwestern Idaho and Southeastern Oregon: Issues in addressing mobility.* [Unpublished master's thesis]. University of Idaho.

Willson, C. A. (2007). A re-evaluation of X-ray fluorescence data from Idaho and southeastern Oregon. *Idaho Archaeologist, 30*, 17–26.

Wright, G. A., Chaya, H., & McDonald, J. (1990). The location of the Field Museum Yellowstone (F.M.Y., 90) Group obsidian source. *Plains Anthropologist, 35*, 71–74. https://doi.org/10.1080/2052546.1990.11909556.

Zar, J. H. (2010). *Biostatistical Analysis* (5th ed.). Prentice Hall.

Zerga, D. (1988). *Intermountain Antiquities Computer System: Site 26EK7320.* Bureau of Land Management.